D0853781

OUTLANDER KITCHEN

OUTLANDER KITCHEN

The Official Outlander Companion Cookbook

Theresa Carle-Sanders

Delacorte Press
New York

Published in the United States by Delacorte Press,
an imprint of Random House, a division of Penguin Random House LLC, New York.

DELACORTE PRESS and the HOUSE colophon are registered trademarks of Penguin Random House LLC.

Some of the recipes contained in this work were originally published on the author's blog,
Outlander Kitchen, outlanderkitchen.com.

This work contains excerpts from the following novels by Diana Gabaldon,
published by Delacorte Press, an imprint of Random House, a division of
Penguin Random House LLC: *Outlander*, copyright © 1991 by Diana Gabaldon;
Dragonfly in Amber, copyright © 1992 by Diana Gabaldon; *Voyager*, copyright © 1994
by Diana Gabaldon; *Drums of Autumn*, copyright © 1997; *The Fiery Cross*, copyright ©
2001 by Diana Gabaldon; and *A Breath of Snow and Ashes*, copyright © 2005 by
Diana Gabaldon. Reprinted by permission of Delacorte Press, an imprint of
Random House, a division of Penguin Random House LLC.

Photographs on pages x, xiii, 2, 5, 7, 9, 10, 11, 18, 23, 25, 28, 30, 32, 42,
47, 53, 54, 70, 77, 80, 81, 84, 88, 97, 100, 102, 103, 107, 117, 124, 130 (top), 144, 152, 160,
161, 168, 193, 198, 200, 202, 208, 220, 222, 225, 228, 233, 234, 239, 247, 251, 253, 257, 259, 268, 273,
293, 296, 300, 305, 307, and 310 are by Theresa Carle-Sanders, copyright © 2016 by Theresa Carle-Sanders
All other photographs are by Rebecca Wellman, copyright © 2016 by Rebecca Wellman Photography

LIBRARY OF CONGRESS CATALOGING-IN-PUBLICATION DATA

Names: Carle-Sanders, Theresa, author.
Title: Outlander kitchen : the official Outlander companion cookbook / Theresa Carle-Sanders.
Description: First edition. | New York : Delacorte Books, [2016]
Identifiers: LCCN 2016000515| ISBN 9781101967577 | ISBN 9781101967584 (ebook)
Subjects: LCSH: Cooking. | Gabaldon, Diana. Outlander. | LCGFT: Literary cookbooks.
Classification: LCC TX714 .C37315455 2016 | DDC 641.5—dc23 LC record available at
http://lccn.loc.gov/2016000515

Printed in the United States of America on acid-free paper

randomhousebooks.com

4 6 8 9 7 5

Book design by Virginia Norey

To Howard, My Englishman.
You look and sound a lot like Frank,
but your heart, and love, is pure Jamie.

CONTENTS

FOREWORD

Food disappears all the time . . .

Especially when you have small children, teenage boys, husbands, girlfriends, or holiday guests, but even when you're home alone, the siren song of savory snacks echoes faintly behind the refrigerator door.

The fact is that every living thing has to eat—and people being the inventive creatures they are, we seldom settle for grubs from under the nearest rock or even raw salmon swatted out of a stream. No, we like our food varied, imaginative, tasty. And usually cooked. Hence the constant demand for something new and delicious.

My first encounter with Theresa Carle-Sanders was some years ago, when she emailed me to ask my permission to use brief quotes from my novels in conjunction with her website. A professional chef with a beautiful (and mouthwatering) website, she had become intrigued with all the mentions of food in the *Outlander* novels, and wanted to explore some of these dishes: inventing or adapting recipes, then posting the results with instructions, photos, and videos, with a relevant quote from one of the novels alongside.

"Cool!" I said. "Why not?"

There's something rather odd about the *Outlander* novels. People who read them seem to be creatively inspired to do all manner of wonderful things.

To this point in my career, I'd had people ask permission to name racehorses, show dogs, and even a housing development after my books, or the people, places, and objects in them. Creative fans had composed ballads, symphonies, and band arrangements based on the books; there was even a CD, *Outlander: The Musical*. People make amazing jewelry, Christmas ornaments, standing-stone birthday cakes, and lighted Halloween pumpkins carved with a back view of Jamie Fraser in the nude. To say nothing of soaps, candles, herbal concoctions, "Lord John Grey" tea, and "La Dame Blanche" wine. A cooking website—even one with recipes like Stephen Bonnet's Balls—seemed refreshingly normal.

Speaking *of* Stephen Bonnet's Balls . . . I met Theresa for the first time in the flesh when she came to a book signing at a writers' conference in British Columbia, bearing a green glass pot filled with said balls—delicious pretzel balls, filled with bittersweet chocolate. Had I had any doubts as to her bona fides as a chef, they would have vanished in an instant—just like Stephen Bonnet's Balls did. . . .

For several years now, I've watched with fascination (and the occasional salivary spasm) as Theresa has gone from Mrs. Fitz's Porridge to Rolls with Minced Pigeon and Truffles, Roast Beef for a Wedding Feast, and Murphy's Mock-Turtle Soup (with plenty of sherry, to be sure). A wonderful cook and an equally talented food writer, her recipes and adaptations are nearly as entertaining to read as they are to eat.

With so much excellent material available, Theresa had been wanting to do an official *Outlander Kitchen* cookbook—and I was all for it. We were advised, though, that it would be best to wait until the television show—then in the early negotiating stages—was aired, in order to assure the best visibility for the new project. The STARZ original show *Outlander* is the latest and most visible part of the evolving creative phenomenon, and I'm happy to say that it's not only been a delight in itself but has definitely paved the way for this wonderful cookbook finally to reach its audience.

Food is, of course, a matter of passionate interest to everyone. Tastes may differ, but not the basic need, the appetite for food. And one needs no explanation for the swift disappearance of any food prepared from this delicious and imaginative collection.

Congratulations, Theresa!

—Diana Gabaldon

INTRODUCTION

I have always been a reader. And a cook.

My mom read to me in the cradle, priming me for a life of adventure both on and off the pages. Decades before anyone had heard of the 100-Mile Diet, my dad was a champion of fresh, local ingredients. I tagged along wherever he went, whether to Chinatown for live prawns fresh from the boats, the farm stands outside Vancouver for just-picked fruits and vegetables, or to the neighborhood bakery for bread on weekend mornings. I was his Sunday-breakfast sous-chef almost every weekend until I moved out on my own.

I filled out an application for culinary school right out of high school, but instead I listened to my wanderlust and spent five years traveling across much of Europe and Asia between bouts of work and study. By the time I got back from my last trip, now with a long-distance English fiancé, dreams of cooking school had been forgotten, and I was told by many around me that it was time to grow up and get a job.

No one, least of all me, really remembers how, but seven years later, at thirty years old, I found myself an operations manager for a multinational transportation company. A good job—even an enviable one—my boss was great, my employees too. I had a competitive salary, benefits package, and even my very own, much-prized parking space in Vancouver's downtown core.

There are no words to describe how incompatible I was for that job. The 24/7, at-all-costs pursuit of guaranteed on-time package delivery did not call to my soul, and my dissatisfaction spilled over into my personal life. I went from a

happy, somewhat-sociable bookworm to an anxious, prematurely gray thirtysomething who hid at home between shifts, unable even to enjoy the comfort of my books.

Eventually, after a drama-filled encounter with an unhappy customer put me over the edge one afternoon, I gathered my courage and, with the encouragement of my husband, Howard, threw that job away, as well as the stress, grief, and cell phone that went with it. I cashed in my retirement savings to temporarily replace my salary, began a daily yoga practice, remembered how to breathe deeply, and walked into a bookstore for the first time in years. That's where I discovered *Outlander* and its creator, Diana Gabaldon.

Since then, the Frasers have accompanied me on every step of this less-than-conventional path that Howard and I chose; our spontaneous move to Pender Island in the Salish Sea between Vancouver and Victoria; the years of menial jobs we worked to build a life here; the unexpected death of my father; and my journey to a weeklong silent retreat in Maine, where, sitting on a rise in the middle of an empty meadow, staring at fields of grass under a sun mid-sky, the missing piece finally slotted into place.

Outlander and its sequels also came with me three short weeks after I got home from Maine, when I moved back to Vancouver and in with my mother to finally attend culinary school almost twenty years after filling out my original application.

Claire and Jamie were also most certainly walking beside me a couple of years later, when a certain tray of rolls with pigeon and truffles from Madame Jeanne's popped into my head while hiking in the woods with the dog. By the time I got home I had a recipe half written in my head, and an idea for a food-related interview with Diana. I emailed that interview, and a request to use the pigeon roll excerpt from *Voyager*, off to her Canadian publicist that afternoon. Diana's very generous response the next day was the birth of *Outlander Kitchen*.

Life got even more interesting in 2013 when the STARZ channel announced a TV adaptation of the *Outlander* series. After I made a trip down to San Diego Comic-Con and posted a series of five suggested *Outlander Kitchen* menus for the television premiere, STARZ asked me to produce a themed recipe for each episode, which they shared across their social media. *OK*'s followers on Facebook and Twitter subsequently grew by thousands, sometimes in a single day.

Along the way, I've interacted with hundreds of Outlanders online, and have met a few dozen in person. I've made connections with fans from all over the world, many of whom I now count among my best friends. *Outlander Kitchen* recipes have been translated into Spanish, German, Italian, and even Japanese!

I have the best job in the world. I work at home, following my passion, with the dog underfoot either at my desk or in front of the stove. Howard is a fabulous taste tester with a gifted palate, and he definitely washes his fair share of the dishes. I still walk in the woods every day, and I am constantly learning something new about history and food through the ages.

I also get a fair share of sideways glances when people ask me what I do.

"An eighteenth-century Scottish cookbook based on a time-travel story, you say? That's a great idea." <eye roll>

My response has always been that *Outlander Kitchen* is not a Scottish cookbook, nor a historical one. It's an *Outlander* cookbook, meaning we have two centuries and several different countries' cuisines to explore, along with a diverse cast of characters, many of whom scream their kitchen inspiration to me from the pages of Diana's books.

And that sounds a lot more fun to my twenty-first-century, book-geek self than attempting the traditional recipe for *powsowdie*, found on the buffet table for Flora MacDonald's visit to River Run in *A Breath of Snow and Ashes*. It starts out much like any other number of dishes from the period, and involves scalding a freshly procured sheep's head in boiling water before scraping out its nostril hairs with a spoon.

Of course, that is historical cuisine at its extreme. A number of recipes, such as the Cock-a-Leekie (page 58), served on the tattie fields of Lallybroch, and the Veal Patties in Wine Sauce (page 99) at Jared's house in Paris, have stood the test of time very well; *OK*'s versions of these historical recipes were taken, with minor adaptations, from eighteenth-century cookbooks.

Other period-appropriate recipes are my own creations, including Pheasant and Greens at Ardsmuir (page 108), which uses ingredients available to an eighteenth-century man of means, such as Lord John, and incorporates classic French techniques conceivably adopted by Scottish cooks during Scotland's nearly four-hundred-year *Auld Alliance* with France, which left a lasting influence on Scottish cuisine and culture.

There is, however, a limit to how much historical accuracy a twenty-first-century cookbook can absorb, especially if it has any hope of finding a regular home on your kitchen counter rather than a shelf in your living room. After all, this is supposed to be fun, aye? And while it is fun to eat like Jamie for an afternoon, you don't want to eat like him every day—trust me. With that in mind, the majority of the historical recipes to follow have been transformed with a little, or a lot of, modern-day finesse.

For the turtle soup from *Voyager*, arguably the most beloved *Outlander* dish of them all, I decided upon a Victorian mock-turtle soup, as turtle is unlikely to make it onto most people's grocery list, including my own. It was only when I began to research the mock version, however, that I found we would all be shopping for calf heads and pigs' trotters instead. (I should have known better, given all those grotesque illustrations of the Mock Turtle in *Alice in Wonderland*.)

What's a twenty-first century cook to do? Well, it took three attempts, but in the end I'm thrilled with *OK's Drunken Mock-Turtle Soup* (page 61), which uses oxtail, a whole bottle of sherry, a combination of historical recipes for real turtle soup from New Orleans and Philadelphia, and Vietnamese fish sauce to produce what the book's photographer, Rebecca Wellman, an accomplished cook and food stylist, described as a "delicious, European version of hot-and-sour soup."

A number of the dishes are naturally gluten-free, or easily adapted, by virtue of the fact that oats grew well on the poor soil of the Highlands, while wheat did not, as well as the fact that corn was the first grain grown in quantity in the colonies. I won't deny there's a lot of butter and cream to follow, especially for a cookbook in these days of alternative diets, but at the same time, there is also a respectable selection of vegetarian-friendly dishes, which were hard to find in the backcountry of the eighteenth-century South, where pork and its fat reigned, as per the White Sow.

Recipes evolve, as do our taste buds. I've done my best to balance historical accuracy with modern tastes, ingredients, and time constraints—most of us today simply do not have the hours to spend in the kitchen that our foremothers did—but I've included a few unapologetically modern recipes such as Sweet Tea–Brined Fried Chicken (page 112), which throws most southern fried chicken traditions out the window to make room for tasty, crunchy, and juicy boneless fried chicken with less mess. I also use baking soda and powder, invented in the nineteenth century, to give lift and lightness to bannocks and biscuits that would otherwise be dense to the point of inedibility for most palates today.

Welcome to my Outlander Kitchen. Take a seat by the fire, pour yourself a dram, and fall through the stones with me on a culinary journey from Lallybroch to The Ridge and back again. Awaken your senses with an aromatic bowl of Peppery Oyster Stew (page 164), deepen your connection to long-beloved characters with a dish of Auld Ian's Buttered Leeks (page 202), and embark on a time-traveling adventure, using your own Outlander Kitchen as a portal.

Ith do leòr! (Eat your fill!)

OUTLANDER KITCHEN

My Outlander Kitchen

Pantry

A time-traveling kitchen requires a versatile pantry. Many ingredients we have come to depend on in the twentieth and twenty-first centuries were not common, or even in existence, in the eighteenth. Other ingredients that were staples two hundred years ago have been lost to our industrialized food system that, in many ways, values convenience over taste and nutrition.

That said, aside from the game meats and a few spices, you won't find a lot of exotic ingredients in *Outlander Kitchen*. I did most of my shopping while writing it in my small island's (population 2,200) grocery store. For the rest, I ventured into the big city and its specialty shops and superstores. When that failed, I always found what I was looking for online, a few short days away by mail.

Remember that a recipe is a guideline, not a blueprint. Use what you have and find inspiration for substitutions in your pantry, rather than buying ingredients that you may use only once. For my part, I've tried to avoid pantry one-hit wonders—ingredients you buy for a single recipe and never use again. In most cases, if I call for an exotic spice or condiment, you'll find it in at least one other recipe; for example, rosewater is used to flavor the Almond Squirts (page 272) as well as the Buttermilk Lamb Chops with Rosewater Mint Sauce (page 136).

Read the recipe through at least once before you go shopping, then again before you start cooking. Prep all of your ingredients before you begin, and I promise you will find that everything goes much more quickly and smoothly, and that cooking along with your favorite books can actually be an enjoyable way to spend a couple of hours, or even a whole afternoon.

Below are a few notes about common *Outlander Kitchen* pantry staples.

Butter In restaurant and industrial kitchens, where the recipes are made to serve dozens or even hundreds, the differences between salted and unsalted butter make a big difference. At home, I use salted and unsalted butter interchangeably for most things—the difference is negligible when you're cooking for smaller numbers. Unless I specify one or the other in a recipe, use what you have on hand.

Buttermilk A frequent ingredient in the recipes that follow, and a staple in my fridge. From time to time, however, I find myself without any and have a craving for Mrs. Bug's Buttermilk Drop Biscuits (page 246). Although not quite the real thing, either of these substitutions works in a pinch:

- *Stir together 1 cup milk and 1 tablespoon lemon juice or vinegar. Let stand 15 minutes at room temperature until thickened and curdled.*
- *Stir together ¾ cup plain yogurt or sour cream and ¼ cup milk. Let stand 10 minutes at room temperature.*

Cornstarch Primarily used as a thickener, cornstarch is known as corn flour in most places outside North America.

Cream Use whipping cream (30 to 35% fat) and heavy cream (36% and up) interchangeably in *Outlander Kitchen* recipes. Substitute double cream (up to 48% fat) for extra richness. The more fat cream has, the more stable its whipped peaks, and the more heat and acid it can withstand before curdling. Other recipes call for light cream, also known as "single" and "table" cream, which are all different names, depending on your geographic location, for cream that has about 18 to 20% fat.

Eggs I always use large eggs. Once separated, yolks should be used immediately, but the whites will keep in the fridge up to five days or in the freezer up to a month. Use them to bulk out a Bacon, Asparagus, and Wild Mushroom Omelette (page 45), for a sweet batch of Almond Squirts (page 272), or beat one with a drop of water and a pinch of salt to make an egg wash for pastry.

Flour All-purpose flour in North America is sold as plain flour just about everywhere else. When baking with whole wheat flour, I use stone-ground flour exclusively.

Herbs I use fresh herbs liberally, just like cooks of the past, to add flavor and aroma. Even those with black thumbs find most herbs relatively easy to grow in a variety of climates. Most of my herb garden regularly survives the relatively mild winters of the Pacific Northwest, but others in more extreme climates keep small pots of herbs on a windowsill during cold months, or buy what they need from the produce section. When fresh herbs are unavailable, substitute about half the amount of dry.

Nutmeg This much-prized seed of a tree native to the Spice Islands of Indonesia was popular for centuries as a spice, medicine, and preservative. Preground nutmeg is tasteless. Buy it whole and grate it, as needed, on a rasp.

Oatmeal Unlike in most of North America, where oatmeal refers to cooked oat porridge, in Britain, oatmeal refers to a meal, from coarse to fine, ground from hulled oats. Traditionally ground on a millstone, it is used extensively in Scottish cooking to make everything from a dense parritch to scones and haggis. I make my own oatmeal by grinding rolled oats in my food processor or coffee grinder. See Grinding Grains, Nuts, and Seeds (page 10).

Oats Advances in oat processing in the late nineteenth century resulted in the development of steel-cut oats, as well as rolled oats. I keep both types in my pantry, and while I tend to prefer steel-cut's texture and nuttiness for my morning parritch, rolled is what I reach for when I am baking.

Oil While I use the generic term "vegetable oil" in all of my recipes, I specifically use sunflower or safflower oil for salad dressings and to pan-fry; to deep fry, I use peanut, avocado, or coconut oil. When a recipe calls for olive oil, I use extra-virgin.

Pepper Pepper was ridiculously expensive historically, and it was used sparingly, yet there were more varieties available to a cook in a wealthy eighteenth-century kitchen than most of us keep now. Expand your horizons with Jamaican or Balinese long pepper, and pick up some ground white pepper to keep cream sauces and pale dishes unmarred by black flakes.

Salt My mother calls me a snob for my shelf of salt, and she's probably right. There *is* a time and place for every salt, but I use kosher salt the vast majority of the time. I prefer it for its flaky texture and lack of processing. Because its large flakes take up more space in a measuring spoon, it takes more kosher salt than regular table salt to season a dish, so if you are using table salt, use about half the amount of the kosher salt called for.

Stock Homemade stock is a relatively inexpensive source of protein, nutrition, and flavor that is undervalued and underused in many kitchens today. Most people cite time as the number one reason they avoid making it, and I can't argue that stock does take some time. But if you are going to be around the house anyway, why not start a pot? Once it's simmering, turn on the exhaust fan and walk away, remembering to check back every thirty minutes or so. All of that said, at the end of a long, hard day, any of the following recipes can be made with packaged stock. Look for no-salt or reduced-salt varieties, or use a very light hand with the salt during cooking.

Sugar Unless otherwise noted, any mention of sugar refers to granulated. Confectioners', or powdered, sugar is also known as icing sugar outside the United States.

Whisky Scottish regulations require all bottles bearing the label "scotch" to contain whisky distilled in Scotland from malted barley (or, less commonly, rye or wheat), and aged in oak casks for a minimum of three years. Single malt whisky is produced entirely from barley malt in one distillery, while blended whisky generally contains whisky from many distilleries.

Whiskey American whiskey is defined under the law as that which is distilled from a fermented mash of cereal grain (barley, corn, wheat, rye, etc.) and aged, at least briefly, in new charred-oak casks. Arguably the most popular style of American whiskey is bourbon, made from a mash containing at least 51% corn.

White vermouth (dry) My shelf-stable substitute for white wine in cooking. It is convenient to have on hand when you need a little wine to deglaze a pan but don't want to open a bottle.

Yeast I use instant yeast (also known as fast-rising, rapid-rise, quick-rise, or bread machine yeast) exclusively. It is easier to use, as it does not require proofing in water like active-dry yeast, and I find its results more consistent.

Equipment

The multicentury kitchen is also stocked with a wide, yet selective variety of tools, some electric, some hand-powered; most are multitasking instruments that don't take up drawer space without good reason.

I'm sure my use of a stand mixer and food processor may seem (ever so slightly) anachronistic to some. When I started *Outlander Kitchen*, I did everything old-school, but soon, warning twinges from my carpal-tunnel wrists put the kibosh on kneading

dough by hand and finely dicing a field's worth of vegetables. In my defense, eighteenth-century cooks in wealthy castle kitchens would have had at least a few "kitchen aides" at their disposal, and I think it's safe to say that my food processor is better treated, and much cleaner, than your average scullery maid.

Beyond the basics in a modern kitchen, I use the following list of tools regularly in my everyday cooking.

Bench scraper Choose one with a straight edge to scrape the counter and cut the dough, and another with a curved edge to clean your bowls.

Coffee grinder Faster than a mortar and pestle for large batches of dried or roasted whole spices, and a quick way to grind a small amount of grains or nuts into meal. Buy a dedicated grinder just for spices, grains, and nuts. To clean it, pulse 2 tablespoons of grain, such as rice, barley, or oats, into a coarse powder. Discard the ground material and brush out the grinder and lid.

Food processor Big ones can be expensive, but if that's out of your reach, consider a smaller, less-expensive model and chop your ingredients in batches.

Immersion blender An inexpensive way to puree soups and sauces in the pan. Even if you have both a blender and a food processor, an immersion blender is a quick stick that gets the job done without leaving you with major cleanup.

Instant-read thermometer Test meat temperatures, make candy, and deep-fry to your heart's content.

Kitchen rasp A multipurpose tool that gets a lot of use in my *Outlander Kitchen*, and a tool Mrs. Bug could have used herself, if only she had thought to ask Arch for his. It is the fastest way to add garlic to a dish and zests a lemon in fifteen seconds flat.

Kitchen scale Weighing ingredients is more accurate and faster than measuring their volume, which is why you'll find a scale in pretty much all professional kitchens.

Knives The most important tools in any kitchen and a basic that warrants a bit of discussion. If you are just starting out, spend as much as you can on a good chef's knife—hold it in your hand, find its point of balance, feel its weight—try several until you find the one for you. A long serrated knife and a cheap paring knife complete a basic set. I always recommend a knife skills class at a local cooking school. In addition to technique and safety, you'll also learn how to keep your knives sharp.

Mortar and pestle Choose the best-quality, heaviest set you can afford (and lift). Make sure it is deep enough to bash some seeds and herbs around without everything scattering all over the counter.

Oven thermometer Ovens in all price ranges are notoriously off-temperature, so it's important to know whether yours runs hot or cold.

Parchment paper Essential for evenly browned baked goods and quick, easy cleanups. Find it beside the aluminum foil and plastic wrap on store shelves.

Pots and pans Another basic worthy of discussion. A decent-quality set of stainless steel pans will last you decades. Look for them on sale, and pick up a better set than you could otherwise afford. I got rid of all of our nonstick frying pans years ago and use cast iron exclusively. I like it for its even heat and ability to go into the oven. Keep your cast iron well seasoned, and it's effectively nonstick without the danger of the surface flaking off and ending up on your plate, and eventually your digestive system. (I really don't like that stuff.)

Slow cooker Choose the one that's right for you; I've gone back to a basic unit with just a plug and a high/low switch to avoid paying for unnecessary electronic controls that malfunction prematurely and render an otherwise perfectly good appliance useless. (I really don't like those things either.)

Soft-bristled nylon brush Give your vegetables a scrub before cooking. I have a second one that I use to scrub my nails like a surgeon before I start any task in the kitchen.

Stand mixer By no means essential, but very nice to have, especially if you do a lot of baking. Attachments abound for these labor-savers, including meat grinders, ice cream makers, and pasta rollers.

Tea ball Pick up a large one in your local Chinatown, kitchen store, or online, and use it to hold together a bouquet garni in a pot of stock or soup. Small ones are handy too.

Glossary and Techniques

Some are more experienced in the kitchen than others, but the vast majority of *OK* recipes are written for everyone. A few, like Vegetable Stew (page 174) and Tortellini

Portofino (page 190), have long lists of ingredients and several involved steps, but even these are achievable by the beginner cook. Remember to read the recipe through at least once, and prepare the ingredients as directed before you begin.

Below is a list of terms and techniques that I use throughout the cookbook. Even if you're an experienced cook, give this section a quick read-through to make sure that we're all speaking the same culinary language.

Blanching and Boiling

Water used to blanch or boil vegetables, grains, and pasta should be salty. Not too salty, but well seasoned, which takes 1½ to 2 teaspoons of salt per quart of blanching water. The salt adds flavor and also helps to preserve the bright color of your favorite green vegetables.

Grinding Grains, Nuts, and Seeds

To grind oats and other softer grains in a coffee grinder (or larger amounts in a food processor), pulse three to five times for coarse meal, where there are still a few larger flakes among the finer grind, suitable for Pumpkin Seed and Herb Oatcakes (page 219). Pulse six or more times for fine meal, closer to the texture of flour.

Harder grains, such as barley, require more grinding time. Grind them in smaller batches in a coffee grinder to avoid scratching and clouding the bowl of your food processor. Use a fine metal sieve to separate the coarser remains for another run through the grinder, and to prevent overgrinding everything into a paste.

Use the same technique to grind nuts and seeds. Sliced or slivered nuts are faster to grind than whole nuts. Avoid crossing that fine line between finely ground seeds and seed butter; check and scrape the bottom of the grinder's bowl with a small silicone spatula every few pulses. Sieve the contents through a fine metal strainer and return the larger pieces to the grinder for another trip through the blades.

Knife Skills

The best thing you can do to make your time in the kitchen easier and more enjoyable is to take a knife skills class at a nearby culinary school. Two or three hours spent learning technique and safety (including how to keep your knives sharp) is time well spent, whether you're just here to cook your way through your favorite series of books or are getting serious about cooking more from scratch.

The photos on this page illustrate the cutting techniques I was taught during my first week at culinary school, using the ubiquitous onion as an example. To prepare, cut off both ends of the onion, then cut it in half vertically. Peel and place the onion cut side down on a cutting board.

To chop, dice, and mince, use a sharp knife to slice the onion horizontally, parallel to the cutting board, from the bottom to the top, without cutting all the way through. Next, make vertical slices from left to right. Finally, slice crosswise in the other direction. Repeat with the second half.

- *Chop: ½-inch-square pieces*
- *Dice: ¼-inch-square pieces*
- *Mince: as fine as you can get*

To julienne, or cut the onion into thin, matchstick-like strips, work right to left—unless you're left-handed—and angle your knife to make graduated ⅛- to ¼-inch-thick slices up the onion. When you get to the middle and your knife is at 90 degrees to the cutting board, clear away the cut onions and tip the freshly cut edge of the onion down to the cutting board. Working right to left, finish julienning the first half of the onion. Repeat with the second half. This cut of onions is used more often in professional kitchens than sliced because the uniform slivers cook more evenly than rings of all different sizes.

Cut the ingredients uniformly, according to the instructions in the recipe, and the dish will cook evenly and in the time given.

Tempering

To add eggs to a hot liquid, stir some of the hot liquid into the beaten eggs to raise their temperature gently and prevent them from scrambling. When the eggs are warmed, stir everything back into the pot.

Thickeners

The most common thickener is a *roux*, an equal amount of butter and flour cooked together, usually at the beginning of a recipe, such as in a cream sauce or gravy. Roux range from light to brown, depending on how long they are cooked; the darker the roux, the less thickening power it has.

French for "kneaded butter," a beurre manié is an equal amount of butter and flour mixed together and left uncooked. It is generally added just before serving to thicken and add gloss to a soup or stew.

Whichever you are using, always remember this simple rule to ensure lump-free thickening: Add a hot roux/beurre manié to cold liquid, or a cold roux/beurre manié to hot liquid. Did you get that? Works every time.

Finally, a *liaison* is a gluten-free mixture of egg yolks and cream used mostly to enrich, but it also thickens soups and stews near the end of cooking. Once you have added the liaison to the pan, do not allow it to boil or the eggs will curdle.

Conversion Tables

In addition to the approximate metric equivalents for weights and packages included in the ingredient list for each recipe, below are a number of practical conversions, rounded for convenience, that are commonly used in an international kitchen:

Temperature

250°F = 120°C = Gas Mark ½
275°F = 135°C = Gas Mark 1
300°F = 150°C = Gas Mark 2
325°F = 165°C = Gas Mark 3
350°F = 175°C = Gas Mark 4
375°F = 190°C = Gas Mark 5
400°F = 200°C = Gas Mark 6
425°F = 220°C = Gas Mark 7
450°F = 230°C = Gas Mark 8
475°F = 250°C = Gas Mark 9
500°F = 260°C = Gas Mark 10

Length

⅛ inch = .25 centimeters (cm)
¼ inch = .5 cm
½ inch = 1.25 cm
1 inch = 2.5 cm
6 inches = 15 cm
12 inches (1 foot) = 30 cm

Volume

½ teaspoon = ¹⁄₁₂ fluid ounce (fl oz.)
⠀⠀ = 3 milliliters (ml)
1 teaspoon = ⅙ fl oz. = 5 ml
1 tablespoon = ⅓ fl oz. = 15 ml
¼ cup = 2 fl oz. = 60 ml
⅓ cup = 2⅔ fl oz. = 80 ml
⅔ cup = 5⅓ fl oz. = 160 ml
¾ cup = 6 fl oz. = 180 ml
1 cup = 8 fl oz. = 240 ml
1 pint = 2 cups = 16 fl oz. = 500 ml
1 quart = 4 cups = 32 fl oz. = 1 liter
1 gallon = 4 quarts = 3.75 liters

Weight

½ ounce = 15 grams
1 ounce = 30 grams
2 ounces = 55 grams
4 ounces = ¼ pound = 115 grams
8 ounces = ½ pound = 225 grams
12 ounces = ¾ pound = 340 grams
16 ounces = 1 pound = 450 grams

"The food was either terribly bad or terribly good," Claire had said, describing her adventures in the past. *"That's because there's no way of keeping things; anything you eat has either been salted or preserved in lard, if it isn't half rancid—or else it's fresh off the hoof or out of the garden, in which case it can be bloody marvelous."*

—*Drums of Autumn,* chapter 35, "Bon Voyage"

Chapter 1

Basic Recipes

Stock

Broth and bannocks, broth and bread. A quick and common meal for everyone from crofters to castle inhabitants throughout Outlander, as well as the real world. Stock was an essential kitchen staple for hundreds of years, when everything was home-made, food supplies were often stretched, and nothing was ever wasted. Especially the bones.

Culinarily speaking, there is a difference between stock and broth. Stock is made from bones and a few aromatics, while broth is stock that has been seasoned with salt and spices, and possibly enriched with meat, to make it deliciously drinkable all on its own. Because we use it primarily as a base for soup and sauces, we use stock rather than broth in *Outlander Kitchen*.

No matter what animal's bones it is made from, meat and poultry stock can be divided into two broad types: white and brown. A white stock is made from raw bones and has almost no color, while a richly colored brown stock is made from bones roasted with tomato paste.

Ideally, white stock is used in cream soups, light sauces, and anywhere else where a neutral color is desired, like Slow-Cooked Chicken Fricassee (page 115). Brown stock finds its home in dark soups and stews such as Jenny's Hare Pie (page 151), pan sauces and gravies, and in mugs, seasoned to taste for sipping. In reality, for most recipes, you can use white and brown stock interchangeably, depending on what you have on hand.

Whether from bird, beast, or vegetable, follow these rules to concoct the perfect pot of stock.

- *For a crystal-clear stock, trim all the bones of excess skin, fat, and meat and cover them with cold water. After the initial boil of the bones, keep the stock at a slow simmer and skim it regularly with a slotted spoon. Never cover a stock with a lid, nor stir it.*

- *A generally acceptable ratio of bones to water for stock is 50% bones by weight. For example, to make 2 quarts of stock, you need about 2 pounds of bones.*

- *Avoid disturbing the bones and vegetables in the bottom of the pot and keep the liquid clear by ladling the finished stock through a strainer lined with several layers of cheesecloth.*

- *Cool your freshly made stock quickly to avoid food-borne illness. Pour the hot liquid into a glass or metal container, and immerse that in another container or sink filled with ice or cold water. Refrigerate immediately when cooled.*

- *NEVER SALT A STOCK. When you use your stock in a soup or sauce, or serve it, steaming in mugs for those coming out of the cold, that is the time to season it with salt and maybe a little freshly cracked pepper.*

Hot Broth at Castle Leoch
(Brown Chicken Stock)

"Ye need not be scairt of me," he said softly. "Nor of anyone here, so long as I'm with ye." He let go and turned to the fire.

"You need somethin' hot, lass," he said matter-of-factly, "and a bit to eat as well. Something in your belly will help more than anything." I laughed shakily at his attempts to pour broth one-handed, and went to help. He was right; food did help. We sipped broth and ate bread in a companionable silence, sharing the growing comfort of warmth and fullness.

Finally, he stood up, picking up the fallen quilt from the floor. He dropped it back on the bed, and motioned me toward it. "Do ye sleep a bit, Claire. You're worn out, and likely someone will want to talk wi' ye before too long."

—*Outlander,* chapter 4, "I Come to the Castle"

The pure liquid nutrition of homemade stock or broth is infinitely superior to anything you can buy in the store—zero salt and additives, but rich with protein to fortify even the most exhausted time travelers.

To serve as is, heat to boiling and season with salt and pepper, or use as the base for any number of soups, stews, and sauces, including Ragoo'd Pork (page 126).

Makes about 2 quarts

Ingredients

2 pounds (900 grams) raw chicken bones, trimmed of skin and fat

1 medium onion, chopped (see Knife Skills, page 11)

1 small carrot, chopped

1 celery stalk, chopped

1 tablespoon tomato paste

2 bay leaves

2 fresh thyme sprigs

6 fresh parsley sprigs

6 whole peppercorns

Method

Move a rack to the middle rung and heat the oven to 400°F.

Arrange the bones in a single layer in a roasting pan, and roast until they begin to brown, about 20 minutes. Add the onions, carrots, and celery to the pan and toss well. Use a pastry brush or spoon to spread the tomato paste onto the bones and vegetables. Roast for another 15 minutes, or until the vegetables are just beginning to brown.

Meanwhile, make a bouquet garni. Wrap the bay leaves, thyme, parsley, and peppercorns in a square of cheesecloth and tie with string, or enclose the items in a large tea ball.

Use a slotted spoon to transfer all the bones and veggies (and a minimum of the fat) into a stockpot. Add 2 quarts cold water, plus more, if necessary, to cover the bones by 2 inches. Bring to a boil over high heat, and immediately reduce the heat to low for a slow simmer.

Skim the surface of the stock with a slotted spoon to remove impurities and fat. Add the bouquet garni to the pot and continue to cook at a slow simmer, uncovered, for 2 hours. Skim and top up the water as needed to keep the bones and veggies well covered. Do not stir.

Ladle the finished stock through a strainer lined with several layers of dampened cheesecloth or a clean cotton or linen dishcloth into a glass or metal container. Gently press on the solids to extract all the liquid.

Cool quickly, refrigerate overnight, and discard the hardened fat from the surface of the cold stock before storing in the fridge up to 5 days. Freeze up to 6 weeks.

Notes

- *Chicken necks and backs make a rich, full-bodied stock. For an extra-delicious and nutritious boost of gelatin, include a few chicken feet too.*
- *To use cooked poultry carcasses in this recipe, brush the bones and vegetables with the tomato paste and roast for 15 minutes before continuing with the recipe.*
- *To make brown beef stock, replace the chicken bones with the same weight of beef bones and increase the initial roast time to 30 minutes before adding the vegetables and tomato paste. Simmer the beef bones for 6 to 8 hours to extract the maximum richness and flavor.*

MURPHY'S BEEF BROTH
(White Beef Stock)

"Wot, not the broth, too?" Murphy said. The cook's broad red face lowered menacingly. "Which I've had folk rise from their deathbeds after a sup of that broth!"

He took the pannikin of broth from Fergus, sniffed at it critically, and thrust it under my nose.

"Here, smell that, missus. Marrow bones, garlic, caraway seed, and a lump o' pork fat to flavor, all strained careful through muslin, same as some folks bein' poorly to their stomachs can't abide chunks, but chunks you'll not find there, not a one!"

—*Voyager,* chapter 41, "We Set Sail"

Use this pale nectar, full of flavor and body, as the base for lightly colored soups and sauces that will heal a weary body and soothe a tired soul, such as Kale Brose with Bacon (page 65).

Makes about 1 gallon

Ingredients

5 pounds (2.3 kilograms) beef bones, trimmed of fat

2 garlic cloves, halved

1 tablespoon caraway seeds

2 bay leaves

12 whole peppercorns

1 large onion, chopped (see Knife Skills, page 11)

1 medium carrot, chopped

2 celery stalks, chopped

Method

In a stockpot, cover the bones with cold water and bring to a boil over high heat. After the water has boiled rapidly for 2 minutes, drain. Rinse the bones clean with cold water. Return the bones to the stockpot, cover with 1 gallon cold water, plus more, if necessary, to cover the bones by 2 inches, and bring to a boil over high heat.

Meanwhile, make a bouquet garni. Wrap the garlic, caraway seeds, bay leaves, and peppercorns in a square of cheesecloth and tie with string, or enclose the items in a large tea ball.

Reduce the heat to low and skim the surface of the stock with a slotted spoon to remove impurities and fat. Add the onions, carrots, celery, and bouquet garni. Simmer gently for 6 to 8 hours, skimming the surface of the stock occasionally and topping up the water as needed to keep the bones and veggies well covered. Do not stir.

Ladle the finished stock through a strainer lined with several layers of damp cheesecloth, or a clean, damp cotton or linen dishcloth, into a glass or metal container. Gently press on the solids to extract all the liquid.

Cool quickly, refrigerate overnight, and discard the hardened fat from the surface of the cold stock. Store, covered, in the refrigerator up to 5 days, or in the freezer up to 6 weeks.

Notes

- *The richest beef stock is made from knuckle, shank, and long leg bones full of marrow. Use marrow bones cut to 2- or 3-inch lengths for maximum richness and flavor.*
- *To make white chicken stock, replace the beef bones with the same weight of raw chicken bones (necks, backs, and feet are best) and reduce the simmering time to 2 hours.*

VEGETABLE STOCK

"When you make bashed neeps," I said, "be sure to boil the tops along with the turnips. Then save the pot liquor and give it to the children; you take some too—it's good for your milk."

Maisri Buchanan pressed her smallest child to her breast and nodded solemnly, committing my advice to memory. I could not persuade most of the new immigrants either to eat fresh greens or to feed them to their families, but now and then I found opportunity to introduce a bit of vitamin C surreptitiously into their usual diet—which consisted for the most part of oatmeal and venison.

—*Drums of Autumn,* chapter 70, "The Gathering"

If you don't have a lot of time to spend in the kitchen, this is the stock for you. It's done in under an hour, including the *oignon brûlé* (burnt onion) that mimics the rich, amber hue of a brown meat stock. Use in vegetarian soups and stews like Cream of Nontoxic Mushroom Soup (page 69) or as a poaching liquid for vegetables or fish.

This is a delicious, light-tasting vegetable stock made from commonly found, vitamin-packed vegetables and aromatics, as well as a few optional ingredients to boost color and flavor.

Makes about 2 quarts

Ingredients

2 large leeks (white and light-green parts only), cut into 1-inch pieces

1 tablespoon vegetable oil

2 medium carrots, chopped (see Knife Skills, page 11)

2 celery stalks, chopped

4 to 6 fennel stalks, chopped

1 cup mushrooms or mushroom stems, chopped

½ medium onion, cut crosswise, skin on

3 garlic cloves, whole

6 fresh parsley sprigs

2 fresh thyme sprigs

2 bay leaves

6 whole peppercorns

1 whole red chile pepper (optional)

1 2-inch piece dried mushroom, such as porcini, morel, or shiitake (optional)

1 sun-dried tomato (not in oil) (optional)

1 6-inch piece kombu (dried kelp) (optional)

Method

Rinse the chopped leeks thoroughly in a bowl of cold water before scooping them out with a slotted spoon, leaving the silt and sand behind. Shake dry in a clean dish-cloth or salad spinner.

In a large stockpot, heat the oil over medium heat. Add the leeks, carrots, celery, fennel, and mushrooms. Cook gently, stirring occasionally until soft, about 10 minutes. Cover with 2 quarts of cold water, increase the heat to medium-high, and bring to a boil.

Meanwhile, make the *oignon brûlé*, or burnt onion. Heat a small cast-iron pan or grill pan over medium-high heat. Place the onion on the dry pan, cut side down. Cook until blackened, 5 to 7 minutes.

Also make a bouquet garni. Wrap the garlic, parsley, thyme, bay leaves, peppercorns, and chile, dried mushroom, sun-dried tomato, and kombu, if desired (see Notes), in a square of cheesecloth and tie with string, or enclose the items in a large tea ball.

Reduce the heat under the stockpot to low and add the burnt onion and bouquet garni. Simmer for 30 minutes. Ladle the finished stock through a strainer lined with several layers of damp cheesecloth, or a clean, damp cotton or linen dishcloth, into a glass or metal container. Gently press on the solids to extract all the liquid.

Cool quickly and store in the refrigerator up to 1 week, or in the freezer for 6 weeks.

Notes

- *The optional ingredients add color and flavor to your stock. Use none, one, or all.*
- *For a quick lunch or light dinner, cook store-bought frozen wontons or dumplings in stock, season (I like a little soy sauce and chile oil), garnish with chopped scallions, and serve.*

SHORT CRUST PASTRY

A multipurpose pastry crust for sweet or savory fillings that is easy to work with and substantial enough to hold up outside the pan for recipes such as Rolls with Pigeon and Truffles (page 82), yet tender enough to yield easily under your fork as the base for Governor Tryon's Humble Crumble Apple Pie (page 250).

Makes one 12-inch crust or two 8-inch crusts

Ingredients

3 cups all-purpose flour

1 tablespoon sugar

1½ teaspoons kosher salt

1 cup (2 sticks) cold butter

½ cup ice water

1 large egg yolk

1 teaspoon lemon juice or vinegar

Method

BY HAND: Stir together the flour, sugar, and salt in a large bowl. Grate the butter into the flour and work it in with your fingertips until the butter is reduced to pea-size lumps and the flour is the color of cornmeal. Make a well in the bottom of the bowl. Whisk together the ice water, egg yolk, and lemon juice. Pour the liquid mixture into the well and use your fingertips to bring the dough together into a shaggy ball.

IN A FOOD PROCESSOR: Combine the flour, sugar, and salt in a large bowl. Pulse three times to combine. Cut the butter into ½-inch cubes and scatter into the flour. Pulse five or six times, until you have mostly pea-size lumps. Whisk together the ice water, egg yolk, and lemon juice. Add to the bowl and pulse five more times.

Pour the dough and any loose flour from your bowl or food processor onto the counter and knead quickly and lightly into a ball. Divide the dough in half and form into two 1-inch-thick disks. Wrap tightly and refrigerate for at least 30 minutes.

Store in the fridge up to 2 days, or in the freezer up to 1 month.

To roll out, lightly dust the counter with flour. Use even pressure to roll the dough out from the center in all four compass directions, north, south, east, and west. Turn and loosen the dough occasionally as you continue to roll the pastry out into

a circle or square shape that is an even ⅛ inch thick (unless otherwise directed in the recipe).

Cut out shapes as directed, or roll the pastry lightly up onto the rolling pin and transfer to a tart pan or pie plate.

Notes

- *If it's very humid, hold back a couple of tablespoons of water when you first mix the dough. Add more water gradually if needed.*
- *If the dough is chilled for more than 30 minutes, it may have to rest on the counter for a few minutes before it will be soft enough to roll.*
- *The leftover egg white can be whisked with a teaspoon of water and a pinch of salt for use as an egg wash before parbaking. It won't result in quite as golden a crust as a whole-egg wash, but it's a great way to avoid waste.*

BLITZ PUFF PASTRY

The folding of the dough creates dozens of buttery layers, which, when baked, are forced upward by the steam released from the melting butter. The result is a light, flaky pastry that can be used in both sweet and savory treats, such as Warm Almond Pastry with Father Anselm (page 255) and Goat Cheese and Bacon Tarts (page 74).

Makes about 2 pounds (900 grams), or two 12 x 18-inch sheets

Ingredients

3 cups all-purpose flour

1½ teaspoons kosher salt

1¼ cups (2½ sticks) cold unsalted
   butter, cut into ½-inch cubes

½ cup ice water

1 teaspoon lemon juice or vinegar

Method

BY HAND: In a large bowl, mix together the flour and salt. Blend in the butter with a pastry cutter or two forks until all the cubes are well broken up. Make a well in the bottom of the bowl and pour in the ice water and lemon juice. Use your hands to bring the dough together into a rough ball. Work quickly, so the heat of your hands doesn't melt the butter. Add water a tablespoon at a time, as needed, to make a soft, shaggy dough that just stays together—it's better that the dough appear slightly dry than wet and sticky.

IN A STANDING MIXER: In the bowl of a standing mixer fitted with the paddle attachment, mix the flour and salt on low speed. Add the butter and mix on medium-low until the butter just begins to break up, about 1 minute. Add the ice water and lemon juice, and continue to mix on medium-low, adding water a tablespoon at a time, as needed, to make a soft, shaggy dough that just stays together, 60 to 90 seconds—it's better that the dough appear slightly dry than too wet and sticky.

Transfer the dough from your bowl or standing mixer to a lightly floured counter and knead lightly into a smooth ball. Form into a flat rectangle about 1 inch thick, wrap tightly, and refrigerate for at least 30 minutes.

On a lightly floured counter, use even pressure to roll from the center of the dough all the way out to each corner. Turn and loosen the dough occasionally as you continue to roll out the corners to a rectangle measuring approximately 12 x 24 to 30 inches. Fold in thirds lengthwise, like a business letter, to complete one single fold. Use the rolling pin to gently mark an X in the top of the dough to help the layers adhere to one another.

If the dough is still cold and firm, repeat another fold immediately. Wrap and refrigerate for 30 to 60 minutes. If the dough is becoming soft or sticky, cover and return to the fridge before completing the second fold.

Repeat the folding process for a total of four to six single folds, doing up to two single folds back-to-back. Rest and chill the dough for 30 to 60 minutes in between each set. After all the folds have been completed, rest the dough for a minimum of 60 minutes, and up to overnight, before rolling out the final sheet.

Unless you have a long stretch of open counter to roll the dough out in one sheet, cut the dough in half crosswise with a sharp knife and roll out two separate final sheets. On a lightly floured counter, use even pressure to roll from the center of the dough all the way out to each corner. Turn and loosen the dough occasionally as you roll out each half of the dough to a sheet approximately 12 x 18 inches and ⅛ inch thick. If it becomes difficult to roll, cover the pastry with plastic and rest it for 5 minutes in the refrigerator before resuming.

Use as directed in recipes calling for puff pastry.

Notes

- *The lemon juice or vinegar prevents the dough from oxidizing and allows you to keep it in the fridge up to 2 days without developing brown spots.*
- *Finished sheets of pastry can be lightly floured, gently folded, wrapped tightly, and stored in the fridge up to 2 days, or in the freezer up to 1 month.*
- *This recipe is easier than traditional homemade puff pastry, though still 3 to 4 hours' work—but worth the effort—and it wins hands down in a side-by-side taste test against the frozen, store-bought stuff.*

CROWDIE CHEESE

A modern adaptation of Scotland's most ancient cheese. At one time, every crofter in the Highlands made it by souring freshly skimmed milk beside a warm fire, then cooking it gently until it curdled. The whey was drained away, leaving a crumbly, unripened white cheese.

A common currency accepted as rent in the Highlands before Culloden, crowdie is the crud in Mrs. Bug's Gingerbread and Fresh Crud (page 283), as well as being delicious on oatcakes, bannocks, scones, and sandwiches.

Makes about 1 cup

Ingredients

1 quart whole milk

2 tablespoons lemon juice or vinegar

1 teaspoon kosher salt

Method

In a large, nonreactive saucepan (not aluminum) over medium heat, heat the milk. Stir occasionally, scraping along the bottom and sides of the pot to prevent the milk from scorching.

Heat the milk until it simmers and foams, 195°F on an instant-read thermometer, about 20 minutes. Do not allow the milk to boil. Remove the pan from the heat and drizzle in the vinegar. Stir once and leave undisturbed for 5 minutes.

Check that the milk has curdled, meaning that the white curds have separated from the translucent whey. If not, stir in another tablespoon of vinegar and wait another 5 minutes. Once the curds and whey have separated, allow the pot to sit undisturbed for 30 minutes.

Line a colander with four layers of cheesecloth or a clean cotton or linen dishcloth. Gently ladle the curds into the colander and drain until the crowdie is like wet cottage cheese, about 30 minutes. To speed up the draining, use a rubber spatula to gently fold the curds over each other occasionally, but do not press down on the curds.

Gather the corners of cloth together and tie around a sink faucet or a wooden spoon handle set over a tall pot. Hang the cheese for 30 minutes and twist the bag gently once or twice to expel the last of the whey.

Scrape the cheese into a bowl and stir in the salt. Store, covered, in the refrigerator up to 5 days.

Notes

- *Use the cooled whey in place of milk to make Brown Buns at Beauly (page 224) or in smoothies, feed it to the chickens and pigs, or, at the very least, pour it into the compost.*
- *Add more flavor to your crowdie by folding chopped fresh herbs such as basil, dill, or oregano, or aromatics like lemon zest, rosewater, freshly ground pepper . . . shall I go on?*

BASIC SALAD DRESSING

A light, adaptable oil-and-vinegar based dressing that is as at home on iceberg lettuce as it is on the salad of bitter leaves in Pheasant and Greens at Ardsmuir (page 109).

Makes about ½ cup

Ingredients

3 tablespoons extra-virgin olive oil

3 tablespoons vegetable oil

2 tablespoons red wine vinegar

2 teaspoons Dijon mustard

½ teaspoon kosher salt

¼ teaspoon freshly ground pepper

Method

In a small bowl or a jar with a tight-fitting lid, combine all the ingredients and whisk or shake until well combined. Taste, and season if necessary.

Dress your salad sparingly—the greens should just glisten. A soggy salad is no one's cup of tea.

Store in the refrigerator, tightly sealed, up to 1 week.

Notes

- *I prefer to lighten the taste of my dressing by combining olive and vegetable oils. Alone, olive oil is powerful stuff, and it can smother the taste of a delicate salad.*
- *The Dijon mustard acts as an emulsifier to temporarily keep the dressing from separating. Whisk or shake to recombine.*
- *Switch up the vinegar for a different dressing. Balsamic, white wine, champagne, and rice vinegar are some of my favorites. You can also substitute some or all of the vinegar with citrus juice, such as lemon, lime, or orange.*
- *For more flavor, add a few dashes of sesame oil, grated or minced garlic, the zest of a lemon, lime, or orange, or chopped fresh herbs such as dill, basil, or mint. (Note that if you add fresh garlic, it reduces the dressing's shelf life in the fridge to 2 days.)*

Chapter 2

~◡~

BREAKFAST

Mrs. FitzGibbons's Overnight Parritch

Potato Fritters

A Coddled Egg for Duncan

Bacon, Asparagus, and Wild Mushroom Omelette

Mrs. Bug's Cinnamon Toast

Yeasted Buckwheat Pancakes

Young Ian's Sage and Garlic Sausage

Mrs. FitzGibbons's Overnight Parritch

"Himself?" I said. I didn't care for the sound of this. Whoever Himself was, he was likely to ask difficult questions.

"Why, the MacKenzie to be sure. Whoever else?"

Who else indeed? Castle Leoch, I dimly recalled, was in the middle of the clan MacKenzie lands. Plainly the clan chieftain was still the MacKenzie. I began to understand why our little band of horsemen had ridden through the night to reach the castle; this would be a place of impregnable safety to men pursued by the Crown's men. No English officer with a grain of sense would lead his men so deeply into the clan lands. To do so was to risk death by ambush at the first clump of trees. And only a good-sized army would come as far as the castle gates. I was trying to remember whether in fact the English army ever had come so far, when I suddenly realized that the eventual fate of the castle was much less relevant than my immediate future.

I had no appetite for the bannocks and parritch that Mrs. FitzGibbons had brought for my breakfast, but crumbled a bit and pretended to eat, in order to gain some time for thought. By the time Mrs. Fitz came back to conduct me to the MacKenzie, I had cobbled together a rough plan.

—*Outlander,* chapter 5, "The MacKenzie"

Traditionally made from oatmeal (see page 5), and stirred with a spurtle (clockwise, to keep the devil away), parritch, or porridge, evolved from pottage, a thick vegetable and grain stew that served as the mainstay of the European diet until the seventeenth century.

This less-dense version is made with steel-cut or rolled oats (see Note). Start it just before you go to bed, and finish it in the morning for an easy, nutritious, and creamily delicious breakfast in minutes.

Serves 4 to 6 (makes 3 cups)

Ingredients

1 cup steel-cut oats

¼ teaspoon kosher salt

1½ cups whole milk

2 teaspoons butter

½ teaspoon cinnamon

Method

Just before you go to bed, bring 1 cup of water to a boil in a covered pot. Stir in the oats and salt, cover the pot, turn off the heat, and leave it overnight.

In the morning, add the milk and butter to the pot and bring to a boil over medium heat. Reduce flame to medium-low and simmer gently until tender, stirring occasionally, 15 to 20 minutes.

Stir in the cinnamon and serve hot, topped with savory butter and salt or, for the sweet-toothed, honey or brown sugar, and/or fresh or dried fruit.

Note

• *To substitute rolled oats, reduce the milk to 1 cup and the cooking time to 7 to 10 minutes.*

POTATO FRITTERS

"Abel, a charaid!" Jamie had paused to greet the last of the men from Drunkard's Creek. "Will ye ha' eaten yet the day?"

MacLennan had not brought his wife to the Gathering, and thus ate where luck took him. The crowd was dispersing around us, but he stood stolidly in place, holding the ends of a red flannel handkerchief pulled over his balding head against the spatter of rain. Probably hoping to cadge an invitation to breakfast, I thought cynically.

I eyed his stocky form, mentally estimating his possible consumption of eggs, parritch, and toasted bread against the dwindling supplies in our hampers. Not that simple shortage of food would stop any Highlander from offering hospitality—certainly not Jamie, who was inviting MacLennan to join us, even as I mentally divided eighteen eggs by nine people instead of eight. Not fried, then; made into fritters with grated potatoes, and I'd best borrow more coffee from Jocasta's campsite on the way up the mountain.

We turned to go, and Jamie's hand slid suddenly downward over my backside. I made an undignified sound, and Abel MacLennan turned round to gawk at me. I smiled brightly at him, resisting the urge to kick Jamie again, less discreetly.

—*The Fiery Cross,* chapter 1, "Happy the Bride the Sun Shines On"

Crisp and golden on the outside, soft and savory in the middle. Add a fruit salad on the side for a balanced and filling breakfast in under 30 minutes. Sprinkle the fruit salad with Crowdie Cheese (page 31) for a no-fuss, dressed-up Sunday brunch.

Serves 4 to 6

Ingredients

2 pounds (900 grams or 2 to 3 medium) russet potatoes

1 medium onion, halved

6 tablespoons all-purpose flour

3 large eggs

1½ teaspoons kosher salt

½ teaspoon freshly ground pepper

Vegetable oil

Method

Move a rack to the middle rung and heat the oven to 250°F.

Grate the potatoes and onion halves into a large bowl. Mix in the flour, eggs, salt, and pepper and stir well to combine.

Heat ½ inch of vegetable oil in a large, heavy pan over medium-high flame. When the oil is hot and shimmering, add rounded tablespoons of potato batter, being sure not to overcrowd the pan. Fry until the bottoms are golden, about 3 minutes, and flip. When golden on the second side, drain on a paper towel–lined plate, and keep warm in the oven while you repeat with the remaining batter.

Serve hot, with your choice of sour cream, applesauce, ketchup, or my favorite, plain, with another sprinkle of salt and pepper.

Note

- *Mix about a link's worth of raw sausage, such as Young Ian's Sage and Garlic Sausage (page 52), into the mix for a carnivore-suitable breakfast without the expense of a lot of meat, or the hassle of extra pans to wash up.*

A Coddled Egg for Duncan

"Phaedre! Have you seen Mr. Innes this morning?" Jocasta's body servant was flying past, her arms full of tablecloths, but came abruptly to a halt at my call.

"Ain't seen Mister Duncan since breakfast, ma'am," she said, with a shake of her neatly capped head.

"How did he seem then? Did he eat well?" Breakfast was an ongoing affair of several hours, the resident guests serving themselves from the sideboard and eating as they chose. It was more likely nerves than food poisoning that was troubling Duncan's bowels, but some of the sausage I had seen on the sideboard struck me as highly suspect.

"No, ma'am, nary a bite." Phaedre's smooth brow puckered; she was fond of Duncan. "Cook tried to tempt him with a nice coddled egg, but he just shook his head and looked peaked. He did take a cup of rum punch, though," she said, seeming somewhat cheered at the thought.

—*The Fiery Cross*, chapter 39, "In Cupid's Grove"

Though Duncan's, like all other eggs in the eighteenth century, was coddled in the shell, one of my favorite specialized kitchen accessories is the egg coddler, a lidded porcelain or glass pot, first made in England at the end of the nineteenth century.

These creamy, dreamy eggs just beg for a stack of toast soldiers alongside for dipping.

Serves 1

Ingredients

½ teaspoon butter

1 or 2 large eggs

2 to 3 teaspoons flavorings (see Notes)

Kosher salt and freshly ground pepper to taste

Method

Bring a saucepan of water to a low boil. Meanwhile, brush the inside of a single or double egg coddler with butter and crack in the egg(s). Add your chosen flavorings and season with salt and pepper. Screw the lid on the coddler fingertight, and place in the pan of gently boiling water. The water should cover the lid, unless otherwise directed in the instructions for your coddler.

Cover and cook in gently boiling water, 5 to 8 minutes for soft eggs with milky inner whites and warm yolks, or 9 to 12 minutes for medium, with firm outer and inner whites and semi-liquid yolks. A double coddler, with 2 eggs, will take longer, about 10 minutes for soft and up to 15 minutes for medium.

Porcelain and glass coddlers cook and hold heat differently, so timings will vary. Porcelain heats up slowly, but holds that heat much longer outside the water than glass. Eggs in porcelain will continue to cook even after removed from the water, while glass, which heats very quickly, will start to cool immediately after removal from the pot.

Notes

- *Some of my favorite flavor combinations include scallions and shredded Parmesan, chopped tomato and smoked Gruyère, crumbled bacon and cubed cheddar, capers and chopped dill, sautéed mushrooms and tarragon.*
- *Less is more—don't overload your coddler and drown out the eggs with extras—a tablespoon of combined flavorings is all you need.*
- *Small mason jars with lids make excellent stand-ins for coddlers.*

Bacon, Asparagus, and Wild Mushroom Omelette

I abandoned Ian and Rollo to the juggernaut of Mrs. Bug's benevolence—let Ian try telling her he didn't want bread and milk—and sat down to my own belated supper: a hot, fresh omelette, featuring not only cheese, but bits of salty bacon, asparagus, and wild mushroom, flavored with spring onions.
—*A Breath of Snow and Ashes,* chapter 5, "The Shadows Which Fire Throws"

I chose shiitakes for year-round availability, but if you've bought some chanterelles or porcini for Cream of Nontoxic Mushroom Soup (page 69), set a few aside and make this for a mouthwatering, stick-to-your-ribs breakfast or quick, satisfying dinner.

Serves 1

Ingredients

2 slices thick-cut bacon

3 asparagus stalks

6 shiitake mushrooms

3 large eggs

Pinch of kosher salt

1 tablespoon butter

½ ounce (15 grams) cheddar cheese, shredded (about 2 tablespoons)

1 scallion, white and green parts, sliced thin

Freshly ground pepper to taste

Method

Cut the bacon crosswise into ¼-inch-thick pieces. Snap the woody ends off the asparagus and slice into 1-inch pieces. Discard the stems from the shiitakes and cut the caps in half.

In a small frying pan, fry the bacon over medium heat until crisp. Remove with a slotted spoon and drain on a paper towel. Pour away all but 2 teaspoons of the bacon fat and fry the asparagus and the mushrooms in the same pan until tender, about 3 minutes. Add the bacon, stir, and keep warm over low heat.

Lightly whisk the eggs and salt together with a fork. Melt the butter in a 7- or 8-inch cast-iron or nonstick sauté pan over medium heat. Swirl the pan to coat the bottom with butter, then add the eggs. Use a spatula to draw the edges of the eggs toward the center of the pan, scrambling them lightly. Shake and tilt the pan to keep the eggs in an even layer.

After about 45 seconds, when the edges of the egg just begin to set, sprinkle the cheese over one half of the eggs. Top the cheese with the bacon, asparagus, mushrooms, scallion, and pepper. Run the spatula around the edge of the pan to loosen. When the eggs are set but still moist on top, about 1 more minute, fold the plain half of the omelette over the filling and slide onto a plate.

Serve immediately with a toasted slice of Honey-Buttermilk Oat Bread (page 232).

Notes

- *A classic French omelette is moist in the middle and very lightly colored on the bottom.*
- *Add another egg and a little more filling, and you have an omelette that's the perfect size for two people with smaller appetites to share.*
- *Shiitake stems can be frozen, and make an umami-rich addition to Vegetable Stock (page 24).*

MRS. BUG'S CINNAMON TOAST

"Do you think he'll come?" Breakfast had been eaten, and no sign yet of Thomas Christie. After a night of broken sleep, in which I dreamed repeatedly of ether masks and surgical disasters, I wasn't sure whether I wanted him to come or not.

"Aye, he'll come." Jamie was reading the *North Carolina Gazette*, four months out of date, while munching the last of Mrs. Bug's cinnamon toast. "Look, they've printed a letter from the Governor to Lord Dartmouth, saying what an unruly lot of seditious, conniving thieving bastards we all are, and asking General Gage to send him cannon to threaten us back into good behavior. I wonder if MacDonald knows that's public knowledge?"

"Did they really?" I said absently. I rose, and picked up the ether mask I had been staring at all through breakfast. "Well, if he does come, I suppose I'd best be ready."

—*A Breath of Snow and Ashes,* chapter 23, "Anesthesia"

Of course, you could just sprinkle some sugar and cinnamon on a piece of buttered toast, but it really tastes better this way. Mrs. Bug would have a had a crock of this on the kitchen table, to feed Himself's cravings throughout the day, just as my Danish grandmother kept hers on hand to feed mine.

Makes ½ cup

Ingredients

½ cup (1 stick) softened butter

¼ cup light or dark brown sugar,
    lightly packed

2 to 3 teaspoons cinnamon

Method

In a small bowl, using a fork, mash together the butter, brown sugar, and cinnamon. Keep the mixture covered on the counter up to a week, or in the fridge for 2 to 3 weeks. It can be kept in the freezer indefinitely.

Spread on hot toast or spoon atop a bowl of Mrs. FitzGibbons's Overnight Parritch (page 36).

Note

• *Try adding a pinch of freshly ground cardamom to your butter. A member of the ginger family, it combines well with cinnamon. Common in Scandinavian baking, the key with cardamom is to use a light hand—a pinch was all my grandmother ever used.*

YEASTED BUCKWHEAT PANCAKES

"That little bitch! I want to just grab her and choke the truth out of her!" Her hand closed convulsively on the neck of the syrup bottle, and he reached to take it from her before she should break it.

"I understand the impulse," he said, "but on the whole—better not."

She glared at him, but relinquished the bottle. "Can't you do something?" she said.

He'd been asking himself that since he'd heard the news of Malva's accusation.

"I don't know," he said. "But I thought I'd go and talk to the Christies, at least. And if I can get Malva alone, I will."

Thinking of his last tête-à-tête with Malva Christie, though, he had an uneasy feeling that she wouldn't be easily shaken from her story.

Brianna sat down, scowling at her plate of buckwheat cakes, and began slathering them with butter. Her fury was beginning to give way to rational thought; he could see ideas darting behind her eyes.

—*A Breath of Snow and Ashes,* chapter 81, "Benefit of the Doubt"

Despite its name, buckwheat is not a grain but a plant related to rhubarb, domesticated thousands of years ago across Europe and Asia. It was one of the first crops brought to North America by Europeans, because it does well in poor, unimproved soil, but its cultivation fell sharply in the twentieth century, as farmers increasingly planted subsidized wheat and corn crops.

The seeds of the buckwheat plant are dried and ground into a wheatlike but gluten-free flour with a pleasant, earthy flavor that makes for much more interesting breakfast fodder than your average twenty-first-century pancakes made with simply white flour.

Makes twelve 4- to 5-inch pancakes

Ingredients

1½ cups whole milk

2 tablespoons butter

1 cup buckwheat flour

½ cup all-purpose flour

2 tablespoons light brown sugar,
    lightly packed

¾ teaspoon instant yeast

½ teaspoon kosher salt

1 large egg, lightly beaten

Method

In a small saucepan, warm the milk and butter gently over medium-low heat until the butter just melts.

In a large bowl, stir together the buckwheat flour, all-purpose flour, sugar, yeast, and salt. Add the warm milk and egg to the dry ingredients and whisk until well combined into a thinnish batter. Scrape down the bowl, cover with a plate or plastic wrap, and set aside in a warm place until bubbling and thickened, about an hour.

Heat an ungreased griddle or cast-iron pan over medium heat and ladle the batter into small circles that spread to 4 or 5 inches. Cook until the top surface is covered with broken bubbles, about 2 minutes. Flip and cook until golden on both sides and cooked through, 1 to 2 minutes.

Keep warm in a low oven and serve with plenty of butter and syrup, jam, or honey.

Notes

- *Mix up the ratio between the all-purpose flour and the buckwheat to find the perfect combination for your family. The more all-purpose flour, the lighter and fluffier the pancakes will be.*
- *My favorite place in my kitchen to keep things warm is the oven, with just the interior light on.*
- *You can also make the batter the night before. Cover and refrigerate overnight. Remove the bowl from the fridge about 30 minutes before cooking. Thin the batter with a bit of milk if necessary.*

Young Ian's Sage and Garlic Sausage

"Well d'ye see, Auntie," Ian said carefully, "we do mean to question the fellow."

"And we will have answers," Fergus said, eyes on the spoon with which he was stirring his coffee.

"And when Uncle Jamie is satisfied that he has told us what he can . . ."

Ian had laid his newly sharpened knife on the table beside his plate. He picked it up, and thoughtfully drew it down the length of a cold sausage, which promptly split open, with an aromatic burst of sage and garlic. He looked up then, and met my eyes directly. And I realized that while I might still be me—Ian was no longer the boy he used to be. Not at all.

—*A Breath of Snow and Ashes,* chapter 30, "The Captive"

This caseless breakfast sausage comes together in a snap and is easy to put your signature on, with different ground meats, fillers, and seasonings.

Cold sausage sandwiches on Raisin Muffins (page 241) make a hearty Fraser's Ridge lunch when served alongside bowls of Kale Brose with Bacon (page 65).

Makes about 1 pound

Ingredients

1 pound (450 grams) ground pork

½ cup filler, such as cornmeal, ground oats, breadcrumbs, etc.

3 garlic cloves, grated or minced

1 tablespoon chopped fresh sage or 1 teaspoon dried

1½ teaspoons kosher salt

½ teaspoon freshly ground pepper

½ teaspoon mustard powder

Method

Combine all the ingredients in a large bowl. Mix well with your hands until the ingredients are well distributed and the meat is a smooth consistency.

In a frying pan over medium heat, first cook a small sausage patty to taste, and adjust seasonings as required. Form into ½-inch-thick patties to cook immediately. Alternatively, you can form the mixture into a long sausage about 2 inches in diameter, wrap tightly in plastic, and turn the ends of the wrap in opposite directions until tight and firm, taping the ends to secure if necessary. Refrigerate for at least 30 minutes before slicing into ½-inch-thick slices.

Heat a frying pan over medium heat and fry slices until golden on both sides and cooked through, 3 to 5 minutes per side. Serve hot or cold.

Keep raw sausage in the fridge for 3 days or in the freezer up to 1 month. Refrigerate cooked sausage up to 5 days.

Notes

- *Ground almonds make a tasty, protein-packed, and gluten-free filler.*
- *To chop the sage, stack the leaves in an even pile, then roll as you would a cigar. Fold the cigar in half and cut the thinnest slivers you can with a sharp knife.*
- *It takes just a little more time to make a triple (or bigger) batch and freeze in 1-pound batches. Use in Bangers and Mash with Slow-Cooked Onion Gravy (page 132), Scotch Eggs (page 129), or make a lamb version for Conspirators' Cassoulet (page 122).*

Chapter 3

SOUPS

Geillis's Cullen Skink

Cock-a-Leekie

Drunken Mock-Turtle Soup

Kale Brose with Bacon

Marsali's Beef (*Buffalo*) Tea

Cream of Nontoxic Mushroom Soup

GEILLIS'S CULLEN SKINK

"Oh, Arthur knew," she said. "He wouldna admit it, to be sure—not even to himself. But he knew. We'd sit across the board from each other at supper, and I'd ask, 'Will ye have a bit more o' the cullen skink, my dear?' or 'A sup of ale, my own?' And him watching me, with those eyes like boiled eggs, and he'd say no, he didna feel himself with an appetite just then. And he'd push his plate back, and later I'd hear him in the kitchen, secret-like, gobbling his food standing by the hutch, thinking himself safe, because he ate no food that came from my hand."

—Outlander, chapter 25, "Thou Shalt Not Suffer a Witch to Live"

This luscious smoked-fish soup is named for its hometown of Cullen in northeastern Scotland, on the shores of the Moray Firth. The word "skink" comes from the German *schinke,* meaning shin. While the textbook skink is a soup made from a shin of beef, Highland fisherfolk adapted the recipe to use the regional ingredients they had in plenty, such as smoked haddock and leeks.

More substantial than a soup but not as thick as a chowder, serve with a crusty loaf of bread or Mrs. Bug's Buttermilk Drop Biscuits (page 246) for a filling lunch. Add a salad to that, and you've got dinner.

Serves 6

Ingredients

1 pound (450 grams) finnan haddie (see Note) or any skinless, cold-smoked white fish such as haddock, cod, or halibut

1 bay leaf

2 medium leeks (white parts only), sliced thin

2 tablespoons butter

Kosher salt and freshly ground pepper

2 medium potatoes, peeled and diced (see Knife Skills, page 11)

3 cups whole milk

3 scallions (white and light-green parts only), sliced thin on the diagonal

Method

In a medium saucepan, cover the fish (cut to fit if necessary) and the bay leaf with 3 cups cold water. Bring to a low boil over medium heat and cook gently until just tender, about 5 minutes. Remove the bay leaf and fish to a plate. Strain the cooking liquid and reserve it for later, along with the bay leaf. Debone the fish, flake with a fork, and set aside.

Rinse the chopped leeks thoroughly in a bowl of cold water. Scoop them out with a slotted spoon or your hands, leaving the silt and sand behind. Shake dry in a clean dishcloth or salad spinner.

In a saucepan, melt the butter over medium heat. Add the leeks and a pinch of salt and pepper. Cook, stirring occasionally, until softened, 3 to 4 minutes. Add the potatoes, as well as the reserved cooking liquid and bay leaf. Simmer over medium-low heat until the potatoes are tender, 10 to 15 minutes.

Remove about 1 cup of the leek and potato mixture with a slotted spoon and set aside. Discard the bay leaf.

Add the milk and half of the fish to the pot. Heat over medium flame until hot, then puree with an immersion blender or countertop blender. Alternatively, you can mash the solids with the back of a fork to puree. Keep warm, but do not allow to boil.

Season to taste and serve, dividing reserved fish and leek and potato mixture among bowls, garnished with the scallions.

Keep leftovers in the fridge up to 3 days. Do not freeze.

Note

- *Although any cold-smoked white fish will make a delicious bowl of soup, an authentic cullen skink requires finnan haddie, which is haddock caught off the Moray Firth and lightly cold-smoked using green wood and peat. Order it from a local specialty fish shop or online.*

COCK-A-LEEKIE

"We'll be having supper here by the field," he told them. "Let's be fetching a bit of wood for a fire, Tom and Willie, and Mrs. Willie, if ye'd be so kind as to bring your big kettle? Aye, that's good, one of the men will help ye to bring it down. You, Kincaid—" He turned to one of the younger men, and waved off in the direction of the small cluster of cottages under the trees. "Go and tell everyone—it's potatoes for supper!"

And so, with the assistance of Jenny, ten pails of milk from the dairy shed, three chickens caught from the coop, and four dozen large leeks from the kailyard, I presided over the preparation of cock-a-leekie soup and roasted potatoes for the laird and tenants of Lallybroch.

—*Dragonfly in Amber*, chapter 32, "Field of Dreams"

Quintessentially Scottish, though most likely medieval French in origin, cock-a-leekie is a popular soup served throughout the winter in Scotland, and a common addition to the table on St. Andrew's Day (November 30), Hogmanay (December 31), and Burns Night (January 25).

The ingredients and instructions below, including the prunes, come almost straight from a mid-eighteenth-century cookbook, and are proof that when simple dishes with a few ingredients are prepared well, they can outshine the most complex *nouvelle cuisine*.

Serves 6 or more

Ingredients

1 (3- to 4-pound or 1.3 to 1.8 kilograms) whole chicken

4 large leeks (white and light-green parts only), cut into 1-inch pieces

6 fresh parsley sprigs

6 whole peppercorns

2 whole cloves

6 whole prunes

2 teaspoons kosher salt, plus additional

½ teaspoon freshly ground pepper (see Notes)

Method

Cut the wings from the chicken and refrigerate or freeze for another purpose. Tie the legs together so that the chicken holds its shape in the pot. In a stockpot, cover the chicken with up to 3 quarts of cold water and bring to a boil on high heat.

Rinse the chopped leeks thoroughly in a bowl of cold water and then scoop them out with your hands or a slotted spoon, leaving the silt and sand behind. Shake dry in a clean dishcloth or salad spinner.

Also make a bouquet garni. Wrap the parsley, peppercorns, and cloves in a square of cheesecloth and tie with string, or enclose the items in a large tea ball.

Once the chicken has come to a boil, reduce to a simmer over medium-low heat. Skim the surface of the stock with a slotted spoon to remove impurities and fat. Add half of the leeks and the bouquet garni and continue to cook, uncovered, at a slow simmer, for 2 hours. Do not stir.

Remove the chicken from the pot to cool on a plate. Discard the bouquet garni. Skim the surface of the soup before adding the remaining leeks, prunes, salt, and pepper to the pot. Simmer until the leeks and prunes are tender, 30 to 45 minutes. Shred the leg and thigh meat and add to the pot 5 minutes before serving. Reserve the breast meat for another purpose (see Notes).

Season to taste and serve with a fresh loaf of Brown Buns at Beauly (page 224). Store leftovers in the fridge up to 3 days.

Notes

- *Early recipes call for Jamaican long pepper, a spicier, more aromatic cousin of our common peppercorn. That, or other varieties of long pepper, which can be found in specialty shops or online, will add an extra layer of depth to this simple dish.*
- *Make chicken salad from the breast meat and serve it with the soup for a delicious dinner. Alternatively, it makes great chicken fried rice.*
- *Save the bones and boil them in more cold water for an hour to make a* remouillage, *a weaker, second stock that is used to make soups and sauces. Our dog slurps it up with his dry dog food for dinner.*

DRUNKEN MOCK-TURTLE SOUP

"Bolt the door? What d'ye think I'm going to do? Do I look the sort of man would take advantage of a woman who's not only wounded and boiling wi' fever, but drunk as well?" he demanded. He stood up, nonetheless.

"I am not drunk," I said indignantly. "You can't get drunk on turtle soup!" Nonetheless, I was conscious that the glowing warmth in my stomach seemed to have migrated somewhat lower, taking up residence between my thighs, and there was undeniably a slight lightness of head not strictly attributable to fever.

"You can if ye've been drinking turtle soup as made by Aloysius O'Shaughnessy Murphy," he said. "By the smell of it, he's put at least a full bottle o' the sherry in it. A verra intemperate race, the Irish."

—*Voyager*, chapter 56, "Turtle Soup"

Once a popular English delicacy enjoyed only by the wealthy, early versions of turtle soup were commonly made with sea turtles, such as the hawksbill, pulled aboard by the crew of the *Artemis*. New Orleans and Philadelphia both gave birth to their own regional turtle soup recipes that were as iconic in the eighteenth and nineteenth centuries as gumbo and cheese steak are today.

This original version of mock-turtle soup, first created in the mid-eighteenth century by the English as a cheaper imitation accessible to the masses, uses meaty oxtail, a mixture of traditional turtle soup ingredients, and a few modern secrets to a make a rich, dark, and substantial dish that is the perfect showcase first course for your next Outlandish gathering.

Serves 6 or more

Ingredients

3 pounds (1.3 kilograms) lean oxtail, cut into 2-inch lengths

1 tablespoon kosher salt, plus additional

1 teaspoon freshly ground pepper, plus additional

4 bay leaves

4 fresh thyme sprigs

6 whole allspice berries (optional)

12 whole cloves

1 tablespoon butter

1 tablespoon olive oil

1 bottle (750 ml) dry sherry

1 small onion, whole

2 quarts Brown Chicken or Beef Stock
  (page 20)

1 large onion, chopped (see Knife Skills,
  page 11)

4 medium celery stalks, chopped

1 large carrot, chopped

1 medium green pepper, chopped

1 garlic head, cloves peeled and
  quartered

¼ cup vegetable oil

⅓ cup flour

2 tablespoons Vietnamese or
  Thai fish sauce

3 tablespoons cornstarch or
  tapioca starch

6 medium Roma tomatoes, cored,
  seeded, and diced

2 tablespoons lemon juice

¼ teaspoon cayenne pepper

½ teaspoon freshly grated nutmeg

4 large hard-boiled eggs, chopped

Scallions (white and light-green parts
  only), sliced thin

Method

Season the oxtail pieces with salt and pepper.

Make a bouquet garni. Wrap the bay leaves, thyme, allspice, and (if desired) cloves into a square of cheesecloth and tie with string, or enclose the items in a large tea ball.

In a large frying pan over medium-high heat, bring the butter and olive oil to a bubble but don't let it darken. Brown the oxtail pieces on both sides in batches, 4 to 5 minutes per side. Remove the meat from the pot and discard the fat.

Deglaze the pan with ½ cup of sherry, scraping up the brown bits from the bottom of the pan. Boil 30 seconds, then add the oxtail, bouquet garni, whole onion, and stock. Bring to a boil over high flame, reduce the heat and simmer, without stirring, but skimming the surface of fat and scum occasionally, until the meat is tender, 3 hours.

Strain the stock, discarding the onion and bouquet garni. You should have about 6 cups of stock. Set the oxtail pieces on a plate until cool enough to handle, and shred the meat while still warm, discarding the fat and gristle.

Combine the onion, celery, carrot, green peppers, and garlic in a food processor and pulse 6 to 8 times, until finely chopped but not mush. If you don't have a food processor, mince the vegetables as finely as possible.

Wash the stockpot and return to medium flame. Heat the vegetable oil until it shimmers and gradually add the flour, stirring constantly to form a smooth paste.

Continue to stir, scraping the bottom and the corners of the pot regularly to avoid burning the flour, until the roux is deep golden-brown, 10 to 15 minutes.

Immediately add the vegetable mixture and cook until tender, about 5 minutes, stirring constantly. Increase flame to medium-high, deglaze the pan with ½ cup of sherry, and boil for 30 seconds. Add the strained stock, shredded meat, and fish sauce, bring to a boil over high, then reduce the heat and simmer for 30 minutes, stirring occasionally.

Stir the cornstarch into 1 cup of sherry and add to the soup, stirring to combine. Add the tomatoes, lemon juice, cayenne pepper, and nutmeg and simmer over medium heat until slightly thickened, 5 to 7 more minutes.

To serve, garnish with the chopped egg and scallions. Pass the remaining sherry at the table for your guests to add to their bowls as desired.

Keep leftovers in the fridge up to 3 days.

Notes

- *Make things easier for yourself and divide the labor over two days; make the oxtail broth in advance, then finish the soup the day you plan to serve it.*
- *Those oxtail bones still have life in them! After you've stripped them of their meat, cool and refrigerate or freeze for later use in another, weaker but still nutritious, stock.*
- *The roux should darken evenly, with the occasional dark-brown speck in the mixture. Black specks mean the flour is burned and the roux is garbage. Begin again at lower heat.*
- *The fish sauce deepens the flavor of the oxtail broth but won't make it taste fishy—it's an umami thing—trust me.*

KALE BROSE WITH BACON

To distract myself from the cold trickles running down my neck, I began a mental inventory of the pantry. What could I make for dinner, once I arrived?

Something quick, I thought, shivering, and something hot. Stew would take too long; so would soup. If there was squirrel or rabbit, we might have it fried, rolled in egg and cornmeal batter. Or if not that, perhaps brose with a little bacon for flavoring, and a couple of scrambled eggs with green onions.

—*Drums of Autumn*, chapter 23, "The Skull Beneath the Skin"

Brose is a fast and filling parcooked porridge. For hundreds of years it was made by covering grain, such as oat or barley meal, with boiling water and allowing it to stand for a short time before being consumed. *Kail* brose used the nutrient-rich liquor in which fatty salt-beef and greens had been boiled instead of plain water.

This twenty-first-century version adds Claire's bacon and uses beef or chicken stock to make a hearty and nutritious soup that comes together in under 30 minutes. Serve with Pumpkin Seed and Herb Oatcakes (page 219) for a modern lunch with ancient roots in the Highlands.

Serves 4 to 6

Ingredients

4 slices thick-cut bacon, cut crosswise in ¼-inch strips

½ to ¾ cup coarsely ground rolled oats (see Grinding Grains, Nuts, and Seeds, page 10)

2 quarts White Beef or Chicken Stock (page 22)

1 large bunch kale, stemmed and shredded

Kosher salt and freshly ground pepper to taste

Method

In a large saucepan, crisp the bacon over medium heat. When browned, pour off all but 1 teaspoon of fat, leaving the bacon in the pan. Add the oats and stir for 1 minute to toast. Add the stock, increase the flame to high, and bring to a boil. Lower the heat and simmer 5 minutes. Add the kale and simmer until tender, 10 more minutes.

Season with salt and pepper and serve.

Store leftovers in the fridge up to 5 days.

Notes

- *The more oats you use, the thicker your brose will be.*
- *Omit the bacon and switch to Vegetable Stock (page 24) to make this soup vegan.*
- *Switch it up and substitute coarsely ground barley for the oats.*

MARSALI'S BEEF *(Buffalo)* TEA

"How is it, man?" he said quietly.

Jamie moved his head on the pillow, dismissive of discomfort. "I'll do."

"That's good." To my surprise, Roger grasped Jamie's shoulder in a brief gesture of comfort. I'd never seen him do that before, and once more I wondered just what had passed between them on the mountain.

"Marsali's bringing up some beef tea—or rather, buffalo tea—for him," Roger said, frowning slightly as he looked at me. "Maybe you'd best be having some, too."

"Good idea," I said. I closed my eyes briefly and took a deep breath.

Only when I sat down did I realize that I had been on my feet since the early morning. Pain outlined every bone in my feet and legs, and I could feel the ache where I had broken my left tibia, a few years before. Duty called, though.

"Well, time and tide wait for no maggot," I said, struggling back to my feet. "Best get on with it."

—*The Fiery Cross,* chapter 92, "I Get By with a Little Help from My Friends"

A common eighteenth- and nineteenth-century restorative, there are as many recipes for beef tea as there are old wives' tales claiming instant rejuvenation from just one cup.

In this version, beef is steeped low and slow in a bain-marie, or hot-water bath. The result is what the French call *l'essence de boeuf,* or beef essence—concentrated and distilled liquid beef.

Makes about 1 cup

Ingredients

1 pound (450 grams) bottom round steak, about 1 inch thick

2 fresh thyme sprigs (optional)

Salt to taste

Method

Roll the steak around the thyme sprigs (if using) and place in a pint-size jar with a lid. Add ½ cup cold water and screw the lid on fingertight.

Roll up a 12-inch square piece of aluminum foil into a tight cigar. Twist into a ring just slightly smaller than the diameter of your jar, wrapping the ends around each other to secure.

Arrange the jar in a tall saucepan or stockpot on top of the aluminum ring so that the bottom of the jar does not touch the bottom of the pan. Add enough cold water to the pot to come up to about 2 inches below the top of the jar.

Bring the water to a simmer over medium heat. Reduce flame to medium-low, cover the pot, and slowly steep the meat for 2 to 4 hours. Strain, pressing firmly on the meat to extract all the liquid. Season with salt.

Serve hot or cold.

Store in the refrigerator up to 3 days.

Notes

- *If you don't have a pot and lid tall enough to cover your jar, create an aluminum foil tent to keep the heat in.*
- *Traditional recipes say to toss the beef, as all its nourishment has been steeped away, but it shreds beautifully, and with added seasonings, it makes a tasty filling instead of cheese for Diana Gabaldon's Cheese Enchiladas (page 184).*

CREAM OF NONTOXIC MUSHROOM SOUP

"Girl Scout handbook," Brianna said. She glanced at the men, but no one was near enough to hear. Her mouth twitched, and she looked away from the body, holding out her open hand. *"Never eat any strange mushroom,"* she quoted. *"There are many poisonous varieties, and distinguishing one from another is a job for an expert.* Roger found these, growing in a ring by that log over there."

Moist, fleshy caps, a pale brown with white warty spots, the open gills and slender stems so pale as to look almost phosphorescent in the spruce shadows. They had a pleasant, earthy look to them that belied their deadliness.

"Panther toadstools," I said, half to myself, and picked one gingerly from her palm. *"Agaricus pantherinus*—or that's what they will be called, once somebody gets round to naming them properly. *Pantherinus*, because they kill so swiftly—like a striking cat."

I could see the gooseflesh ripple on Brianna's forearm, raising the soft, red-gold hairs. She tilted her hand and spilled the rest of the deadly fungus on the ground.

—*A Breath of Snow and Ashes,* chapter 2, "Dutch Cabin"

A decadent adaptation of a classic cream soup from Auguste Escoffier, an important chef, restaurateur, and food writer who greatly influenced the development of modern French cuisine in the late nineteenth and early twentieth centuries.

Instead of a roux, this recipe uses a gluten-free *liaison* of egg yolks and cream to thicken the soup slightly just before serving.

Serves 6

Ingredients

2 tablespoons butter

2 tablespoons olive oil

1 pound (450 grams) fresh wild mushrooms, such as chanterelles, morels, or porcini, diced (see Knife Skills, page 11)

2 large shallots, diced

1 medium celery stalk, diced

1 garlic clove, grated or minced

1 teaspoon kosher salt, plus additional

½ teaspoon ground white pepper, plus additional

¼ cup brandy

4 cups Vegetable Stock (page 24)

½ cup whipping cream

2 large egg yolks

Method

Heat the butter and oil in a large saucepan over medium flame. When bubbling, add the mushrooms, shallots, celery, garlic, salt, and pepper. Cook, stirring occasionally, until the mushrooms are soft and their water has evaporated, 8 to 12 minutes.

Deglaze with the brandy and reduce until almost dry, about 3 minutes. Puree in a food processor until smooth. Return to the pan, add the stock, and bring to a boil over medium-high flame. Reduce the heat and simmer 30 minutes.

Gently beat the cream and yolks together in a medium bowl. Stir in a ladle of mushroom soup to temper the yolks, then pour everything back into the pot and heat gently. Do not allow to boil. Adjust seasonings if necessary.

Serve with Bannocks at Carfax Close (page 230) spread with butter and cheese. Store leftovers in the fridge up to 5 days. Do not freeze.

Notes

- *Portobello mushrooms are my favorite substitute outside the wild-mushroom seasons of spring and fall. Remove the stems from the portobellos and use a spoon to scrape away and discard the gills to avoid a dark gray, unappetizing-looking soup.*
- *No food processor? Use an immersion blender to puree the soup after you've added the stock but before you add the liaison.*
- *Freeze this soup prior to adding the yolks and cream.*

Chapter 4

APPETIZERS

Goat Cheese and Bacon Tarts

Murtagh's Gift to Ellen *(Puff Pastry Boar Tusks)*

Cheese Savories *(Gougères)*

Rolls with Pigeon and Truffles

Mr. Willoughby's Coral Knob

Beer-Battered Corn Fritters

Mushroom Pasties

GOAT CHEESE AND BACON TARTS

It was a savoury made of goat's meat and bacon, and he saw Fergus's prominent Adam's apple bob in the slender throat at the smell of it. He knew they saved the best of the food for him; it didn't take much looking at the pinched faces across the table. When he came, he brought what meat he could, snared rabbits or grouse, sometimes a nest of plover's eggs—but it was never enough, for a house where hospitality must stretch to cover the needs of not only family and servants, but the families of the murdered Kirby and Murray. At least until spring, the widows and children of his tenants must bide here, and he must do his best to feed them.

"Sit down by me," he said to Jenny, taking her arm and gently guiding her to a seat on the bench beside him. She looked surprised—it was her habit to wait on him when he came—but sat down gladly enough. It was late, and she was tired; he could see the dark smudges beneath her eyes.
—*Voyager,* chapter 4, "The Dunbonnet"

Vegetarian options were tough to come by in the eighteenth century, and goat meat can be hard to find for some in the twenty-first, so I'm claiming food-from-fiction license with this switch-up from a meat pie to one-bite puff pastry rounds topped with a savory goat cheese spread.

A delicious addition to the snack table at your next book club meeting or office party.

Makes 36

Ingredients

4 slices thick-cut bacon, cut crosswise into ¼-inch strips

½ recipe Blitz Puff Pastry (page 29), chilled, or 1 pound (450 grams) frozen puff pastry, thawed

8 ounces (225 grams) goat cheese

1 tablespoon poppy seeds

3 tablespoons olive oil

Zest of 1 lemon, grated or minced

1 large egg

2 tablespoons butter

36 small fresh sage leaves, or 18 large ones, cut in half lengthwise

Method

Move a rack to the top-middle rung and heat the oven to 400°F.

In a frying pan, crisp the bacon over medium heat. Drain on paper towels.

On a lightly floured counter, roll the pastry out to a 16-inch square. Cover with plastic wrap and allow to rest for 10 minutes.

Meanwhile, combine the goat cheese, bacon, poppy seeds, 1 tablespoon of the olive oil, and lemon zest in a small bowl and stir well. Cover and refrigerate.

Lightly beat the egg with 1 teaspoon cold water to make an egg wash.

Use a 3-inch round cutter to cut 36 rounds from the pastry. Transfer to a parchment paper–lined baking sheet and brush with the egg wash. Bake until puffed and golden, 12 to 15 minutes. Cool completely on the baking sheet.

Reduce the oven to 300°F.

In a small frying pan, heat the remaining 2 tablespoons olive oil and the butter until bubbling over medium heat. Fry the sage leaves in batches until crisp. Drain on a paper towel–lined plate and repeat with the remaining sage leaves.

Top each puff pastry round with a teaspoonful of the goat cheese mixture and a fried sage leaf. Heat in the oven for 5 minutes and serve.

Notes

- *If you don't allow the pastry to rest before cutting the rounds, they will shrink and become misshapen in the oven.*
- *Store the leftover egg wash up to a day in the fridge and combine it with 2 more eggs to make a Bacon, Asparagus, and Wild Mushroom Omelette (page 45).*

MURTAGH'S GIFT TO ELLEN
(Puff Pastry Boar Tusks)

MacRannoch was studying the wizened little man, trying to subtract thirty years from the seamed countenance.

"Aye, I know ye," he said at last. "Or not the name, but you. Ye killed a wounded boar single-handed with a dagger, during the tynchal. A gallant beast too. That's right, the MacKenzie gave ye the tushes—a bonny set, almost a complete double curve. Lovely work that, man." A look perilously close to gratification creased Murtagh's pitted cheek momentarily.

I started, remembering the magnificent, barbaric bracelets I had seen at Lallybroch. My mother's, Jenny had said, given to her by an admirer. I stared at Murtagh in disbelief. Even allowing for the passage of thirty years, he did not seem a likely candidate for the tender passion.

—*Outlander,* chapter 36, "MacRannoch"

Use purchased frozen puff pastry to make short work of these fun, edible boar tusk bracelets, or spend an afternoon in the kitchen folding and rolling up a recipe of Blitz Puff Pastry (page 29), and use the other half of the recipe to make the Goat Cheese and Bacon Tarts (page 74).

Makes 12

Ingredients

12 slices prosciutto or bacon
½ recipe Blitz Puff Pastry, chilled, or
    1 pound (450 grams) frozen puff
    pastry, thawed

1 large egg
24 asparagus tips (about 2 inches long)
½ ounce (about ¼ cup or 15 grams)
    shredded Parmesan cheese

Method

Move a rack to the middle rung and heat the oven to 425°F.

    Line two baking sheets with parchment paper. Cut the prosciutto or bacon slices in half lengthwise, so that you have twenty-four long, narrow strips.

    On a lightly floured counter, roll the puff pastry out to a 12-inch square, ⅛ inch thick. Use a sharp knife to cut the pastry into twelve strips, each 1 inch wide. The cleaner the cuts, the more evenly the pastry will puff.

Beat the egg with 1 teaspoon water. Brush two or three strips on both sides with the egg wash and cover the remaining strips with plastic wrap to prevent them from drying.

Hold an asparagus tip on one end of a pastry strip while wrapping the prosciutto around both, securing the asparagus to the pastry. Repeat on the other end with another asparagus tip and bacon strip.

Gently twist the pastry ends in opposite directions, then lay the spirals on the prepared baking sheet in a horseshoe shape, with the asparagus tips pointing toward each other. Cover with plastic wrap and repeat with the other pastry strips.

Dab the pastry with a little extra egg wash, sprinkle with grated Parmesan, and bake until golden, 12 to 15 minutes. Rotate and turn the pan at 8 minutes, reshaping the tusks if necessary. Work quickly to get the oven door closed as soon as possible.

Cool slightly on a wire rack. Though these are best served warm from the oven, they can be baked a few hours ahead and crisped up at 350°F just before serving.

Notes

- *The warmer puff pastry gets, the trickier it becomes to handle. If things are getting slippery, cover everything with plastic wrap and refrigerate for 10 to 15 minutes.*
- *The tusks can be prepared in the morning, wrapped well, and refrigerated until you're ready to bake.*
- *Make a batch of asparagus soup from the leftover stalks, a chopped onion, and a quart of Vegetable Stock (page 24). Puree, then thicken the soup with roux and finish with cream, salt, and pepper.*

CHEESE SAVORIES
(Gougères)

"Indeed, Monsieur le Comte?" Silas Hawkins raised thick, graying brows toward our end of the table. "Have you found a new partner for investment, then? I understood that your own resources were... depleted, shall we say? Following the sad destruction of the *Patagonia*." He took a cheese savory from the plate and popped it delicately into his mouth.

The Comte's jaw muscles bulged, and a sudden chill descended on our end of the table. From Mr. Hawkins's sidelong glance at me, and the tiny smile that lurked about his busily chewing mouth, it was clear that he knew all about my role in the destruction of the unfortunate *Patagonia*.
—*Dragonfly in Amber*, chapter 18, "Rape in Paris"

Gougères are made from *pâte à choux*, a centuries-old, double-cooked pastry dough versatile enough to make into éclairs, profiteroles, beignets, gnocchi, and more. Traditionally served at Burgundy vineyards as an accompaniment during wine tastings, these light-as-air cheese puffs would have been at home in any eighteenth-century Parisian parlor or dining room, and make delicate finger food for your next happy hour.

Makes 24

Ingredients

½ cup (1 stick) butter, cut into cubes

½ teaspoon kosher salt

½ teaspoon mustard powder (optional)

1 cup all-purpose flour

4 large eggs

6 ounces (170 grams or about 1½ cups) shredded cheese, such as Gruyère or aged cheddar

Method

Move a rack to the middle rung and heat the oven to 425°F.

In a medium saucepan, combine the butter, salt, mustard powder (if desired), and 1 cup warm water and bring it to a rolling boil over medium-high heat.

Reduce the heat to low and vigorously stir in the flour with a wooden spoon until the mixture forms a smooth paste that pulls away from the sides of the pan, 1 to 2 minutes.

BY HAND: Transfer the dough to a large bowl and beat with the wooden spoon until slightly cooled, about 2 minutes. Beat in the eggs one at a time, ensuring that each egg is well absorbed and the dough smooth before adding the next. Scrape down the bowl as needed. When all the eggs are incorporated, you will have a smooth, creamy batter that hangs from the spoon in a ragged V. Gently fold in the cheese.

IN A STANDING MIXER: Transfer the dough to the bowl of a machine fitted with the paddle attachment. Beat the dough on medium-low for about 1 minute, until the steam dissipates. With the machine on, add the eggs one at a time, waiting until each egg is absorbed and the dough smooth before adding the next. Scrape down the bowl as needed. When all the eggs are incorporated, you will have a smooth, creamy batter that hangs from the paddle in a ragged V. Reduce to low speed and mix in the cheese.

Line two cookie sheets with parchment. Fill a piping bag fitted with a medium-size round tip to pipe out mounds about the size of Ping-Pong balls, at least 1 inch apart. Alternatively, drop the dough by teaspoonfuls onto the sheet. Wet your fingertip with cold water and smooth down any peaked tops.

Bake one sheet at a time. (If there is room, refrigerate the second sheet while the first bakes.) To prevent the dough from collapsing, do not open the oven door for the first 15 minutes. After 15 minutes, turn the sheet in the oven, reduce the oven

temperature to 350°F, and continue baking until the gougères are golden, light-weight, and hollow-feeling, another 10 to 15 minutes. Cool slightly on a wire rack.

Reheat the oven to 425°F before baking the second batch.

Best served warm from the oven, however, they can be baked a few hours ahead and crisped up at 350°F just before serving.

Notes

- *Strong, aged cheeses work best for this recipe. Let's just say mozzarella gougères won't knock your socks off. Gruyère is traditional, and my favorite.*
- *When I say LARGE eggs, I really mean it for this recipe—not extra large. If you can't find large, buy medium instead. Too much egg will cause the puffs to cave in. And if they do cave in, don't sweat it! They'll still be delicious . . . just with character.*
- *Gougères can be any size you like, from marble-size (to garnish soup) to big tennis balls (which make pretty fancy sandwiches). Adjust baking times as required.*
- *To prepare in advance, freeze the piped, uncooked dough, then bake directly from frozen as directed in the recipe.*

ROLLS WITH PIGEON AND TRUFFLES

Jamie nodded, picking up a sort of hot stuffed roll.

"I should be surprised if he had not," he said dryly. "While there's likely more than one man willing to do me harm, I canna think it likely that gangs o' them are roaming about Edinburgh." He took a bite and chewed industriously, shaking his head.

"Nay, that's clear enough, and nothing to be greatly worrit over."

"It's not?" I took a small bite of my own roll, then a bigger one. "This is delicious. What is it?"

Jamie lowered the roll he had been about to take a bite of, and squinted at it. "Pigeon minced wi' truffles," he said, and stuffed it into his mouth whole.

"No," he said, and paused to swallow. "No," he said again, more clearly. "That's likely just a matter of a rival smuggler. There are two gangs that I've had a wee bit of difficulty with now and then." He waved a hand, scattering crumbs, and reached for another roll.

—*Voyager,* chapter 28, "Virtue's Guardian"

Fragrant and savory rolls made by Madame Jeanne's undoubtedly French cook to satisfy the discerning clientele of her fine establishment. The pigeon has been replaced with easier-to-find chicken thighs and the truffles with less-expensive, umami-rich dried mushrooms. Shallots and thyme are eternal in French cuisine, and pork fat would have most certainly been added to make up for the leanness of the pigeon.

Serve one or two alongside a bowl of Cream of Nontoxic Mushroom Soup (page 69) for a homey and satisfying meal, or cut them into 1-inch lengths for one-bite sausage rolls sure to be a hit at your next cocktail party.

Makes eighteen 2-inch sausage rolls

Ingredients

½ ounce (15 grams) dried morel or porcini mushrooms

1 pound (450 grams) boneless, skinless chicken thighs, chopped

2 strips bacon, cut crosswise into ¼-inch strips

1 large celery stalk, chopped (see Knife Skills, page 11)

1 large shallot, chopped

1 tablespoon fresh thyme leaves

1 teaspoon kosher salt

½ teaspoon freshly ground pepper

¾ cup panko-style breadcrumbs

1 recipe Short Crust Pastry (page 27), chilled

1 large egg

Method

Cover the dried mushrooms in boiling water and soak for 5 minutes. Lift the mushrooms from the water with a fork to leave the grit at the bottom of the dish. Press down on the mushrooms in a small strainer to remove as much moisture as possible. Chop coarsely.

Combine the mushrooms, chicken, bacon, celery, shallots, thyme, salt, and pepper in the bowl of a food processor. Pulse eight to ten times, until the mixture is well combined and the texture of sausage meat. Scoop the sausage mixture into a bowl and mix in the breadcrumbs with your hands until well combined.

On the counter, lay a piece of plastic wrap at least 24 inches long. Form half of the mixture into a long 18-inch log on top of the wrap and roll it up tightly in the plastic. Turn the ends of the wrap in opposite directions until very tight and secure with tape if necessary. Repeat with another piece of plastic wrap and the other half of the sausage mixture. Freeze both logs for 15 minutes while you roll out the pastry.

Move a rack to the lower-middle rung and heat the oven to 425°F. Beat the egg with 1 teaspoon water to make an egg wash.

On a lightly floured board, roll out the pastry into a rectangle 10 x 18 inches. Cut the pastry in half lengthwise so that you have 2 pieces measuring 5 x 18 inches. Unwrap one of the chilled logs and place along the long edge of the pastry. Brush the edge farthest from you with the egg wash, then roll the sausage log in the pastry, leaving about a ½-inch overlap. Pinch the seam firmly closed, then roll the seam to the counter and rock the sausage gently to flatten and even out the join. Repeat with the other sausage log and remaining pastry.

Brush the tops and sides of the pastry with the egg wash. Using a sharp knife, cut each log into nine 2-inch pieces, and place seam side down on a parchment paper–lined baking sheet. Bake until golden brown, 25 to 30 minutes.

Cool at least 15 minutes on a wire rack before serving.

Store leftovers in the fridge up to 3 days. Warm slightly in a 300°F oven to recrisp the pastry.

Notes

- *Freeze the assembled, unbaked rolls up to 1 month. Thaw overnight in the fridge before baking as directed.*
- *Substitute any dark poultry meat for the chicken thighs, including duck, game hen, quail, or even actual pigeon. (Look for squab, which is the common culinary name for farm-raised pigeons less than four weeks old.)*

MR. WILLOUGHBY'S CORAL KNOB

"I wrote all my poems to Woman—sometimes they were addressed to one lady or another, but most often to Woman alone. To the taste of breasts like apricots, the warm scent of a woman's navel when she wakens in the winter, the warmth of a mound that fills your hand like a peach, split with ripeness."

Fergus, scandalized, put his hands over Marsali's ears, but the rest of his hearers were most receptive.

"No wonder the wee fellow was an esteemed poet," Raeburn said with approval. "It's verra heathen, but I like it!"

"Worth a red knob on your hat, anyday," Maitland agreed.
—*Voyager,* chapter 46, "We Meet a Porpoise"

A perennial staple at picnics, potlucks, and church socials in the American South, pimento cheese was actually first developed in New York at the turn of the nineteenth century, and gained popularity across the nation as a new, mass-produced, and modern food. Originally a combination of Spanish pimiento peppers and newly invented cream cheese, its popularity fell in the North after World War II.

Since then, Southerners, in addition to purchasing pimento cheese, have made their own homemade versions, although there is little reference to it in cookbooks, even in the South, before the 1990s.

Makes about 3 cups

Ingredients

1 cup mayonnaise

1 teaspoon hot paprika

1 cup diced pimentos or roasted red peppers (reserve 2 tablespoons for garnish)

8 ounces (225 grams or about 1 cup) aged cheddar cheese, shredded

8 ounces (225 grams or about 1 cup) Monterey Jack cheese, shredded

1 to 2 tablespoons grated onion

Tabasco to taste (optional)

Method

In a large bowl, mix together the mayonnaise and paprika. Add the pimentos, cheeses, and onions. Beat together well with a wooden spoon to develop a slightly creamy texture. Taste and season with a dash or two of Tabasco, if desired. Cover with plastic and refrigerate for at least 2 hours, and up to overnight, to allow the flavors to blend and mellow.

Pack the mixture into a small bowl and invert onto a plate. Top with a small mound of the reserved pimentos (the *knob*).

Serve with crackers or baguette slices, or try it in a grilled cheese, stirred into grits, or atop a sandwich of Rosamund's Pulled Pork with Devil's Apple BBQ Sauce (page 120).

Keep leftovers in the fridge up to 3 days.

Note

• *The hot paprika may raise the hackles of some pimento cheese purists, but along with a little coral color, it also adds depth of flavor. If you can't find hot paprika, use sweet instead.*

BEER-BATTERED CORN FRITTERS

"I'll go and have a bit of a blether with him, aye?" Roger touched her back in brief affection. "He could maybe use a sympathetic ear."

"That and a stiff drink?" She nodded toward the house, where Robin McGillivray was visible through the open door, pouring what she assumed to be whisky for a select circle of friends.

"I imagine he will have managed that for himself," Roger replied dryly. He left her, making his way around the convivial group by the fire. He disappeared in the dark, but then she saw the door of the cooper's shop open, and Roger silhouetted briefly against the glow from within, his tall form blocking the light before vanishing inside.

"Wanna drink, Mama!" Jemmy was wriggling like a tadpole, trying to get down. She set him on the ground, and he was off like a shot, nearly upsetting a stout lady with a platter of corn fritters.

—*A Breath of Snow and Ashes,* chapter 6, "Ambush"

Light and crispy bundles of corn that make the perfect accompaniment for an afternoon of drinks on the deck, or in front of the game, with friends.

Makes about 24

Ingredients

2 cups corn kernels (fresh, frozen, or canned)

1 cup all-purpose flour

⅔ cup cornmeal

2 tablespoons grated onion

1 tablespoon sugar

1 teaspoon baking powder

1 teaspoon kosher salt, plus additional

¼ teaspoon cayenne pepper, plus additional

1 large egg

1 cup ale or beer (see Notes)

Vegetable oil

Honey, to serve

Method

Combine the corn, flour, cornmeal, onions, sugar, baking powder, salt, and cayenne pepper in a medium bowl. In a separate bowl, whisk the egg into the ale, then add to the dry ingredients. Stir well to combine.

In a heavy-bottomed saucepan over medium-high heat, bring 2 inches of vegetable oil to 360°F. Drop tablespoonfuls of batter into the hot oil and fry until puffed and golden, turning once, 2 to 3 minutes.

Drain on paper towels and repeat until all the batter is fried.

Serve, slightly cooled, drizzled with honey and sprinkled with a little extra salt and cayenne pepper. Best eaten shortly after cooking.

Notes

- *To use fresh corn, choose two medium-size cobs and blanch in boiling salted water for 3 minutes. Cool in an ice bath, then drain and pat dry before carefully slicing the kernels off the cob with a sharp knife. Frozen corn or drained canned corn can be used as is.*
- *I prefer to use a Scottish ale, but any low-hops beer will do. Hops become more bitter when cooked, so are best avoided.*

MUSHROOM PASTIES

"You have all you want, Miss Bree." He smiled, whipping the napkin away to display a selection of savories.

She inhaled beatifically. "I want them all," she said, taking the tray, to Tommy's amusement. Roger, seizing the chance, murmured his own request to the slave, who nodded, disappeared, and returned within moments with an open bottle of wine and two goblets. Roger took these, and together they wandered down the path that led from the house to the dock, sharing tidbits of news along with the pigeon pies.

"Did you find any of the guests passed out in the shrubbery?" she asked, her words muffled by a mouthful of mushroom pasty. She swallowed, and became more distinct. "When Da asked you to go and look this afternoon, I mean."

—*The Fiery Cross,* chapter 47, "The Lists of Venus"

Medieval pasties, from the Old French *pasté*, meaning a pie baked without a dish, were consumed exclusively by the wealthy. Later, in the seventeenth and eighteenth centuries, pasties filled with less-expensive ingredients became popular with miners in Cornwall as a meal that could be eaten without cutlery.

These small, two-bite vegetarian hand pies are big on rich, savory flavor and make great hors d'oeuvres at a stand-up party, or a delicious lunch when served beside a bowl of Cock-a-Leekie (page 58).

Makes 18 to 20

Ingredients

3 tablespoons butter

2 tablespoons olive oil

2 medium shallots, minced

1 pound (450 grams) button mushrooms, minced (see Knife Skills, page 11)

1 large garlic clove, grated or minced

1½ teaspoons fresh thyme leaves

½ cup dry white wine

2 tablespoons whipping cream (optional)

1 teaspoon kosher salt, plus additional

½ teaspoon freshly ground pepper

1 recipe Short Crust Pastry (page 27), chilled

1 large egg

Method

In a large saucepan, heat the butter and olive oil over medium heat until bubbling. Add the shallots and stir occasionally until soft and translucent, about 3 minutes. Add the mushrooms and cook, stirring occasionally, until they have released their water and it has evaporated but the mushrooms remain unbrowned, 8 to 12 minutes.

Add the garlic and thyme and stir until fragrant, about 1 minute. Deglaze the pan with the white wine and reduce until the pan is almost dry, about 2 minutes. Stir in the cream (if desired) off the heat and season with salt and pepper. Cool completely.

Move a rack to the upper-middle rung and heat the oven to 400°F.

Roll half of the pastry out into a circle ⅛ inch thick. Use a 3- or 4-inch cutter to cut out rounds. Brush the top edge of a pastry circle sparingly with water. Carefully mound 1 tablespoon of the mushrooms onto the top half and fold the bottom half over to make a half-moon. Press the edges firmly together, crimp (see Notes) to seal well, and, with a sharp knife, make a slit in the top of each pie to vent the steam.

Wrap and refrigerate for at least 30 minutes, and up to overnight. Arrange on a parchment paper–lined baking sheet. Lightly beat the egg with 1 teaspoon water and brush onto the pasties. Bake until golden, about 30 minutes.

Cool at least 10 minutes before serving.

Notes

- *The pasties are much easier to fold and crimp if the mushroom mixture is cold from the refrigerator. Prepare the mushrooms up to 3 days in advance.*
- *To crimp the pie shut, roll and press the edge of the dough under itself as you work left to right. (You can find good instructional videos on YouTube.)*
- *Freeze uncooked pasties up to 2 weeks. Defrost in the refrigerator overnight, and bake as directed.*

Chapter 5

༄

BEEF

Roast Beef for a Wedding Feast

At the inn, food was readily available, in the form of a modest wedding feast, including wine, fresh bread, and roast beef.

Dougal took me by the arm as I started for the stairs to freshen myself before eating.

"I want this marriage consummated, wi' no uncertainty whatsoever," Dougal instructed me firmly in an undertone. "There's to be no question of it bein' a legal union, and no way open for annulment, or we're all riskin' our necks."

"Seems to me you're doing that anyway," I remarked crossly. "Mine, especially."

Dougal patted me firmly on the rump.

"Dinna ye worry about that; ye just do your part." He looked me over critically, as though judging my capacity to perform my role adequately.

"I kent Jamie's father. If the lad's much like him, ye'll have no trouble at all. Ah, Jamie lad!" He hurried across the room, to where Jamie had come in from stabling the horses. From the look on Jamie's face, he was getting his orders as well.

—*Outlander,* chapter 15, "Revelations of the Bridal Chamber"

Most modern wedding receptions involve some clinking cutlery, a toast from the best man, and a cheesy cover band—the buffet is usually a little more generous as well—but if you were hurled back two hundred years in time, forced to marry a virtual stranger, hungover, in someone else's strong-smelling dress and a language other than your own, all on no more than a couple of glasses of port for breakfast, I'm willing to bet you'd accept roast beef, bread, and wine with a little more grace than your average bridezilla.

The top round cut makes an economical and delicious roast for a Sunday or special occasion dinner. It cooks in under an hour to leave plenty of time for visiting with guests and family.

Serves 6 or more

Ingredients

1 tablespoon olive oil

6 garlic cloves, minced or grated

2 teaspoons kosher salt

1 teaspoon freshly ground pepper

1 teaspoon minced fresh rosemary leaves

3- to 4-pound (1.3 to 1.8 kilograms)
    top round beef roast

Method

Mix together the olive oil, garlic, salt, pepper, and rosemary in a small bowl. Smear the paste all over the roast, lightly rubbing it into the meat. Set the roast on a wire rack in a roasting pan and cover loosely with plastic. Rest on the counter for an hour to marinate and take the chill off the meat.

Move a rack to the middle rung and heat the oven to 350°F.

Roast the meat for 28 to 31 minutes per pound for medium rare (145°F on an instant-read thermometer), 30 to 34 minutes per pound for medium (160°F), and 40 to 45 minutes per pound for well-done (170°F). (Rare is not recommended for this cut of meat.)

Loosely tent the cooked roast with foil and allow it to rest for 15 minutes. Use the pan juices to make gravy, or skim the surface of fat, strain, season, and serve the jus alongside the roast.

Slice and serve hot with your favorite sides, or re-create Jamie and Claire's wedding feast with a loaf of Honey-Buttermilk Oat Bread (page 232) and copious amounts of wine to wash it all down.

Keep leftovers in the fridge up to 3 days.

Notes

- *You can mash and grind the garlic, salt, peppercorns, and rosemary in a mortar and pestle. Mix in the olive oil to form a paste for the meat.*
- *Rest the roast after you remove it from the oven and before you carve it to ensure the juices are reabsorbed into the center of the meat. During the resting period, a roast's internal temperature will also rise by a few degrees. Always remove a roast from the oven a few minutes before it reaches the desired temperature.*

GYPSY STEW

I was cautious, but we were welcomed with expansive motions, and invited to share the Gypsies' dinner. It smelt delicious—some sort of stew —and I eagerly accepted the invitation, ignoring Murtagh's dour speculations as to the basic nature of the beast that had provided the stew meat.

They spoke little English, and less Gaelic; we conversed largely in gestures, and a sort of bastard tongue that owed its parentage largely to French. It was warm and companionable in the caravan where we ate; men and women and children all ate casually from bowls, sitting wherever they could find space, dipping the succulent stew up with chunks of bread. It was the best food I had had in weeks, and I ate until my sides creaked. I could barely muster breath to sing, but did my best, humming along in the difficult spots, and leaving Murtagh to carry the tunes.

—*Outlander*, chapter 34, "Dougal's Story"

In lieu of potatoes, which weren't found in Highland vegetable plots until the last quarter of the eighteenth century, this stew is filled with leeks, root vegetables, and kale. Turnips, I have recently learned, arrived in Scotland with potatoes, so, technically, they shouldn't be in here either, but this stew has become an *Outlander Kitchen* classic over the years, so in they stay.

A succulent beef stew made rich with stout and hearty with a fine collection of (mostly) traditional early-eighteenth-century Scottish vegetables.

Serves 6 to 8

Ingredients

2 pounds (900 grams) stew beef,
  cut into 2-inch cubes

¼ cup plus 2 tablespoons all-purpose
  flour

2 teaspoons kosher salt, plus additional

1 teaspoon freshly ground pepper,
  plus additional

¼ teaspoon cayenne pepper

3 medium leeks (white and light-green
  parts only), cut into 1-inch pieces

3 tablespoons vegetable oil

4 large cloves garlic, minced or grated

1½ cups stout or other dark beer

1 bunch kale, stemmed and shredded

3 medium carrots, cut into 1-inch pieces

1 small turnip, peeled and cut into
    1-inch cubes
½ small rutabaga (yellow turnip), peeled
    and cut into 1-inch cubes
2 fresh thyme sprigs

2 fresh rosemary sprigs
2 bay leaves
4 to 6 cups Brown Chicken or Beef Stock
    (page 20)
2 tablespoons butter

Method

Pat the beef dry with paper towels. In a large bowl, combine the ¼ cup flour, salt, ground pepper, and cayenne pepper. Toss the beef in the flour until the cubes are lightly dusted on all sides.

Rinse the chopped leeks thoroughly in a bowl of cold water. Scoop them out with your hands or a slotted spoon, leaving the silt and sand behind. Shake dry in a clean dishcloth or salad spinner.

In a stockpot or Dutch oven, heat the oil over medium-high flame until shimmering. Brown the beef in batches, being careful not to overcrowd the pot, until the cubes have a dark golden crust all over, 2 to 3 minutes per side.

When the last batch of beef has been removed from the pot, add the leeks, garlic, and stout. Scrape up the brown bits with a wooden spoon, and boil for 3 minutes. Add the meat (and its juices), kale, carrots, turnips, rutabaga, herbs, and stock to cover. Stir and bring to a boil. Reduce the heat to low and simmer, partially covered, until the meat is fork-tender, about 90 minutes. Remove the stems from the rosemary and thyme as well as the bay leaves.

Just before serving, use a fork to blend together the remaining 2 tablespoons flour with the butter. Stir this beurre manié into the hot stew and cook for another 5 to 7 minutes, until slightly thickened and glossy. Season with salt and pepper.

Serve hot with Brown Buns at Beauly (page 224) or ladle over Spoon Bread (page 236).

Store leftovers in the fridge up to 3 days.

Notes

- *The world's bestselling stout is Guinness, but with so many micro- and small-batch local breweries, you should be able to find other varieties. Experiment!*
- *If you don't cook with alcohol, replace the stout with more stock.*
- *This stew has a lot more meat in it than its eighteenth-century counterpart would have, and you can stretch it further by increasing the amount of vegetables, including potatoes, and/ or by adding ½ cup barley. Add more stock or water as required.*

VEAL PATTIES IN WINE SAUCE

Jared, who was consuming veal patties in a businesslike way, paused to swallow, then said, "Dinna trouble yourself about that, my dear. I've made up a list for you of useful acquaintances. I've written letters for ye to carry to several friends there, who will certainly lend ye assistance."

He cut another sizable chunk of veal, wiped it through a puddle of wine sauce, and chewed it, while looking thoughtfully at Jamie.

Having evidently come to a decision of some kind, he swallowed, took a sip of wine, and said in a conversational voice, "We met on the level, Cousin."

I stared at him in bewilderment, but Jamie, after a moment's pause, replied, "And we parted on the square."

—*Voyager,* chapter 40, "I Shall Go Down to the Sea"

During the seventeenth and eighteenth centuries, the Portuguese archipelago of Madeira was an important port of call for ships on the way to the Americas and the East Indies. Merchants such as Jared loaded their ships with supplies and Madeira wine, which was fortified with brandy to extend its life on long voyages. As the ships passed through the tropics, the casks of Madeira heated and cooled repeatedly, inadvertently deepening and improving the wine's flavor.

Today, Madeira's unique winemaking process involves heating the wine for an extended period of time, as well as deliberately exposing the wine to increase evaporation. Its taste has changed very little in three hundred years, making this sauce virtually the same one served at the house in the rue Tremoulins.

Serves 6

Ingredients

1½ cups White Beef Stock (page 22)

1 cup dry Madeira

¼ cup (4 tablespoons) butter

6 veal leg cutlets, pounded thin, about
    2 pounds (900 grams) (see Notes)

1½ teaspoons kosher salt

½ teaspoon freshly ground pepper

1 cup all-purpose flour

2 tablespoons olive oil

2 tablespoons chopped fresh parsley

Method

In a saucepan, boil the stock and Madeira together over medium-high heat until reduced by half, about 25 minutes. Stir in 2 tablespoons of butter and keep warm over low heat.

Pat the veal dry with paper towels and season with salt and pepper. Dredge each cutlet lightly in the flour.

In a heavy frying pan, heat the remaining 2 tablespoons butter with the olive oil over medium-high flame until bubbling. Cook the veal, in batches if necessary to avoid overcrowding the pan, until golden on both sides, turning once, 2 to 4 minutes per side, depending on their thickness. Rest the meat on a plate, loosely tented with foil, for 5 minutes.

Serve each cutlet in a pool of wine sauce and sprinkle parsley on top.

Notes

- *I prefer leg cutlets for this recipe instead of ground veal patties, but use what is available and affordable, adjusting cooking times as required.*
- *Madeira is a robust wine that keeps indefinitely when stored, tightly capped, in the refrigerator. Splash it into gravies, sauces, stews, and risottos.*
- *No Madeira? Try dry Marsala, an Italian fortified wine from Sicily.*

BRIANNA'S BRIDIES

Brianna thought the gentleman in question looked too stupid to be dishonest, but refrained from saying so, merely shaking her head emphatically.

Young Jamie shrugged philosophically and resumed his scrutiny of the would-be bondsmen, walking around those who took his particular interest and peering at them closely, in a way she might have thought exceedingly rude had a number of other potential employers not been doing likewise.

"Bridies! Hot bridies!" A high-pitched screech cut through the rumble and racket of the hall, and Brianna turned to see an old woman elbowing her way robustly through the crowd, a steaming tray hung round her neck and a wooden spatula in hand.

The heavenly scent of fresh hot dough and spiced meat cut through the other pungencies in the hall, noticeable as the old woman's calling. It had been a long time since breakfast, and Brianna dug in her pocket, feeling saliva fill her mouth.

—*Drums of Autumn,* chapter 35, "Bon Voyage"

Forfar Bridies are said to have first been made by Maggie Bridie, a traveling food seller who sold her hot, savory pies at the Buttermarket in Forfar, Forfarshire (now County Angus). Though it uses the same short crust pastry as a Cornish pasty, a bridie's traditional filling of beef, onion, and suet is lighter in texture than that of its southern cousin, which also contains potato and rutabaga.

I have also included a vegetarian filling, because, while authenticity is important, most people these days understand the benefits of a vegetable-rich diet. If Claire were here, I'm sure she would approve.

Makes 8
(4 meat, 4 veggie)

Ingredients

1 pound (450 grams) sirloin or top round, minced (see Knife Skills, page 11)

2 medium onions, diced

½ cup (1 stick) cold butter or suet, diced

3 teaspoons kosher salt

1 teaspoon freshly ground pepper

1 large potato, peeled and diced

1 small turnip, diced

1 medium carrot, diced

6 ounces (170 grams or about 1 cup) shredded cheddar cheese

½ teaspoon crushed red pepper flakes (optional)

1 recipe Short Crust Pastry (page 27)

1 large egg

Method

In a medium bowl, mix together the minced steak, half the onions, 4 tablespoons butter, 1½ teaspoons salt, and ½ teaspoon pepper. In a separate bowl, mix the potatoes, turnips, carrots, cheese, and red pepper flakes with the remaining onions, butter, salt, and pepper. Cover both bowls with a plate or plastic and refrigerate.

On a lightly floured board, roll out half of the pastry into a circle. Turn and loosen the dough occasionally as you continue to roll the pastry out into a circle or square that is an even ⅛ inch thick. Cut four 6-inch circles from the dough, then roll each circle to lengthen it into a slight oval.

Pile one-fourth of the meat filling (packed ½ cup) onto the top center of each oval, leaving a 1-inch border. Wet the top edge of the pastry sparingly with water, and fold

the bottom half over to make a half-moon. Press the edges firmly together and crimp to seal well (see Notes). With a sharp knife, make a slit in the top of each pie to vent steam.

Repeat with the remaining pastry and the vegetarian filling to make another four pies.

Wrap and refrigerate the filled pies for at least 30 minutes, and up to overnight.

Move the racks to the upper- and lower-center rungs and heat the oven to 400°F.

Lightly beat the egg with 1 teaspoon water. Brush the tops of the bridies sparingly with the egg wash and bake on parchment paper–lined baking sheets for 30 to 40 minutes, until golden brown, turning and rotating the sheets halfway through. Cool at least 10 minutes on a wire rack.

Serve hot or cold. Pack into a basket along with a tartan blanket and flask of Laoghaire's Whiskey Sour (page 304) for an afternoon picnic on an imagined Highland hillside.

Store cooked bridies in the fridge up to 3 days.

Notes

- *Most modern bridies in pie shops contain ground meat, which you are free to use, but the texture of the cooked hand-minced meat is superior and worth the extra effort.*
- *To crimp, roll and press the edge of the dough under itself as you work left to right. You can find good instructional videos on YouTube.*
- *To make cheese straws from the leftover dough, brush the pastry scraps with leftover egg wash, sprinkle sparingly with strong cheese, twist, and bake at 375°F until golden.*

Chapter 6

POULTRY

Claire's Roast Chicken

Pheasant and Greens at Ardsmuir

Sweet Tea–Brined Fried Chicken

Slow-Cooked Chicken Fricassee

CLAIRE'S ROAST CHICKEN

"How's that thumb taste, sweetie?" he inquired. "They say you shouldn't oughta let 'em suck their thumbs, you know," he informed me, straightening up. "Gives 'em crooked teeth and they'll need braces."

"Is that so?" I said through my own teeth. "How much do I owe you?"

Half an hour later, the chicken lay in its pan, stuffed and basted, surrounded by crushed garlic, sprigs of rosemary, and curls of lemon peel. A quick squeeze of lemon juice over the buttery skin, and I could stick it in the oven and go get myself and Brianna dressed. The kitchen looked like the result of an incompetent burglary, with cupboards hanging open and cooking paraphernalia strewn on every horizontal surface. I banged shut a couple of cupboard doors, and then the kitchen door itself, trusting that that would keep Mrs. Hinchcliffe out, even if good manners wouldn't.

—*Voyager,* chapter 3, "Frank and Full Disclosure"

This crispy, juicy, and aromatic roast bird makes a cozy family meal that will transport you from Boston to Lallybroch and back again when served with Fergus's Roasted Tatties (page 206) and Auld Ian's Buttered Leeks (page 202).

Serves 4

Ingredients

3½- to 4-pound (1.5 to 1.8 kilograms) whole chicken

1½ teaspoons kosher salt, plus additional

½ teaspoon freshly ground pepper, plus additional

¼ lemon

2 fresh rosemary sprigs

2 garlic cloves, crushed

2 tablespoons all-purpose flour

1½ cups Brown Chicken Stock (page 20)

Method

Take the chicken out of the fridge 1 hour before you cook it. Pat it dry, inside and out, with paper towels. Mix together the salt and pepper and season the chicken inside and out. Stuff the cavity with the lemon, rosemary, and garlic.

Twist and tuck the wing tips under the back of the chicken to keep them in place during cooking. With a sharp knife, poke a small hole in the loose skin between the breast and thigh on either side. Cross the legs and tuck the end of each through the hole in the skin on the opposite side. Arrange the bird on a wire rack in a roasting pan.

Move a rack to the lower-middle rung and heat the oven to 475°F.

Roast for 30 minutes, rotate the pan, and continue to cook until the skin is golden and the internal temperature reaches 175°F, 20 to 30 more minutes, depending on the size of the bird. Set on a plate, tent loosely with foil, and let it rest 10 to 15 minutes before carving.

To make the gravy, while the bird rests, strain the juices from the bottom of the pan and the inside of the chicken into a small saucepan over medium heat. Skim and discard all but about 1 tablespoon of fat from the surface. When the juices start to boil, whisk in the flour until a smooth paste forms, and cook, stirring, for 2 minutes. Slowly whisk in the chicken stock. Boil gently, stirring almost constantly, until the gravy is thickened enough to coat the back of a spoon. Season to taste with salt and pepper.

Keep the leftover chicken and gravy in the refrigerator up to 3 days.

Notes

- *To measure the internal temperature of the chicken, stick an instant-read thermometer in the meatiest part of the thigh, ensuring that the tip does not touch the bone.*
- *A larger chicken's skin will burn before it is cooked through using this method. To serve more than four adults, roast two chickens simultaneously at 500°F.*
- *Use the carcass to make a batch of Hot Broth at Castle Leoch (page 20).*

PHEASANT AND GREENS
AT ARDSMUIR

John Grey had dressed carefully this evening, with fresh linen and silk stockings. He wore his own hair, simply plaited, rinsed with a tonic of lemon-verbena. He had hesitated for a moment over Hector's ring, but at last had put it on, too. The dinner had been good; a pheasant he had shot himself, and a salad of greens, in deference to Fraser's odd tastes for such things. Now they sat over the chessboard, lighter topics of conversation set aside in the concentration of the midgame.

"Will you have sherry?" He set down his bishop, and leaned back, stretching.

Fraser nodded, absorbed in the new position. "I thank ye."

Grey rose and crossed the room, leaving Fraser by the fire. He reached into the cupboard for the bottle, and felt a thin trickle of sweat run down his ribs as he did so. Not from the fire, simmering across the room; from sheer nervousness.

—*Voyager,* chapter 11, "The Torremolinos Gambit"

A crisp-skinned, tender, pan-fried pheasant breast in a sweet, luscious sauce of orange and apricot, and served with a salad of bitter greens that balances the sauce's sweetness.

Serves 4

Ingredients

4 boneless pheasant breasts, skin on

2 teaspoons kosher salt, plus additional

1 cup dry white wine

½ cup orange juice

10 dried apricots, cut into quarters

2 tablespoons honey

2 tablespoons white wine vinegar

2 short sprigs fresh rosemary

6 whole peppercorns

¼ cup (4 tablespoons) butter

2 cloves garlic, smashed

6 cups mixed greens (arugula, dandelion, mustard greens, baby kale, beet greens, etc.)

1 recipe Basic Salad Dressing (page 33)

Method

Remove the pheasant from the fridge half an hour before cooking. Season generously on both sides with salt and set aside.

In a small saucepan, stir together the wine, orange juice, apricots, honey, vinegar, rosemary, and peppercorns. Bring to a boil over medium-high heat and simmer briskly, until the mixture is syrupy with big bubbles, 12 to 15 minutes. Strain the sauce and return it to the pan to keep warm over low heat.

Blot dry the skin side of the pheasant with paper towels. In a large frying pan, melt 2 tablespoons of the butter over medium-high heat. When the butter is bubbling, add the pheasant breasts, skin side down, and the garlic to the pan, without overcrowding. Press down on each breast to ensure full contact with the cooking surface and sear for 2 minutes.

Use a spoon to baste the tops of the pheasant breasts occasionally with the garlicky browned butter. Cook, without flipping, until the skin sides are crisp and golden, and the internal temperature at the thickest part of the breasts reaches 150°F (medium rare) to 160°F (medium), 5 to 8 minutes. Reduce the heat, if necessary, to avoid burning the skin. Remove the pheasant from the pan and rest skin side up, loosely tented with foil, for 5 minutes.

While the pheasant rests, increase the heat under the sauce to medium and whisk in the remaining 2 tablespoons butter. Season with salt to taste.

Gently toss the greens in a large bowl with about 3 tablespoons of the dressing. Add more if needed, but don't drench the leaves—they should just glisten.

To serve, spoon some of the sauce onto each plate, top with a pheasant breast (sliced if you prefer), a little more sauce, and a small stack of dressed greens on the side.

Notes

- *The ideal doneness for pheasant breast is medium rare to medium. Anything beyond that and the meat becomes tough.*
- *Pheasants are lean birds with a delicious mild gamey flavor. If you prefer, substitute boneless, skin-on chicken breasts and flatten them slightly with a meat mallet.*
- *Finely chop the strained apricots from the sauce to serve as a relish on top of warm Brie, or stir them into a batch of Mrs. Graham's Oatmeal Scones (page 216).*

SWEET TEA–BRINED FRIED CHICKEN

**Food was beginning to be brought out: tureens of powsowdie and hotchpotch—
and an enormous tub of soup à la Reine, a clear compliment to the guest of
honor—platters of fried fish, fried chicken, fried rabbit; venison collops in red
wine, smoked sausages, Forfar bridies, inky-pinky, roast turkeys, pigeon pie;
dishes of colcannon, stovies, turnip purry, roasted apples stuffed with dried
pumpkin, squash, corn, mushroom pasties; gigantic baskets overflowing with
fresh baps, rolls, and other breads . . . all this, I was well aware, merely as pre-
lude to the barbecue whose succulent aroma was drifting through the air: a
number of hogs, three or four beeves, two deer, and, the *pièce de résistance,* a
wood bison, acquired God knew how or where.**

—*A Breath of Snow and Ashes,* chapter 54, "Flora MacDonald's Barbecue"

Fried chicken was likely brought to the southern colonies by Scottish immigrants,
who had a long history of frying chicken in fat, unlike their English and European
counterparts, who baked or boiled the bird. African slaves brought to cook on
plantations came with their own tradition of deep-frying meats, and added their
own spin to the dish using seasonings and spices previously unknown in Scottish
kitchens.

This less-than-traditional version brines boneless chicken pieces in southern
sweet tea and salt. The result is a flavorful, plump, and easy-to-eat fried chicken
that will make a popular addition to your next twenty-first-century picnic or potluck
table.

Serves 6

Ingredients

4 tea bags of black tea, such as orange
   pekoe

1 cup sugar

¼ cup kosher salt, plus 1 teaspoon

2 bay leaves

1 fresh rosemary sprig

12 whole peppercorns

1 quart boiling water

1 tray of ice cubes

6 chicken breasts or 12 thighs (or a mix),
   boneless and skinless

2 cups all-purpose flour

½ cup cornstarch

1 teaspoon freshly ground pepper

1 teaspoon onion powder

½ teaspoon dried thyme

½ teaspoon paprika

2 cups buttermilk

½ teaspoon cayenne pepper

Vegetable oil

Method

In a large heatproof bowl, combine the tea bags, sugar, salt, bay leaves, rosemary, and peppercorns. Pour in the boiling water and stir to dissolve the sugar and salt. Steep for 10 minutes and discard the tea bags. Add the ice cubes and stir. Refrigerate to cool the brine completely.

Cut the chicken breasts in half crosswise. Add the chicken pieces to the brine, cover, and refrigerate for 2 to 3 hours.

In a bowl, mix together the flour, cornstarch, 1 teaspoon salt, pepper, onion powder, thyme, and paprika. In another bowl, combine the buttermilk, cayenne pepper, and a pinch of salt.

Drain the chicken and pat dry with paper towels. Dredge the pieces in the flour and shake off the excess. One at a time, dip each piece into the buttermilk, then dredge again in the flour to coat completely.

In a Dutch oven or deep, heavy frying pan over medium-high heat, bring 3 inches of oil to 350°F. Fry half of the chicken pieces, turning occasionally, until golden brown and cooked through, 7 to 8 minutes. Drain on paper towels and tent with foil to keep warm while you fry the remaining chicken.

Serve hot or cold with Broccoli Salad (page 210) and Corn Muffins (page 244). Store leftovers in the fridge up to 3 days.

Notes

- *Serve with a quick dipping sauce made of equal parts mayonnaise and Dijon mustard, stirred with a squeeze of honey or maple syrup to taste—also a delicious spread for leftover fried chicken sandwiches.*
- *Tea was a scarce commodity in the colonies by the time River Run hosted Flora MacDonald, but I have a theory that Jocasta kept a stash in Hector's mausoleum along with the Jacobites' gold. If you disagree, herbal teas, such as lemon ginger, are an excellent substitute.*

SLOW-COOKED
CHICKEN FRICASSEE

"Less EAT, Mummy!" Jemmy piped up helpfully. A long string of molasses-tinged saliva flowed from the corner of his mouth and dripped down the front of his shirt. Seeing this, his mother turned on Mrs. Bug like a tiger.

"Now see what you've done, you interfering old busybody! That was his last clean shirt! And how dare you talk about our private lives with everybody in sight, what possible earthly business of yours is it, you beastly old gossiping—"

Seeing the futility of protest, Roger put his arms round her from behind, picked her up bodily off the floor, and carried her out the back door, this departure accented by incoherent protests from Bree and grunts of pain from Roger, as she kicked him repeatedly in the shins, with considerable force and accuracy.

I went to the door and closed it delicately, shutting off the sounds of further altercation in the yard.

"She gets that from you, you know," I said reproachfully, sitting down opposite Jamie. "Mrs. Bug, that smells wonderful. Do let's eat!"

Mrs. Bug dished the fricassee in huffy silence, but declined to join us at table, instead putting on her cloak and stamping out the front door, leaving us to deal with the clearing-up. An excellent bargain, if you ask me.

—*A Breath of Snow and Ashes,* chapter 21, "We Have Ignition"

Murdina Bug would have loved the convenience of a slow cooker, our modern equivalent to her iron kettle over the hearth. After all, she had busy days—what with there being eggs to collect, bread to bake, stockings to knit, beer to brew, men to feed—and one less thing to keep watch over would have been a welcome reprieve.

A classic French chicken and vegetable stew with a comforting cream sauce, a traditional fricassee does not include potatoes, but in the spirit of a true one-pot meal, throw in a few anachronistic spuds with everything else.

Serves 6

Ingredients

3 pounds (1.3 kilograms or 10 to 12 pieces) chicken thighs, bone in and skin on

½ cup all-purpose flour

1 teaspoon kosher salt

½ teaspoon freshly ground pepper

2 tablespoons olive oil

¼ cup (4 tablespoons) butter

¾ pound (340 grams) small button mushrooms, wiped clean

1½ pounds (700 grams) yellow potatoes, cut into 2-inch pieces

2 tablespoons lemon juice

1 pound (450 grams) pearl onions, peeled (see Notes), or 1 large onion, julienned (see Knife Skills, page 11)

3 medium carrots, each cut in 4 to 6 pieces

1 garlic head, papery skin discarded

2 bay leaves

2 fresh thyme sprigs

1 cup White Chicken Stock (page 23, Notes)

½ cup dry white wine

2 large egg yolks

½ cup whipping cream

Method

Pat the chicken pieces dry with paper towels. Mix together the flour, salt, and pepper on a plate. Dredge the thighs in flour one at a time, and shake off the excess.

In a large frying pan, heat the olive oil and 2 tablespoons of the butter over medium-high flame. When it's bubbling, add the chicken, skin side down, and fry until golden on the bottom, 3 to 4 minutes. Flip and fry until golden on the second side. To get a good golden crust, do not overcrowd the pan; better instead to fry the chicken in batches, undisturbed.

Arrange the fried chicken pieces in a 4- or 5-quart slow cooker.

Toss the mushrooms and potatoes with the lemon juice. Nestle them, along with the onions, carrots, garlic, the remaining 2 tablespoons butter, bay leaves, and thyme among the chicken pieces. Pour in the stock and wine, and rock the slow cooker gently to settle and mix. Cook over low heat for 6 to 8 hours.

Move a rack to the top rung and heat the oven to 300°F.

When the chicken and vegetables are cooked, turn off the slow cooker. Discard the garlic, bay leaves, and thyme. Use a slotted spoon to move the chicken and vegetables to an ovenproof dish. Keep them warm in the oven while you finish the sauce.

Strain the cooking liquid from the slow cooker into a medium saucepan. Skim off the surface fat, then reduce the liquid over medium-high heat until it measures about 1½ cups. Reduce the heat to medium-low.

In a small bowl, whisk together the egg yolks and cream. Add 2 to 3 tablespoons of the hot cooking liquid to temper the mixture, stir well, then add the cream back into the saucepan and stir constantly until hot and slightly thickened, about 5 minutes. Season to taste and keep warm.

When the sauce is ready, turn the oven to broil and lightly brown and crisp the chicken's skin, 3 to 5 minutes.

To serve, divide the chicken and vegetables on plates and spoon over the sauce.

Keep leftovers in the fridge up to 3 days.

Notes

- *You can use boneless chicken and reduce the cooking time, but the marrow from the bones adds depth, not to mention nutrition, to the finished dish that you won't get if you cook without them.*
- *To peel pearl onions, pour boiling water over them to cover. When the water has cooled enough to handle the onions, cut off the root end, and pop each out of its skin.*

Chapter 7

PORK

Rosamund's Pulled Pork with Devil's Apple BBQ Sauce

Conspirators' Cassoulet

Ragoo'd Pork

Scotch Eggs

Bangers and Mash with Slow-Cooked Onion Gravy

Rosamund's Pulled Pork with
Devil's Apple BBQ Sauce

"Aye, well, but this is the barbecue, isn't it?" Ronnie said stubbornly, ignoring my feeble attempt at humor. "Anyone kens that ye sass a barbecued hog wi' vinegar—that's the proper way of it! After all, ye wouldna put gravel into your sausage meat, would ye? Or boil your bacon wi' sweepings from the henhouse? Tcha!" He jerked his chin toward the white porter basin under Rosamund's arm, making it clear that its contents fell into the same class of inedible adulterants, in his opinion.

I caught a savory whiff as the wind changed. So far as I could tell from smell alone, Rosamund's sauce seemed to include tomatoes, onions, red pepper, and enough sugar to leave a thick blackish crust on the meat and a tantalizing caramel aroma in the air.

—*The Fiery Cross,* chapter 13, "Beans and Barbecue"

North Carolina has a long tradition of barbecue, and it holds an important place in the state's history and cultural identity. Rosamund's recipe, for the most part, is Lexington-style, rather than Ronnie Sinclair's preferred Eastern-style. The ketchup is authentic, at least in modern versions, but the apple cider is my addition to the classic tomato-vinegar mop. It deepens the flavor of the sauce and boosts its sugar content to result in the thick, caramelized crust on the meat that matches Claire's mouthwatering description.

Serves 6 or more

Ingredients

2 tablespoons paprika

6 tablespoons dark brown sugar, firmly packed

5 teaspoons kosher salt

1 teaspoon mustard powder

1 teaspoon onion powder

½ teaspoon dried thyme

1 teaspoon freshly ground pepper

½ teaspoon cayenne pepper

5- to 6-pound (2.3 to 2.7 kilograms) pork butt (shoulder)

1 to 2 tablespoons vegetable oil

1½ cups ketchup   ¾ cup cider vinegar
1½ cups hard or soft apple cider

Method

In a small bowl, combine the paprika, 2 tablespoons brown sugar, 1 tablespoon salt, mustard powder, onion powder, thyme, ½ teaspoon ground pepper, and ¼ teaspoon cayenne pepper and stir to mix well.

Pat the pork roast dry with paper towels. Use your hands to rub the oil all over the roast, then coat it generously with the dry rub. Rest on the counter for 1 to 2 hours.

Meanwhile, in a saucepan, combine the ketchup, apple cider, vinegar, and the remaining ¼ cup brown sugar, 2 teaspoons salt, ½ teaspoon ground pepper, and ¼ teaspoon cayenne pepper. Bring to a boil over medium-high heat, then reduce the heat and simmer briskly until reduced to 3 cups, 10 to 15 minutes.

Set your smoker/grill to between 225°F and 250°F.

Cook the roast with the wood/charcoal of your choice. Start mopping the surface with sauce in the third hour, and every half hour after that, until the internal temperature measures 190 to 195°F on an instant-read thermometer inserted in the thickest part of the roast, 5 to 7 hours, give or take, depending on the size of your roast and the temperature of your smoker or grill.

When it is done, set the meat on a large dish or serving platter and tent it loosely with foil for at least 45 minutes before pulling the meat apart with two forks.

Serve on rolls or Mrs. Bug's Buttermilk Drop Biscuits (page 246) with the remaining sauce and a tangy coleslaw on the side.

Store leftovers in the fridge up to 3 days.

Notes

- *To keep food-borne illness away, pour a small amount of the sauce into a bowl from which you can mop the meat while it's cooking. Replenish as needed, but never dip the brush you're using on the meat into the main batch of sauce.*
- *Removing the meat from the fridge before cooking is an important step; the most tender, evenly cooked, and delicious roasts are started from meat at room temperature.*
- *Just as important is the long resting period after the meat has been cooked but before it has been pulled. The larger the roast, the more time it takes for the juices to migrate back into the center of the meat.*

Conspirators' Cassoulet

"I thought you'd be upset," I said, scooping up a mouthful of succulent cassoulet with a bit of bread. The warm, bacon-spiced beans soothed me, filling me with a sense of peaceful well-being. It was cold and dark outside, and loud with the rushing of the wind, but it was warm and quiet here by the fire together.

"Oh, about Louise de La Tour foisting a bastard on her husband?" Jamie frowned at his own dish, running a finger around the edge to pick up the last of the juice. "Well, I'm no verra much in favor of it, I'll tell ye, Sassenach. It's a filthy trick to play on a man, but what's the poor bloody woman to do otherwise?" He shook his head, then glanced at the desk across the room and smiled wryly.

"Besides, it doesna become me to be takin' a high moral stand about other people's behavior. Stealing letters and spying and trying generally to subvert a man my family holds as King? I shouldna like to have someone judging me on the grounds of the things I'm doing, Sassenach."

—*Dragonfly in Amber,* chapter 13, "Deceptions"

Cassoulet comes from the French *cassole*, the traditional, conical clay pot in which this savory, rib-sticking meat-and-bean stew is cooked. Originally a simple "casserole" of white beans, duck or goose confit, sausages, pork, and whatever other meat was available, this dish of humble beginnings, and its ingredients, is now the cause of much regional debate across southern France.

The *Outlander Kitchen* cassoulet is a combination of traditional ingredients and techniques with a few modern modifications to make this historical dish more accessible to twenty-first-century North Americans.

Serves 6

Ingredients

1 pound (450 grams) dry white beans
   (cannellini, Great Northern, navy)
1 smoked ham hock (about 2 pounds
   or 900 grams)

2 large onions, 1 whole and 1 julienned
   (see Knife Skills, page 11)
6 whole cloves

2 medium stalks celery, each cut
   into 2 pieces
1 medium carrot, cut into 4 pieces
2 bay leaves
1 pound salt pork (450 grams),
   cut into ¾-inch cubes
4 whole chicken legs with thighs
1 pound (450 grams) raw lamb or
   pork sausages with garlic

½ cup white wine or dry vermouth
1 can (14 ounces or 398 ml) whole
   tomatoes, drained
2 tablespoons duck fat, plus additional,
   as required
½ teaspoon freshly ground pepper
1 whole garlic head,
   loose papery skin removed
1 fresh sage sprig

Method

Soak the beans overnight in a large bowl of tepid water.

The next day, in a stockpot, cover the ham hock with cold water, cover, and bring to a boil over high heat. Boil 2 minutes, then drain and discard the water. Cover again with cold water. Stud the uncut onion with cloves. Add it to the pot, along with the celery, carrots, and bay leaves. Bring to a boil, covered with a lid, over high heat. Once at a rolling boil, reduce heat to low and simmer until the ham hock is almost fork-tender, about 90 minutes.

Add the drained beans to the pot, increase the heat to high, and bring to a low boil. Reduce the heat to low, cover, and simmer until the beans are just tender, 45 to 60 minutes, depending on the variety and age of the beans.

Drain and reserve the liquid. Discard the clove-studded onion, carrots, celery, and bay leaves. Pour the beans into a large bowl and shred the meat from the ham hock, discarding the bone, skin, fat, and gristle. Add the meat to the beans.

Move a rack to the middle rung and heat the oven to 350°F.

Place the cubed salt pork in a cold Dutch oven or large cast-iron pan set over medium heat. Cover with a lid and cook until the fat is rendered, stirring very occasionally, 30 to 40 minutes. Remove the lid and cook until the pork is crisp. Scoop the pork onto a plate with a slotted spoon.

Leave all the fat from the salt pork in the pan. (If you do not have at least 3 tablespoons of fat in the pan, add duck fat to make up the difference and heat until shimmering.) Add the chicken legs, skin side down. Cook, undisturbed, until golden brown, 4 to 5 minutes. Flip and brown the other side. Add the legs to the plate with the salt pork. Next, brown the sausages in the fat, turning occasionally until deep golden, about 5 minutes. Cut the sausages in half and pile onto the plate with the rest of the meat.

Discard all but 1 tablespoon of fat from the Dutch oven. Add the julienned onions, stirring constantly, until they soften, about 3 minutes. Deglaze with the wine, scraping up the browned meat bits, until almost dry, about 2 minutes. Add to the bowl with the beans, along with the tomatoes, duck fat, and pepper. Mix well.

Pour half of the bean mixture into a 3-quart *cassole,* ovenproof ceramic bowl, or Dutch oven. Add the salt pork, chicken, and sausage in a mixed layer, then top with the remaining beans. Pour in enough of the reserved pork hock cooking liquid to just come up to the level of the beans and poke the garlic and sage under the surface.

Bake, uncovered, until the cassoulet comes to a simmer and a crust begins to form, about 1 hour. Stir the crust gently back into the cassoulet, bringing moist beans to the top. Add additional pork hock liquid if required to moisten the beans.

Cook for another 2 hours, checking and stirring in the crust one more time. When finished, it should have a thick, golden crust.

Allow to rest for 15 minutes before serving from the pot, breaking the crust at the table.

Store leftovers in the fridge up to 3 days.

Notes

- *Discarding the hock's first boiling water mellows the second boiling to a mild-tasting, slightly smoky stock that won't overpower the other ingredients.*
- *I have replaced a classic cassoulet ingredient, duck confit, with more readily available chicken legs. The optional duck fat replaces the authentic flavor lost by using chicken, but if you have access to duck confit, by all means use that.*
- *In lieu of an authentic cassole, use a Dutch oven or other large ovenproof vessel. Without the traditional conical shape and sloping sides, however, the liquid in the dish will not evaporate and form a crust. You'll still have a rich and delicious cassoulet, just a crustless one.*
- *Use the leftover pork hock stock to make a smoky bowl of Kale Brose with Bacon (page 65).*

RAGOO'D PORK

"Oh, they would," Jamie assured me. "They were most seriously sharpening their knives when I found them at it and told them not to trouble themselves."

I suppressed an involuntary smile at the image of the Beardsleys, bent side by side over a grindstone, their lean, dark faces set in identical scowls of vengeance, but the momentary flash of humor faded.

"Oh, God. We'll have to tell the McGillivrays."

Jamie nodded, looking pale at the thought, but pushed back his bench.

"I'd best go straightaway."

"Not 'til ye've had a bite." Mrs. Bug put a plate of food firmly in front of him. "Ye dinna want to be dealing wi' Ute McGillivray on an empty stomach."

Jamie hesitated, but evidently found her argument to have merit, for he picked up his fork and addressed himself to the ragoo'd pork with grim determination.

—*A Breath of Snow and Ashes,* chapter 46, "In Which Things Gang Agley"

By the eighteenth century, much of the North Carolina and surrounding colonies' diets were based on pork and corn, as both were relatively easy and inexpensive to raise. This "hog and hominy" diet, as it came to be called, stretched across all levels of society, with the average person consuming five pounds of pork for every pound of beef.

Ragoo is from the French *ragoût*, a main-dish stew cooked slowly over low heat. Serve this tender, red-wine braised pork with Beer-Battered Corn Fritters (page 88), or over pasta, like an Italian *ragù*, also borrowed from the French root word.

Serves 6 or more

Ingredients

¼ cup all-purpose flour

1 teaspoon kosher salt, plus additional

½ teaspoon freshly ground pepper

4 to 5 pounds (2 kilograms) boneless
    pork shoulder, cut into 6 to 8 pieces

¼ cup (4 tablespoons) butter

2 bay leaves

2 fresh thyme sprigs

1 fresh rosemary sprig

2 1-inch strips lemon zest

1 large onion, julienned (see Knife Skills, page 11)

1 tablespoon tomato paste

1 cup red wine

1 cup Brown Chicken Stock (page 20)

3 large garlic cloves, whole

1 tablespoon Worcestershire sauce

Method

On a large plate, mix together the flour, salt, and pepper. Dredge the pork pieces in the flour to cover on all sides.

In a Dutch oven or stockpot, melt the butter over medium-high heat. When bubbling, add half of the pork, leaving space between each piece. Fry until brown on all sides, about 3 minutes per side. Reduce the heat if necessary to avoid burning. Move the cooked pork to a plate and repeat with the remaining pieces. Keep the cooking juices in the pot.

Meanwhile, tie the bay leaves, thyme, rosemary, and lemon zest into a square of cheesecloth with string, or enclose them in a large tea ball. Set the bouquet garni aside.

Add the onions to the pot, scraping up the browned meat bits with a wooden spoon. Stirring almost constantly, fry the onions until they are a deep golden color but not browned, 7 to 10 minutes. Add the tomato paste and stir for 1 minute. Deglaze with the red wine, bring to a boil, and stir for 1 minute. Add the stock, the pork and its accumulated juices, the garlic, and the Worcestershire sauce. Bring to a boil over high heat, add the bouquet garni to the pot, reduce the heat to low, and cover. Simmer until the meat is very tender, about 3 hours.

Discard the bouquet garni and skim the clear fat from the surface of the pot. Shred the pork with two forks and toss in the liquid to cover well.

Store leftovers in the fridge up to 3 days.

SCOTCH EGGS

"Ken the difference between a Scottish wedding and a Scottish funeral, do ye?"

"No, what?"

"The funeral has one less drunk."

She laughed, scattering crumbs, and took a Scotch egg. "No," he said, steering her skillfully to the right of the dock, and toward the willows. "Ye'll see a few feet sticking out of the bushes now, but this afternoon, they hadn't had the time to get rat-legged yet."

"You have such a way with words," she said appreciatively. "I went and talked to the slaves; all present and accounted for, and mostly sober, too. A couple of the women admitted that Betty does tipple at parties, though."

"To say the least, from what your Da said. Stinking, he described her as, and I gather he didn't mean only drunk." Something small and dark leaped out of his path. Frog; he could hear them piping away in the grove.

—*The Fiery Cross*, chapter 47, "The Lists of Venus"

The origins of this tasty, protein-packed portable snack are unclear. London's Fortnum & Mason claims to have invented it for rich coach travelers in 1738. Others have speculated that Scotch eggs were inspired by *nargisi kofta*, also known as Narcissus meatballs, a dish of minced meat and boiled eggs from the kitchens of sixteenth-century imperial India. A third, more pedestrian, explanation is the most likely: a portable lunch made from leftovers, a Scotch egg is a variation of a Cornish pasty, bridie, or any other handheld working man's lunch from the early days of industrialized Britain.

Makes 6

Ingredients

7 large eggs

½ cup all-purpose flour

½ teaspoon kosher salt

Pinch of cayenne pepper

1½ cups panko-style breadcrumbs

1½ pounds (700 grams) pork sausage

Vegetable oil

Method

In a large saucepan, cover 6 eggs with cold water and top off with an extra inch. Bring to a full rolling boil over high heat, remove from the heat, and cover for 7 minutes. Drain and cover the eggs with ice water until cool to the touch, then peel them.

In a small bowl, stir together the flour, salt, and cayenne pepper. In another bowl, beat the remaining egg with 1 teaspoon of water to make an egg wash. Fill a third bowl with the breadcrumbs.

Flatten 4 ounces of sausage into a patty in the palm of your hands, and wrap it around a peeled egg. Repeat with the remaining sausage meat and eggs. Roll the sausage-covered eggs in the flour to coat lightly, then in the egg wash, and finally in the breadcrumbs to cover evenly.

In a large frying pan, heat 3 inches of vegetable oil to 350°F. Fry the Scotch eggs until golden, turning occasionally, about 3 minutes. Drain on paper towels. Alternatively, bake in a 400°F oven until light golden and crispy, 25 to 30 minutes.

Serve warm or cold.

Store leftovers up to 3 days in the fridge.

Notes

- *Lightly cracking the hard-boiled eggs before submerging them in ice water makes them easier to peel, especially farm-fresh eggs.*
- *Pork sausage is traditional—but you can use any sausage your heart desires—beef, turkey, even veggie, or make a batch and a half of Young Ian's Sage and Garlic Sausage (page 52) and use that.*
- *Baked Scotch Eggs are not a beautiful golden like those fried in oil, but they do crisp up nicely, to the point where I can honestly say that you're not going to lose a lot of flavor if you forgo the mess and cleanup of deep-fat frying.*

Bangers and Mash with Slow-Cooked Onion Gravy

"Where the hell have you been?" I demanded.

He took time to kiss me before replying. His face was cold against mine, and his lips tasted faintly and pleasantly of whisky.

"Mm, sausage for supper?" he said approvingly, sniffing at my hair, which smelled of kitchen smoke. "Good, I'm fair starved."

"Bangers and mash," I said. "Where have you been?"

He laughed, shaking out his plaid to get the blown snow off. "Bangers and mash? That's food, is it?"

"Sausages with mashed potatoes," I translated. "A nice traditional English dish, hitherto unknown in the benighted reaches of Scotland. Now, you bloody Scot, where in hell have you been for the last two days? Jenny and I were worried!"

—*Dragonfly in Amber,* chapter 33, "Thy Brother's Keeper"

In the past, British sausages—particularly those made under rationing during World War II—were made with an excess of water and would sometimes burst when cooked over a high heat, leading to their nickname, bangers. That won't happen with a modern sausage on either side of the pond, so fear not.

This is English comfort food at its best. The onions for the gravy cook low and slow all day to make an unbelievably flavorful gravy, and the rest comes together quickly for an easy, end-of-day meal that everyone will love.

Serves 6

Ingredients

3 medium onions, julienned (see Knife Skills, page 11)

2 tablespoons vegetable oil, plus 1 teaspoon

½ cup (1 stick) butter

1 fresh thyme or rosemary sprig

Kosher salt to taste

¼ cup all-purpose flour

2 cups Brown Chicken Stock (page 20) or Vegetable Stock (page 24)

8 to 12 pork, beef, or veggie sausages, such as Young Ian's Sage and Garlic Sausage (page 52)

3 pounds (1.4 kilograms or 5 to 6
   medium) yellow potatoes, peeled,
   cut into 2-inch pieces

2 bay leaves
½ cup light cream
Ground white pepper to taste

Method

In a 3-quart (minimum) slow cooker, toss together the onions, 2 tablespoons veg-etable oil, 2 tablespoons butter, thyme, and a pinch of salt. Mound the onions in the center, away from the edges, so that they don't burn. Cook over low heat for 4 to 5 hours, stirring occasionally if you are around.

Move a rack to the middle rung and heat the oven to 400°F.

When the onions are a deep caramel color, discard the thyme. Turn the slow cooker to high and stir in the flour. Cover and cook for 10 minutes. Whisk in the stock and another pinch of salt, cover, and cook, stirring occasionally, while you prepare the rest of the meal.

In a metal baking pan, toss the sausages with the remaining 1 teaspoon vegetable oil. Roast until golden brown, turning occasionally, 25 to 30 minutes. Tent loosely with foil until the potatoes are ready.

While the sausages cook, place the potatoes and bay leaves in a large saucepan with 2 inches of cold, salted water. Cover and bring to a boil over medium-high heat. Reduce to medium and steam, covered, until tender, 25 to 30 minutes. Drain and discard the bay leaves.

Mash the potatoes until smooth, and stir in the remaining 6 tablespoons butter and the cream vigorously with a wooden spoon. Season the potatoes and the onion gravy with salt and pepper.

Mound the mash in the middle of each plate and top with 1 or 2 sausages. Spoon over the onion gravy and serve with green peas or your favorite vegetable.

Notes

- *Don't rush the onions; the darker the caramel of the onions, the richer and more flavorful the gravy.*
- *Caramelized onions freeze very well. I often do up to 10 onions at a time, then freeze them in individual containers for use later.*
- *Avoid turning on the oven and grill the sausages on the BBQ or fry them on the stovetop.*

Chapter 8

LAMB

Buttermilk Lamb Chops with Rosewater Mint Sauce

Shepherd's Pie

Sarah Woolam's Scotch Pies

BUTTERMILK LAMB CHOPS
WITH ROSEWATER MINT SAUCE

"Excellent," Ned said again. He rose, beaming, and bowed to the company. "As our friend Dr. John Arbuthnot says, 'Law is a bottomless pit.' But not more so at the moment than my stomach. Is that delectable aroma indicative of a saddle of mutton in our vicinity, Mrs. Jenny?"

At table, I sat to one side of Jamie, Hobart MacKenzie to the other, now looking pink and relaxed. Mary MacNab brought in the joint, and by ancient custom, set it down in front of Jamie. Her gaze lingered on him a moment too long. He picked up the long, wicked carving knife with his good hand and offered it politely to Hobart.

"Will ye have a go at it, Hobart?" he said.

"Och, no," Hobart said, waving it away. "Better let your wife carve it. I'm no hand wi' a knife—likely cut my finger off instead. You know me, Jamie," he said comfortably.

Jamie gave his erstwhile brother-in-law a long look over the saltcellar.

"Once I would ha' thought, so, Hobart," he said. "Pass me the whisky, aye?"

—*Voyager,* chapter 38, "I Meet a Lawyer"

A saddle of mutton or lamb is a cut not often seen these days, except by preorder from a specialty butcher. It is a boneless roast rolled from the animal's two loins, the tender muscles located on either side of the spine, nestled protectively under the ribs.

More popular these days is a rack of lamb, where the loin is still attached to the ribs. It's easy to prepare, tender and delicious, especially in this simple buttermilk marinade made from ingredients found at eighteenth-century Lallybroch, including the rosewater, which Jenny would have distilled from the petals of Ellen's rosebush.

Serves 6

Ingredients

3 frenched racks of lamb (see Notes), 6 to 8 ribs each, 3 to 4 pounds (1.3 to 1.8 kilograms) total

¼ cup fresh marjoram or oregano leaves

1 tablespoon coriander seeds

1½ teaspoons kosher salt

1 teaspoon whole peppercorns

1 cup buttermilk

1 teaspoon rosewater

1 cup finely chopped fresh mint leaves

3 tablespoons white wine vinegar

1½ tablespoons honey

Vegetable oil for brushing the grill pan (optional)

Method

With a sharp knife, carefully cut between the lamb ribs to divide them into chops of equal thickness. Depending on the number of ribs per rack, you will have eighteen to twenty-four individual chops.

In a mortar, combine the oregano, coriander seeds, salt, and peppercorns. Bash and grind with the pestle until well mixed. In a small bowl, combine the ground herbs and spices with the buttermilk and ½ teaspoon rosewater. Pour over the lamb chops in a baking dish or on a large plate and toss to coat evenly. Cover and refrigerate for 1 to 2 hours.

Combine the chopped mint, vinegar, honey, and the remaining ½ teaspoon rosewater in a small bowl and mix to combine. Refrigerate while the lamb marinates.

Gently shake most of the marinade from the chops and cook by one of the following three methods.

UNDER THE BROILER: Move a rack to the top rung and heat the oven to 450°F. Arrange the chops on a broiler pan or on a wire rack set in a rimmed baking sheet. Turn on the broiler and cook until browned and at the desired doneness, 3 to 4 minutes per side for medium rare.

ON THE STOVETOP: Heat a grill pan on the stove over medium for 5 minutes. Increase the heat to medium-high, lightly brush the pan with oil, and cook the chops until browned, 2 to 3 minutes per side for medium rare.

ON THE BARBECUE: Cook the chops over a medium-high flame until browned, 2 to 3 minutes per side for medium rare.

Arrange the cooked chops on a plate and tent loosely with foil. Rest 5 minutes before serving.

Serve with the mint sauce and Stovie Potatoes (page 182), and pass Atholl Brose for the Bonnie Prince (page 299) around the table after dinner for a seemingly homely, but surprisingly refined, family dinner straight from Lallybroch.

Refrigerate leftovers up to 3 days.

Notes

- *A frenched rack of lamb has had the chine, fat cap, and membranes between the rib bones removed and cleaned. Ask your butcher to do this, or check YouTube for instructional videos on how to do it yourself.*
- *When I french my own rack at home, I broil the fat and gristly bits until crisp, and incorporate them, finely chopped, into a batch of homemade dog biscuits. There's a reason that guy follows me everywhere, aye?*
- *For thicker chops, cut between every second rib, and adjust cooking times.*

SHEPHERD'S PIE

The house was empty when we returned, though Mrs. Bug had left a covered dish of shepherd's pie on the table, the floor swept, and the fire neatly smoored. I took off my wet cloak and hung it on the peg, as though I stood in a stranger's house, in a country where I did not know the custom.

Jamie seemed to feel the same way—though after a moment, he stirred, fetched down the candlestick from the shelf over the hearth, and lit it with a spill from the fire. The wavering glow seemed only to emphasize the odd, echoing quality of the room, and he stood holding it for a minute, at a loss, before finally setting it down with a thump in the middle of the table.
—*A Breath of Snow and Ashes,* **chapter 80, "The World Turned Upside Down"**

Although the dish itself is much older, the name *shepherd's pie* did not appear until the nineteenth century. *Cottage* pie was in use by the turn of the eighteenth century, when the potato was being introduced as an affordable crop for the poor, many of whom lived in cottages. The two terms were used synonymously for a long time, but today it is generally agreed that a shepherd's pie contains lamb, while a cottage pie contains beef.

Nothing quiets a growling wame faster, and this version's red wine base and crown of golden, cream-free duchesse potatoes is an update on the Scottish lamb-and-potatoes classic. Make no mistake; this is not Mrs. Bug's Shepherd's Pie.

Serves 6 or more

Ingredients

2 pounds (900 grams) ground lamb

1 tablespoon minced fresh rosemary

1 tablespoon minced fresh thyme

2 teaspoons kosher salt, plus additional

1 teaspoon freshly ground pepper, plus additional

2 medium onions, grated

2 large carrots or 2 medium parsnips, grated

3 garlic cloves, grated or minced

6 large mushrooms, thinly sliced

2 tablespoons tomato paste

½ cup red wine (optional)

1 cup Brown Beef or Chicken Stock (page 20)

1 tablespoon Worcestershire sauce

2½ pounds (1+ kilograms or 4 to 5 medium) yellow potatoes, peeled and cut into 2-inch pieces

6 tablespoons butter
3 large egg yolks
1 cup shredded Parmesan cheese

Method

Move a rack to the middle rung and heat the oven to 425°F.

Heat an extra-large frying pan or saucepan over medium-high. Add the lamb, rosemary, thyme, 2 teaspoons salt, and 1 teaspoon pepper. Cook, gently breaking up the lamb with the back of a wooden spoon and stirring occasionally. When the lamb is no longer pink, add the onions, carrots, garlic, and mushrooms. Cook until the vegetables are softened, 5 to 7 minutes. Drain off excess fat and return to the stove.

Add the tomato paste and stir constantly for about a minute. Deglaze with the red wine and reduce, stirring and scraping up the brown bits, until almost dry, about 2 minutes. Add the stock and Worcestershire sauce, reduce the heat to medium-low, and simmer for 15 minutes. Season to taste with salt and pepper.

While the meat is cooking, place the potatoes in a large pot with 2 inches of cold, salted water. Cover and bring to a boil over medium-high heat. Reduce to medium and steam, covered, until tender, 25 to 30 minutes. Drain and allow them to steam dry in the saucepan, off the heat, for 2 minutes. Mash, add the butter and egg yolks, then mash again until smooth. Add half of the Parmesan and mix well. Season with salt and pepper to taste.

Spoon the meat mixture into a 2-quart baking dish, spoon the potatoes over the meat, sprinkle with the remaining Parmesan, and bake 25 to 30 minutes, or until the top is golden. Let the meat rest for 10 minutes before serving to allow the juices to settle.

Store leftovers in the fridge up to 3 days.

Notes

- *No lamb? Substitute regular ground beef and enjoy a scrumptious cottage pie.*
- *Because there are only two of us, I divide the recipe into two loaf-size pans and freeze one for dinner down the road.*
- *Yellow potatoes result in a slightly creamier mash, but russets work well if that is what you have on hand.*

Sarah Woolam's Scotch Pies

He was chilled now, from sitting, and pulled his shirt back on. He was hungry, too, but he would wait a bit for the young ones. Not but what they had likely stuffed themselves already, he thought cynically. He could almost smell the meat pies Sarah Woolam made, the rich scent twining in his memory through the actual autumn smells of dead leaves and damp earth.

The thought of meat pies lingered in his mind as he went on with his work, along with the thought of winter. The Indians said it would be hard, this winter, not like the last. How would it be, hunting in deep snow? It snowed in Scotland, of course, but often enough it lay light on the ground, and the trodden paths of the red deer showed black on the steep, bare mountainsides.

—*Drums of Autumn,* chapter 44, "Three-Cornered Conversation"

Also known as a mutton pies, Scotch pies were frowned upon in the Middle Ages by the Scottish Church, viewed as extravagant, sinful, English-style food. In later centuries, they evolved into inexpensive and sustaining snacks for the working class, and today are sold at outdoor events such as football (soccer) matches. The space on top of the pie, created by the raised crust, is often filled with gravy, mashed potato, or Oxford Baked Beans (page 204).

The hot-water pastry used to make hand-raised pies is more often formed around a mold, but I prefer the easier technique below, where the pastry is shaped within the mold, taught to me by a New Zealand culinary instructor.

Makes 6

Ingredients

1 pound (450 grams) lamb or
    beef sirloin, minced (see Knife Skills,
    page 11)

¼ cup Brown Beef or Chicken Stock
    (page 20)

½ small onion, grated

2 teaspoons Worcestershire sauce

2 teaspoons kosher salt

½ teaspoon freshly ground pepper

¼ teaspoon freshly grated nutmeg

¾ cup (12 tablespoons) butter or lard,
    cut into 1-inch cubes

4 cups all-purpose flour

1 large egg

Method

Combine the lamb, stock, onions, Worcestershire sauce, 1 teaspoon salt, pepper, and nutmeg in a bowl and mix well.

In a large saucepan, melt the butter or lard in 1 cup of water over medium-high heat. Remove from the heat and stir in the flour and remaining 1 teaspoon salt with a wooden spoon until a smooth dough forms. Tip onto the counter and quickly, so the hot dough doesn't burn them, knead for 3 minutes.

Divide the pastry into three equal portions and loosely tent two portions under foil while you use the first to make two pies. On a lightly floured counter, roll the pastry out to a 12-inch square, ⅛ inch thick. Cut out two 7-inch circles and two 4-inch circles. Lay one of the larger circles in a 3-inch mold (see Notes), gently pressing into the bottom edge to form a case. Smooth the pastry around the sides, minimizing folds in the pastry as best you can.

Fill the casing with ⅙ of the lamb filling (about 3 ounces), leaving at least

½ inch of space at the top. Lay a smaller circle of pastry over the filling. Press firmly with your fingertips to crimp the lid to the pastry case all the way around. Roll the rolling pin over the top of the cutter to trim the pastry and with a sharp knife, make a slit in the top of the pie to vent steam. Gently tap the pie out of the bottom of the mold. Repeat with the remaining pastry and filling.

Whisk the egg with 1 teaspoon of water. Brush the pastry with the egg wash, arrange the pies on a parchment paper–lined baking sheet and refrigerate for 30 minutes.

Move a rack to the upper-middle rung and heat the oven to 400°F. Bake the pies, rotating the pan once, until golden, 35 to 45 minutes. Cool on a wire rack for at least 15 minutes.

Serve hot or cold. Refrigerate leftovers up to 3 days. Freeze uncooked pies up to 2 weeks—defrost in the refrigerator overnight and bake as directed above.

Notes

- *Most Scotch pies bought in shops contain ground meat, but the superior texture of the cooked, hand minced meat is worth the extra prep time.*
- *Hot-water pastry is much easier to work with on the first roll. While you can gather the scraps and reroll, it is tricky to avoid holes and tears in your pastry.*
- *Three-inch diameter PVC piping cut into 2-inch lengths from the hardware store makes excellent molds for Scotch pies. A round 3-inch biscuit cutter also works, as long as it is at least 1½ inches high.*

Chapter 9

~◦~

GAME

Venison Stew with Tomatoe-Fruits

Jenny's Hare Pie

Venison Stew with Tomatoe-Fruits

Do not, I pray you suffer any Alarm on our account. The Black Bears of this country are wary of Humans, and Loath to approach even a Single Man. Also, our house is strongly built, and I have forbidden Ian to go Abroad after dark, save he is Well-armed.

In the matter of Armament, our situation is much Improved. Fergus has brought back from High Point both a fine Rifle of the new kind, and several excellent Knives.

Also a large boiling kettle, whose Acquisition we have Celebrated with a great quantity of tasty Stew made with Venison, wild Onions from the wood, dried beans, and likewise some Tomatoe-fruits, dried from the Summer. None of us Died or suffered Ill-effects from Eating of this stew, so Claire is likely right, Tomatoes are not Poison.

—*Drums of Autumn,* chapter 34, "Lallybroch"

In eighteenth-century Britain, venison was found only on the tables of the extravagantly rich, whose land holdings were large enough to sustain large herds of grazing deer. In contrast, most Highlanders existed on a subsistence diet of boiled grains and vegetable stews, up until their forced emigration during the Highland Clearances in the years following the Battle of Culloden.

Those who arrived in the colonies found lush, natural larders in backcountry areas such as the fictional Fraser's Ridge in North Carolina, and they quickly incorporated locally grown corn, beans, squash, and collards into their diets. The addition of animal protein, hunted in forests bursting with birds and game, resulted in a much more varied and nutritionally complete diet for all.

Beets, red wine, and juniper join Jamie's list of venison, wild onions, beans, and sun-dried tomatoes to make a rich, satisfying stew that will keep you warm during the cold months of the year.

Serves 6

Ingredients

½ cup dried kidney beans

½ cup sun-dried tomatoes

¼ cup all-purpose flour

1½ teaspoons kosher salt, plus
    additional

½ teaspoon freshly ground pepper, plus
    additional

1½ pounds (700 grams) venison stew
    meat, cut into 2-inch cubes

2 tablespoons olive oil, plus additional

4 slices bacon, cut crosswise into ¼-inch
    strips

1 large onion, cut into ½-inch wedges

1 cup dry red wine

2 cups Brown Chicken or Beef Stock
    (page 20)

1 pound beets (450 grams or about
    4 medium), peeled and cut into
    ½-inch wedges

2 bay leaves

2 fresh rosemary sprigs

12 juniper berries, crushed

2 garlic cloves, halved

Method

In a small saucepan, cover the kidney beans with 2 inches of cold water. Bring to a boil over medium-high heat and boil for 2 minutes. Remove from the heat, cover, and soak for 1 hour. Drain.

Soak the sun-dried tomatoes in 1 cup boiling hot water for 1 hour. Drain, reserving the soaking liquid. Chop the tomatoes roughly.

Move a rack to the bottom rung and heat the oven to 325°F.

Mix together the flour, salt, and pepper in a bowl. Pat the venison dry with paper towels, then dredge the pieces in the flour to coat on all sides.

In a Dutch oven or large saucepan, heat the oil over medium-high flame. In batches, brown the venison on all sides, about 2 minutes per side. Rest the browned meat on a plate and repeat with the remaining venison, using additional oil if required.

When the last batch of venison is gone from the pan, reduce the heat to medium and fry the bacon pieces until golden brown. Add the bacon pieces to the venison and pour off all but 1 tablespoon of bacon fat from the pan.

Add the onions to the pan and cook until slightly softened, scraping up the brown bits from the bottom of the pan, 3 to 5 minutes. Deglaze with the red wine and boil 1 minute, stirring constantly. Add the stock, tomato soaking liquid, venison, bacon, beans, tomatoes, and beets. Increase the heat to medium-high and bring to a rapid boil.

Meanwhile, make a bouquet garni. Wrap the bay leaves, rosemary, juniper berries, and garlic in a square of cheesecloth and tie with string, or enclose the items in a large tea ball.

When the stew is boiling, poke the bouquet garni under the surface and cover the pot. Cook in the oven until the meat, beans, and beets are tender, about 90 minutes. Season with salt and pepper to taste.

Serve hot over Spoon Bread (page 236).

Refrigerate leftovers up to 3 days.

Note

- *Juniper berries are not a true berry, but instead are the female seed cones produced by select species of juniper trees. They pair well with game, particularly wild birds, boar, and venison, and also give gin its distinctive flavor.*

JENNY'S HARE PIE

"If ye've brought meat, we'll have it. If not, it's brose and hough."

He made a face at this; the thought of boiled barley and shin-beef, the last remnants of the salted beef carcass they'd bought two months before, was unappealing.

"Just as well I had luck, then," he said. He upended his game bag and let the three rabbits fall onto the table in a limp tumble of gray fur and crumpled ears. "And blackthorn berries," he added, tipping out the contents of the dun bonnet, now stained inside with the rich red juice.

Jenny's eyes brightened at the sight. "Hare pie," she declared. "There's no currants, but the berries will do even better, and there's enough butter, thank God." Catching a tiny blink of movement among the gray fur, she slapped her hand down on the table, neatly obliterating the minuscule intruder.

"Take them out and skin 'em, Jamie, or the kitchen will be hopping wi' fleas."

—*Voyager,* chapter 5, "To Us a Child Is Given"

Hare, as well as the rabbit Jamie brings to supper here, is a flavorful, low-fat protein, and an excellent alternative to night-after-night chicken. The bacon, berries, and wine combine to make a flavor-filled potpie worthy of a wealthy table in any century.

Ask your butcher to cut the rabbit up for you, or watch an online video to learn how to do it yourself.

Serves 6 to 8

Ingredients

1 hare or rabbit (2 to 3 pounds or 900 to 1,300 grams), cut into 6 to 8 pieces

2 teaspoons kosher salt

½ teaspoon freshly ground pepper

2 strips thick-cut bacon, cut crosswise into ¼-inch pieces

1 medium onion, diced (see Knife Skills, page 11)

1 medium carrot, diced

1 cup Brown Chicken Stock (page 20)

1 cup rosé wine (see Notes)

2 bay leaves

1 fresh rosemary sprig

¼ cup (4 tablespoons) butter

¼ cup all-purpose flour

1 teaspoon mustard powder

¼ teaspoon freshly grated nutmeg

1 recipe Short Crust Pastry (page 27), chilled

¾ cup blackberries or blueberries (see Notes)

1 large egg

Method

Flatten the hare or rabbit pieces with a meat mallet and season well with the salt and pepper.

Heat a Dutch oven or large, deep frying pan over medium and fry the bacon, stirring occasionally, until browned and rendered of its fat. Remove with a slotted spoon and drain on paper towels, leaving the bacon fat in the pan.

Immediately add half of the rabbit pieces to the pan and cook, undisturbed, until

golden, 4 to 5 minutes. Flip and cook until golden on the other side, 3 to 4 more minutes. Rest on a plate and repeat with the remaining rabbit pieces.

Add the rabbit meat back to the pot along with the onions, carrots, stock, wine, bay leaves, and rosemary. Bring to a boil, cover, reduce the heat to low, and simmer until the rabbit is tender, 45 to 60 minutes, stirring gently once or twice.

With a slotted spoon, remove the rabbit pieces from the pan and set aside to cool. Discard the bay leaves and rosemary. When the rabbit is cool enough to handle, remove the meat from the bones in chunks.

In a bowl, use a fork to mash together the butter, flour, mustard powder, and nutmeg into a paste. Stir this beurre manié into the cooking liquid and vegetables in the pan, increase the heat to medium, and cook until the mixture is glossy and slightly thickened, about 5 minutes. Remove from the heat.

Move a rack to the bottom rung and heat the oven to 400°F.

Roll out half of the pastry into a bottom crust ⅛-inch thick, and transfer to a 9-inch deep-dish pie plate. Fill the crust almost to the top with the rabbit meat, berries, reserved cooking liquid, and vegetables.

Roll out the other half of the pastry to ⅛ inch thick and use it to cover the pie. Trim and crimp the crusts together to seal. Use a sharp knife to cut two or three steam vents in the top. Whisk together the egg with 1 teaspoon water for an egg wash and brush it on the top of the pie sparingly.

Bake for 15 minutes, then reduce the heat to 350°F and bake until golden, another 25 to 30 minutes. Remove from the oven and rest for 15 minutes before slicing and serving with the remainder of the rosé.

Refrigerate leftovers up to 3 days.

Notes

- *Starting the pie on a higher heat and at the bottom of the oven will help to crisp up the bottom crust.*
- *Today, the term* claret *refers to a dry, dark red wine from Bordeaux, but originally, a claret was a pale, light-tasting wine—close to what we now call a rosé. Serve the remainder of the bottle to your guests, chilled, with the pie.*
- *Blackthorn berries are commonly known today as sloe berries. I've only ever seen them in the UK, but blackberries or blueberries match well with rabbit and are a great substitute. If you don't have any berries, use a bit of jam instead, dolloping small spoonfuls in among the meat and veggies.*

Chapter 10

❧

Fish and Seafood

Fish Pie at the Lillingtons'

Steamed Mussels with Butter

Fish Fillets Poached in Wine

Peppery Oyster Stew

Baja Fish Tacos at the Celtic Festival

Trout Fried in Cornmeal

FISH PIE AT THE LILLINGTONS'

"River Run?" he said. "You have relations with Mrs. Jocasta Cameron?"

"She's my husband's aunt," I replied. "Do you know her?"

"Oh, indeed! A charming woman, most charming!" A broad smile lifted the Baron's pendulous cheeks. "Since many years, I am the dear friend of Mrs. Cameron and her husband, unfortunately dead."

The Baron launched into an enthusiastic recounting of the delights of River Run, and I took advantage of the lull to accept a small wedge of fish pie, full not only of fish, but of oysters and shrimps in a creamy sauce. Mr. Lillington had certainly spared no effort to impress the Governor.

As I leaned back for the footman to ladle more sauce onto my plate, I caught Judith Wylie's eyes on me, narrowed in a look of dislike that she didn't trouble to disguise. I smiled pleasantly at her, displaying my own excellent teeth, and turned back to the Baron, newly confident.

—*Drums of Autumn,* chapter 7, "Great Prospects Fraught with Peril"

A delicious, hearty pie chock-full of the fish, seafood, and vegetables of your choice, folded in a creamy white sauce, and topped with cheesy mashed potatoes.

A childhood favorite of My Englishman, can be served this British classic for Sunday supper, followed by Governor Tryon's Humble Crumble Apple Pie (page 250) for dessert.

Serves 6

Ingredients

½ cup (1 stick) butter, plus additional for the baking dish

2½ pounds (1.1 kilograms or 4 to 5 medium) yellow potatoes, peeled and cut into 2-inch pieces

1 garlic clove, quartered

¾ cup whipping cream

8 ounces (225 grams or about 2 cups) shredded aged cheddar cheese

2 teaspoons kosher salt, plus additional

1 teaspoon ground white pepper

1 small onion, julienned (see Knife Skills, page 11)

¼ cup all-purpose flour

1 teaspoon mustard powder

2 cups whole milk

2 bay leaves

¼ cup chopped fresh dill

½ cup white wine

3 cups assorted chopped vegetables (such as leeks, peas, carrots, corn, beans)

1½ to 2 pounds (700 to 900 grams) assorted fish and seafood, such as cod, salmon, shrimp, oysters, and crab, cleaned and cut into 2-inch pieces

Method

Move a rack to the middle rung and heat the oven to 375°F. Butter a 3-quart baking dish.

In a large saucepan with 1 inch of salted water, place the potatoes and garlic. Cover and bring to a boil over high heat, then reduce heat for a gentle boil. Cook until the potatoes are fork-tender, 20 to 25 minutes. Drain and allow to steam-dry in the saucepan, off the heat, for 2 minutes. Mash until smooth and stir in 4 table-spoons butter and ¼ cup cream. Stir in the cheddar until melted, season with 1 teaspoon salt and ½ teaspoon white pepper. Cover to keep warm.

While the potatoes cook, melt the remaining 4 tablespoons butter in a large saucepan over medium heat. Add the onions and cook until softened, about 3 minutes. Whisk in the flour and mustard powder until smooth. Cook for 3 minutes, then slowly pour in the milk and remaining ½ cup cream, whisking continuously to avoid lumps. Add the bay leaves and cook, stirring occasionally to prevent scorching, until thick enough to coat the back of a spoon, 7 to 10 minutes. Season with the dill, the remaining 1 teaspoon salt, and the remaining ½ teaspoon white pepper. Cover to keep warm.

In a large frying pan or skillet, bring the wine to a boil over high heat. Add the vegetables and fish, cover and cook steam until the vegetables are not quite tender and the fish is just opaque, 3 to 4 minutes. Drain.

Add the fish and vegetables to the prepared baking dish. Remove the bay leaves and pour on the cream sauce, folding it in gently among the fish and vegetables. Top with the mashed potatoes, using the tines of a fork to fluff up the potatoes with peaks and valleys. Set the baking dish on a rimmed baking sheet to contain spill-overs, and bake until golden and bubbling, about 45 minutes.

Rest on a wire rack for 15 minutes before serving.

Notes

- *I use white pepper to avoid marring the pure white of the cream sauce and potatoes, but if freshly ground black pepper is what you have on hand, use that.*
- *To change things up, add the cheese to the cream sauce, omit the mashed potatoes, and enclose this pie in short crust pastry, following the directions in Jenny's Hare Pie (page 151).*
- *For a quick tartar sauce to go with Trout Fried in Cornmeal (page 170), mix any leftover dill with mayonnaise and gherkins.*

STEAMED MUSSELS WITH BUTTER

I sat on a chest against the taffrail, enjoying the salty breeze and the tarry, fishy smells of ships and harbor. It was still cold, but with my cloak pulled tight around me, I was warm enough. The ship rocked slowly, rising on the incoming tide; I could see the beards of algae on nearby dock pilings lifting and swirling, obscuring the shiny black patches of mussels between them.

The thought of mussels reminded me of the steamed mussels with butter I had had for dinner the night before, and I was suddenly starving. The absurd contrasts of pregnancy seemed to keep me always conscious of my digestion; if I wasn't vomiting, I was ravenously hungry. The thought of food led me to the thought of menus, which led back to a contemplation of the entertaining Jared had mentioned. Dinner parties, hm? It seemed an odd way to begin the job of saving Scotland, but then I couldn't really think of anything better.

—*Dragonfly in Amber,* chapter 6, "Making Waves"

These meaty morsels from the sea are packed in the shell with a colorful and decadent compound butter. Serve with a loaf of crusty bread and a sharply dressed green salad to balance the buttery richness, or with a big plate of Matchstick Cold-Oil Fries (page 208) for an Outlandish take on the Belgian classic, *moules et frites.*

The leftover butter is delicious on toast under a poached egg, stirred into mashed potatoes, or perched atop a grilled steak.

Serves 4 as a main course or 6 as an appetizer

Ingredients

1 cup (2 sticks) softened unsalted butter

1 small shallot, diced

1 to 2 garlic cloves, grated or minced

2 tablespoons tomato paste

3 tablespoons fresh lemon juice

2 tablespoons chopped fresh parsley

2 tablespoons chopped fresh basil

1 teaspoon kosher salt

½ teaspoon freshly ground pepper

¼ teaspoon cayenne pepper

3 to 4 pounds (1.3 to 1.8 kilograms) mussels

1 cup white wine

Method

In a food processor, combine the butter, shallots, garlic, tomato paste, lemon juice, parsley, basil, salt, ground pepper, and cayenne pepper and pulse until well combined, scraping down the sides of the bowl often. Alternatively, in a large bowl, mash the ingredients with a fork until combined.

Inspect the mussels to ensure they are all closed. Discard any with broken shells or open ones that don't close immediately when tapped. Use a small, stiff brush to remove barnacles and/or seaweed.

Arrange half of the mussels in a single layer in a large skillet, add half of the wine, cover, and bring to a boil over medium-high heat. Steam until all the mussels are open, about 3 minutes. Remove the mussels from the pan and repeat with the remaining mussels and wine.

When cool enough to handle, discard the empty half shells and use a knife to loosen the meat from the other halves. Trim the meat of any threadlike "beards."

With a small spoon or knife, cover the meat and fill the shells with compound butter. Arrange on a baking sheet, wrap with plastic, and refrigerate up to 1 day.

Move a rack to the top rung and heat the oven broiler or a grill.

Cook the mussels until the butter is melted and bubbling, 2 to 3 minutes. Serve immediately with lots of fresh crusty bread to soak up all the coral-colored, flavor-filled butter.

Notes

- *This recipe is one of the few where I specify unsalted butter—because the compound butter is full of big flavors, when combined with the mussels, things can get salty very quickly.*
- *When you purchase mussels, choose damp, shiny, fresh-smelling specimens with securely closed shells. (Mussels left undisturbed will open their shells slightly. Tap open shells firmly. If the shell closes, it is still alive. Discard those that don't close.) Avoid mussels with broken or split shells and those that smell off. Store them in the refrigerator layered in damp newspaper or cloth—avoid plastic containers or bags, which will suffocate them. Wait to clean them until just before cooking.*

Fish Fillets Poached in Wine

I might have managed if it weren't for the bloody nightingales. The dining salon was hot and crowded with courtiers and onlookers, one of the stays in my dress frame had come loose and was stabbing me viciously beneath the left kidney each time I drew breath, and I was suffering from that most ubiquitous plague of pregnancy, the urge to urinate every few minutes. Still, I might have managed. It was, after all, a serious breach of manners to leave the table before the King, even though luncheon was a casual affair, in comparison with the formal dinners customary at Versailles—or so I was given to understand.

"Casual," however, is a relative term. True, there were only three varieties of spiced pickle, not eight. And one soup, clear, not thick. The venison was merely roasted, not presented en brochette, and the fish, while tastily poached in wine, was served fileted, not whole and riding on a sea of aspic filled with shrimp.

—*Dragonfly in Amber,* chapter 9, "The Splendors of Versailles"

Delicate white fish, gently cooked in an aromatic wine bath. An easy-to-prepare dish full of simple flavors that shine when served with a rice pilaf and Auld Ian's Buttered Leeks (page 202).

Serves 4

Ingredients

3 tablespoons butter

2 teaspoons chopped fresh dill

1 cup white wine, plus additional

1 teaspoon salt, plus additional

1 large lemon, cut into 3 slices plus
    wedges to garnish

2 onion slices (separated into rings)

2 bay leaves

1 fresh rosemary or thyme sprig

12 whole peppercorns

4 skinless fish fillets, such as cod,
    haddock, tilapia, or halibut

Method

In a small bowl, mix together the butter and dill. Set aside.

In a large saucepan, bring the wine, salt, lemon slices, onion rings, bay leaves, rosemary or thyme, peppercorns, and 1 cup water to a simmer over medium heat.

Gently place the fish in the poaching liquid to cover. Cook at a gentle simmer, reducing the heat if necessary, until the fish is opaque in the center and flakes with a fork. The timing will depend on the density and thickness of the fish. Thin tilapia fillets will take about 5 minutes, while inch-thick halibut may take up to 15 minutes.

Carefully remove the fish with a large slotted spoon or spatula. Serve immediately, in a small pool of the poaching liquid, and garnish with a sprinkle of salt, a lemon wedge, and a pat of dill butter.

Notes

- *Add additional, equal, amounts of wine and water to the pot if necessary to cover the fish.*
- *Other seafoods, such as scallops and shrimp, are also delicious poached.*

PEPPERY OYSTER STEW

"Sawney's what they say in the Highlands," he informed me. "And in the Isles, too. Sandy's more what ye'd hear in the Lowlands—or from an ignorant Sassenach." He lifted one eyebrow at me, smiling, and raised a spoonful of the rich, fragrant stew to his mouth.

"All right," I said. "I suppose more to the point, though—who am I?"

He had noticed, after all. I felt one large foot nudge mine, and he smiled at me over the rim of his cup.

"You're my wife, Sassenach," he said gruffly. "Always. No matter who I may be—you're my wife."

I could feel the flush of pleasure in my face, and see the memories of the night before reflected in his own. The tips of his ears were faintly pink.

"You don't suppose there's too much pepper in this stew?" I asked, swallowing another spoonful. "Are you sure, Jamie?"

"Aye," he said. "Aye, I'm sure," he amended, "and no, the pepper's fine. I like a wee bit of pepper." The foot moved slightly against mine, the toe of his shoe barely brushing my ankle.

—*Voyager,* chapter 27, "Up in Flames"

Oysters and black pepper have been considered aphrodisiacs by myth and legend for thousands of years. Recently, science has found that rare amino acids found in bivalves, including oysters, trigger increased levels of sex hormones. And piperine, the compound responsible for the pungency of black pepper, has been shown to increase blood flow throughout the body, providing an above-table, socially acceptable explanation for Claire's flushed face and Jamie's pink ears.

This recipe comes to you via Lori Zachary at LittleWhiteApron.com, my first and dearest friend to come from my Outlandish food obsession. Also a trained chef, Lori lives in Louisiana, near the Gulf coast, celebrated historically as one of the best sources for oysters in America.

Serves 6

Ingredients

6 tablespoons butter

2 large shallots, diced

2 medium celery stalks, diced

1 teaspoon kosher salt, plus additional

3 garlic cloves, grated or minced

¼ cup flour

¼ teaspoon cayenne pepper

3 cups whole milk

½ cup whipping cream

1 pint (500 ml) shucked, fresh oysters in their own juices (10 to 20, depending on their size)

1 teaspoon freshly ground pepper, plus additional

Method

In a Dutch oven or heavy-bottomed saucepan, melt the butter over medium heat. When the butter is bubbling, add the shallots, celery, and ½ teaspoon of salt. Cook, stirring occasionally until soft, about 5 minutes. Add the garlic and cook until fragrant, 1 to 2 minutes.

Add the flour and cayenne pepper to the vegetables in the pot and stir to combine. Cook for 3 minutes, stirring frequently, lowering the heat to avoid burning if necessary.

Add the milk and cream. Increase the heat to medium-high and continue cooking, stirring regularly, until the mixture is smooth and slightly thickened, 5 to 7 minutes.

Drain the oysters, reserving ½ cup of the juice. Add the juice, ground pepper, and remaining ½ teaspoon salt to the pot, reduce heat to medium-low, and cook 5 minutes. Add the raw oysters, reduce heat to low, and simmer until oysters are cooked, about 5 minutes. Season to taste with more salt and black pepper, if required.

Serve hot with a pat of butter, more ground pepper, and Pumpkin Seed and Herb Oatcakes (page 219) or oyster crackers.

BAJA FISH TACOS
AT THE CELTIC FESTIVAL

"Wow!" She walked round him in a circle, goggling. "Roger, you are gorgeous!" She smiled, a trifle lopsided. "My mother always said men in kilts were irresistible. I guess she was right."

He saw her swallow hard, and wanted to hug her for her bravery, but she had already turned away, gesturing toward the main food area.

"Are you hungry? I had a look while you were changing. We've got our choice between octopus-on-a-stick, Baja fish tacos, Polish dogs—"

He took her arm and pulled her round to face him.

"Hey," he said softly. "I'm sorry; I wouldn't have brought you if I'd known it would be a shock."

"It's all right." Her smile was better this time. "It's—I'm glad you brought me."

"Truly?"

"Yeah. Really. It's—" She waved helplessly at the tartan swirl of noise and color all around them. "It's so—Scottish."

—*Drums of Autumn*, chapter 4, "A Blast from the Past"

In 1969, Bree and Roger's Baja fish tacos would have been an assembly of heavily battered cod and shredded iceberg lettuce, smothered with a bland mayonnaise sauce and wrapped in cardboard tortillas. It's best not to think about the octopuses-on-sticks too much.

In the twenty-first century, soft corn tortillas are filled with seared, spice-rubbed fish fingers, cabbage slaw, and topped with sliced avocado and a citrusy mayo sauce for a fresh-tasting dinner ready in under 30 minutes.

Serves 6

Ingredients

12 small corn tortillas

½ cup mayonnaise

2 tablespoons whole milk

Zest and juice of 1 lime
(see Notes)

1 garlic clove, grated or minced

2½ to 3 pounds (900 to 1,300 grams) skinless white fish fillets, such as halibut, cod, or tilapia

1 tablespoon ground cumin

1 tablespoon ground coriander

2 teaspoons kosher salt, plus additional

½ teaspoon freshly ground pepper, plus additional

¼ teaspoon crushed red pepper flakes

2 cups shredded cabbage

½ small red pepper, sliced

½ small red onion, sliced

½ bunch cilantro, chopped

1 teaspoon vegetable oil

1 avocado, sliced

1 to 2 limes, cut into wedges

Method

Move a rack to the middle rung and heat the oven to 250°F. Stack the tortillas, wrap them in a clean, slightly damp dishcloth, and set them in the oven to warm.

In a small bowl, mix together the mayonnaise, milk, lime zest and juice, and garlic. Cover and refrigerate until ready to serve.

Cut the fish into twelve pieces, 1 to 1½ inches wide. In a small bowl, mix together the cumin, coriander, salt, pepper, and red pepper flakes. Sprinkle the fish pieces liberally on all sides with the spices.

Toss together the cabbage, red peppers, onions, and cilantro and season with salt and pepper.

Heat a heavy-bottomed frying pan or grill pan over medium heat for 3 to 5 minutes. When hot, brush the pan lightly with half of the vegetable oil and add half of the fish pieces. Fry until the bottom half begins to turn opaque. Gently flip the fish and fry until cooked through—the timing will depend on the thickness of the fillets but shouldn't take more than 4 to 5 minutes total. Remove to a plate and tent loosely with foil to keep warm. Wipe the pan, brush with the remaining oil, and repeat with the remaining fish pieces.

Fill each warm tortilla with a small handful of cabbage slaw and a drizzle of sauce, then top with a piece of fish and more sauce. Serve with avocado slices and lime wedges.

Notes

- *Zest the lime before you juice it.*
- *To shred cabbage, quarter it and remove the core from each piece. Peel away four or five of the outer leaves, lay them flat on a cutting board, and cut thin slivers. Shredding on a mandolin is even faster, unless you shave your finger—so make sure to ALWAYS USE THE GUARD.*
- *For even more flavor, grind the spice mix in your mortar and pestle using whole cumin and coriander seeds, and peppercorns, as well as the kosher salt and crushed red pepper flakes.*

TROUT FRIED IN CORNMEAL

He had such glimpses of Claire, of his sister, of Ian . . . small moments clipped out of time and perfectly preserved by some odd alchemy of memory, fixed in his mind like an insect in amber.

And now he had another. For so long as he lived, he could recall this moment. He could feel the cold wind on his face, and the crackling feel of the hair on his thighs, half singed by the fire.

He could smell the rich odor of trout fried in cornmeal, and feel the tiny prick of a swallowed bone, hair-thin in his throat. He could hear the dark quiet of the forest behind, and the soft rush of the stream nearby. And forever now he would remember the firelight golden on the sweet bold face of his son.

—*Drums of Autumn,* chapter 27, "Trout Fishing in America"

When buying whole fish, choose fresh-smelling or odorless specimens with clear, full eyes, firm flesh, bright red gills, and wet, glistening skin. Avoid dry-looking, mushy, bruised, or damaged fish, as they are either old or of poor quality. If you are unable to find whole fish, see the Note below the recipe for instructions for frying fillets instead.

Serve garnished with lemon wedges and a big pile of Matchstick Cold-Oil Fries (page 208) for an old-fashioned and gluten-free fish-and-chip feast.

Serves 4

Ingredients

4 whole trout (10 to 12 ounces or 300 to 350 grams each), cleaned

1 teaspoon kosher salt

½ teaspoon freshly ground pepper

Pinch of cayenne pepper

1 cup cornmeal

Vegetable shortening or oil

Lemon wedges for garnish

Method

Rinse the trout under cold water and pat dry, inside and out, with paper towels.

In a small bowl, mix together the salt, ground pepper, and cayenne pepper. Season the trout inside and out.

Pour the cornmeal into a 13 x 9-inch baking dish and roll the trout, one at a time, in the cornmeal, turning several times to coat well.

In two large frying pans over medium-high flame, place ¼ inch vegetable shortening or oil and heat until shimmering. Fry the fish, two per pan, until crisp and golden on the outside and opaque on the inside, 3 to 4 minutes per side. Watch carefully as the fish are frying and reduce the heat if the fish darkens too quickly.

Drain briefly on paper towels and serve immediately with lemon wedges.

Notes

- *For trout fillets, season and coat in cornmeal as directed, then fry with the flesh side down first until golden, 2 to 3 minutes. Flip and fry the skin side until crisp, about 1 minute.*
- *Not all cornmeal is guaranteed to be gluten-free. Check the packaging before you buy.*

Chapter 11

VEGETARIAN

Vegetable Stew

Jenny's Onion Tart

Manioc and Red Beans with Fried Plantain

Stovie Potatoes

Diana Gabaldon's Cheese Enchiladas

VEGETABLE STEW

"Bloody man," I said aloud. "What have you done, shot a moose?" My voice sounded small in the muffled air, but the thought made me feel better. If he had in fact bagged something large near the end of the day, he might well have chosen to camp by the carcass; butchering a large animal was exhausting, lengthy work, and meat was too hard come by to leave it to the mercies of predators.

My vegetable stew was bubbling, and the cabin was filled with the savory scent of onions and wild garlic, but I had no appetite. I pushed the kettle on its hook to the back of the hearth—easy enough to heat again when he came. A tiny flash of green caught my eye, and I stooped to look. A tiny salamander, frightened out of its winter refuge in a crack of the wood.

—*Drums of Autumn,* chapter 21, "Night on a Snowy Mountain"

A hearty mix of vegetables with a rich and delicious brown-roux base. The cornerstone of Cajun and Creole cuisine, brown roux is used to thicken gumbos and étouffées. It lends this vegetable stew a deep color, body, and flavor missing from many meatless dishes; even the most committed carnivores will approve.

Once you start the roux, you cannot leave the stove for even a moment, so make sure all the ingredients are prepped before you begin.

Serves 6 or more

Ingredients

1 large onion, chopped (see Knife Skills, page 11)

2 large stalks celery, chopped

1 medium red bell pepper, chopped

3 garlic cloves, halved

1 fresh rosemary sprig

2 fresh thyme sprigs

2-inch piece of fresh ginger, peeled and quartered

6 whole peppercorns

1 cup vegetable oil

¾ cup all-purpose flour

1½ pounds (700 grams or 1 small) butternut squash, peeled and seeds removed, cut into 2-inch pieces

1½ pounds (700 grams or about 3 medium) potatoes, peeled and cut into 2-inch pieces

2 large carrots, peeled and cut into 2-inch pieces

2 large parsnips, peeled and cut into
2-inch pieces

½ pound (225 grams) button mushrooms, chopped

1 medium pear, peeled, cored, and cut
into 1-inch pieces

1 small zucchini, cut into 1-inch pieces

1 bunch spinach, stems removed

1 tablespoon kosher salt, plus additional

¼ teaspoon cayenne pepper

Freshly ground pepper to taste

Method

Combine the onions, celery, red peppers, and garlic in a food processor and pulse 6 to 8 times, until finely chopped but not mush.

Make a bouquet garni. Wrap the rosemary, thyme, ginger, and peppercorns in a square of cheesecloth and tie with string, or enclose the items in a large tea ball. Set the bouquet garni aside.

In a stockpot or Dutch oven, heat the oil over medium until shimmering. Sprinkle in the flour gradually, stirring constantly to form a smooth paste. Continue to stir, scraping the bottom and the corners of the pot regularly to avoid burning the flour. Reduce the heat to medium-low after about 10 minutes and continue to cook, stirring constantly, until the mixture is the deep, rich color of milk chocolate, 30 to 40 minutes.

Immediately add the chopped vegetables, being careful of splatters, and mix well. Increase the heat to medium-high, add 1 quart cold water and the squash, potatoes, carrots, parsnips, mushrooms, and pear. Bring to a boil, stirring almost constantly. Reduce heat to medium-low and add the bouquet garni. Simmer, uncovered, for 30 minutes. Add the zucchini, spinach, salt, and cayenne pepper and cook for 15 more minutes. Remove the bouquet garni and season with salt and pepper.

Serve hot with Dumplings in Cross Creek (page 200) or over rice.

Keep leftovers in the fridge up to 5 days.

Notes

- *Have patience with the roux—do not attempt to rush it over a high heat. It should darken evenly, with the occasional dark brown speck in the mixture. Black specks mean the flour is burned and the roux is garbage. Begin again on a lower heat.*
- *Pear, parsnip, and ginger combine to produce a subtle yet complex flavor that is a delicious surprise for many.*
- *Mustard greens, collards, or any bitter green are a tasty substitute for the spinach.*

JENNY'S ONION TART

I caught up with her just outside the barn; she heard my step behind her and turned, startled. She glanced about quickly, but saw we were alone. Realizing that there was no way of putting off a confrontation, she squared her shoulders under the woolen cloak and lifted her head, meeting my eyes straight on.

"I thought I'd best tell Young Ian to unsaddle the horse," she said. "Then I'm going to the root cellar to fetch up some onions for a tart. Will ye come with me?"

"I will." Pulling my cloak tight around me against the winter wind, I followed her into the barn.

—*Voyager,* chapter 38, "I Meet a Lawyer"

A creamy and mild vegetarian version of the classic Alsatian onion tart that combines julienned onions and bacon in an egg-enriched béchamel sauce. Serve it with a salad for a simple yet delectable Sunday brunch.

Makes one 10- to 12-inch tart

Ingredients

¼ cup (4 tablespoons) butter

2 tablespoons olive oil

1 pound (450 grams or 2 to 3 medium) yellow onions, julienned (see Knife Skills, page 11)

1 teaspoon fresh thyme, chopped, or ½ teaspoon dried

Kosher salt to taste

White pepper to taste

2 large eggs, 1 separated

2 tablespoons flour

2 cups whole milk

⅛ teaspoon freshly ground nutmeg

½ recipe Short Crust Pastry (page 27), chilled

Method

In a large frying pan, heat 2 tablespoons butter and the olive oil over medium heat until melted. Add the onions, thyme, salt, and a pinch of white pepper. Cook until the onions are soft and translucent, but with no color, about 15 minutes, stirring occasionally.

Move a rack to the middle rung and heat the oven to 350°F. Whisk together the whole egg and the yolk. In a separate bowl, lightly beat the egg white with 1 teaspoon cold water to make an egg wash.

In a medium saucepan, melt the remaining 2 tablespoons butter over medium heat. When the butter is bubbling, whisk in the flour and cook, stirring constantly, for 2 minutes. Whisk in the milk slowly and heat, stirring occasionally to prevent scorching, until it comes to a boil. Boil gently, stirring constantly, until the mixture thickens substantially, about 2 minutes. Whisk in the beaten egg and yolk and let cool for 10 minutes. Season to taste with salt and pepper.

Roll the short crust dough out to a circle ⅛ inch thick. Transfer to a 10- to 12-inch tart pan and trim. Poke holes all over the bottom of the crust, cover the dough with parchment paper or foil, and fill the crust with pie weights or dried beans. Bake 10 minutes, remove the weights and parchment paper, and return to the oven until the pastry looks dry, about 10 more minutes. Brush the bottom with the egg wash to seal.

Increase the oven temperature to 400°F.

Center the tart pan on a rimmed baking sheet and arrange the onions in an even layer. Pour the béchamel over the top and bake until just set in the center, 30 to 35 minutes.

Serve slightly warm or at room temperature.

Refrigerate leftovers up to 3 days.

Note

- *Crisp and crumble 2 slices of thick-cut bacon over the parbaked crust before topping with the onions and béchamel for a classic Alsatian onion tart.*

MANIOC AND RED BEANS WITH FRIED PLANTAIN

"Would one of Ermenegilda's dresses fit you, I wonder?"

I didn't know whether to answer this or not. Instead, I merely smiled politely, and hoped what I was thinking didn't show on my face. Fortunately, at this point Mamacita came back, carrying a steaming clay pot wrapped in towels. She slapped a ladleful of the contents on each plate, then went out, her feet—if she had any—moving invisibly beneath the shapeless skirt.

I stirred the mess on my plate, which appeared to be vegetable in nature. I took a cautious bite, and found it surprisingly good.

"Fried plantain, mixed with manioc and red beans," Lawrence explained, seeing my hesitation. He took a large spoonful of the steaming pulp himself and ate it without pausing for it to cool.

—*Voyager*, chapter 50, "I Meet a Priest"

Mamacita's dish of manioc and red beans is a simplified and vegetarian version of the Caribbean comfort food called "oil down," a stew of vegetables, salted fish and/or beef, chicken, dumplings, pig's tail, et cetera, in coconut milk.

The crunchy garlic- and-ginger-spiked green plantain fritters are also a variation of local recipes, and contrast beautifully with the smooth, starchy texture of the manioc.

Serves 6

Ingredients

1 teaspoon whole allspice berries

5 garlic cloves, halved

2 fresh thyme sprigs

1 jalapeño pepper, halved

1½ to 2 pounds (700 to 900 grams) manioc (also known as cassava, tapioca, or yuca)

¼ cup coconut or vegetable oil, plus additional for frying

1 large onion, julienned (see Knife Skills, page 11)

1 teaspoon turmeric

1 can (14 ounces or 400 ml) coconut milk

1½ teaspoons kosher salt, plus additional

1 can (14 ounces or 398 ml) kidney beans, drained

1 tablespoon peeled, minced fresh ginger

1 teaspoon whole peppercorns

1½ to 2 pounds (700 to 900 grams) unripe (green) plantains

Method

Crush the allspice berries lightly in a mortar with a pestle, or on a cutting board with the side of a knife. To make a bouquet garni, wrap the allspice, 1 garlic clove, the thyme, and the jalapeño together in a square of cheesecloth and tie with string, or enclose the items in a large tea ball. Set the bouquet garni aside.

Peel the manioc, remove the large central vein, and cut into 2-inch chunks.

In a large saucepan, heat the oil over medium flame until shimmering. Add the onions and fry until soft and translucent, 3 to 5 minutes. Stir in the turmeric and cook 30 seconds. Add the manioc, coconut milk, bouquet garni, and ½ teaspoon salt. Stir to combine. Bring to a boil, reduce heat to medium-low, cover, and simmer until the manioc is tender, 35 to 40 minutes. Mash the root pieces lightly with the back of a fork and add the beans. Continue to cook, uncovered, until most of the liquid has been absorbed, another 5 to 10 minutes. Season to taste, cover, and keep warm over low.

Meanwhile, combine the remaining garlic, the ginger, and the peppercorns with the remaining 1 teaspoon salt in a mortar. Pound to a smooth paste with the pestle.

Cut the ends off the plantains and slit the skin lengthwise. Remove the peel in chunks. Shred the plantain on the biggest holes of a grater into a bowl. Add the garlic paste and mix until well combined.

In a large frying pan, heat 2 inches of oil to 340°F over medium-high flame. Drop the plantains by tablespoons into the hot oil, being careful not to overcrowd the pan. Fry until just golden (not brown), turning once, 3 to 5 minutes. Drain on paper towels, sprinkle lightly with salt, and keep warm in the oven.

Serve both hot, with rice and a big pitcher of Mamacita's Sangria (page 306) for a Caribbean feast worthy of Father Fogden.

Notes

- *If you don't have a mortar and pestle, smash the garlic with the side of a knife and cover with the salt. Add the ginger and continue to smash with the side of your knife until you have a paste. Mix 1 teaspoon freshly ground pepper into the paste.*
- *No allspice? Stir in ½ teaspoon cinnamon, a pinch of ground cloves, and a pinch of freshly grated nutmeg with the turmeric.*

STOVIE POTATOES

"Survey?" Brianna took two of the little potato dumplings and sat down beside Roger, automatically passing him one. "It's for surveying?"

"Among other things." Jamie turned the astrolabe over and gently pushed the flat bar, making the notched sights revolve. "This bit—it's used as a transit. Ye'll ken what that is?"

Brianna nodded, looking interested.

"Sure. I know how to do different sorts of surveying, but we generally used . . ."

I saw Roger grimace as he swallowed, the roughness of the stovie catching at his throat. I lifted my hand toward the water pitcher, but he caught my eye and shook his head, almost imperceptibly. He swallowed again, more easily this time, and coughed.

—*The Fiery Cross,* chapter 77, "A Package from London"

There are millions of Scots and their descendants around the world, most with their own recipe for stovies, from the Scots verb *to stove,* meaning "to stew." This classic and simple fare of potatoes cooked slowly with stock and fat is traditionally made on a Monday to use up the leftovers from Sunday dinner. Below is a vegetarian version, including turnips and carrots to add variety and color.

Serves 4 as a main dish or 6 as a side

Ingredients

2 tablespoons butter

2 tablespoons olive oil

1 large onion, cut into ½-inch slices

2 garlic cloves, quartered

Kosher salt to taste

Freshly ground pepper to taste

4 to 6 large bay leaves

2 pounds (900 grams or 3 to 4 medium) russet potatoes, peeled and cut into 1-inch wedges

½ small turnip, peeled and cut into ½-inch wedges

1 large carrot, peeled and cut into 2-inch pieces

3 fresh rosemary sprigs

¼ cup Vegetable Stock (page 24)

Method

Heat the butter and olive oil in a large pot over medium until bubbling. Add the onions, garlic, salt, and pepper. Cook, stirring frequently, until the onions start to soften, 3 minutes.

Empty the contents of the pan into a bowl. With the pot off the heat, line the bottom with the bay leaves. Add a layer of potatoes, a few turnip and carrot pieces, some of the onions and garlic, and a sprig of rosemary. Season generously with salt and pepper. Repeat with the remaining vegetables, rosemary, and more salt and pepper, finishing with a layer of seasoned potatoes.

Return the pot to the stove, pour in the stock, and bring to a rapid boil over medium-high heat. Cover with a tight-fitting lid, reduce to low, and cook for about 1 hour, until everything is very tender and the bottom of the pot is almost dry. Discard the bay leaves and rosemary and season to taste with salt and pepper.

Serve hot with Oxford Baked Beans (page 204).

Keep leftovers in the refrigerator up to 5 days.

Notes

- *For a slightly more exotic flavor, substitute curry leaves or kaffir lime leaves for the bay leaves.*
- *To make a meat-eaters main dish, layer in shredded leftover cooked meat such as Roast Beef for a Wedding Feast (page 94) or crisped and crumbled bacon.*

Diana Gabaldon's Cheese Enchiladas

A family recipe straight from Diana and her late father, Tony Gabaldon. Get everything prepped and organized before you start to roll your enchiladas to avoid getting sauce on every surface of the kitchen.

Makes 12

Ingredients

3 tablespoons vegetable oil, plus additional for frying

4 garlic cloves, grated or minced

3 tablespoons all-purpose flour

2 cups tomato sauce (Diana uses El Pato brand, which has red chile pepper already in it)

Red chile pepper to taste (minced fresh, frozen, or flakes)

½ teaspoon kosher salt

1 dozen corn tortillas

1 pound (450 grams) cheddar cheese (see Notes), shredded, plus additional

1 small onion, minced (see Knife Skills, page 11)

Method

In a heavy-bottomed saucepan, heat the oil over medium flame. When it is shimmering, add the garlic, stirring constantly until just golden, 1 to 2 minutes. Sprinkle in the flour and stir to form a smooth paste. Cook, stirring constantly, for 2 to 3 minutes. Add the tomato sauce and stir quickly to avoid lumps, then add 2 cups water and stir to combine. Taste and add red chile as desired (see Notes). Cook over medium-low heat until thickened enough to coat the back of a spoon, about 5 minutes. Season with salt, cover, and keep warm over low heat.

Move a rack to the middle rung and heat the oven to 375°F.

Arrange a 13 x 9-inch baking dish and a clean dinner plate on the counter next to the stove, along with the tortillas, cheese, and onions. Pour enough of the enchilada sauce into the bottom of the baking dish to coat the bottom lightly.

In a small frying pan, heat ½ inch vegetable oil over medium-high flame until shimmering. With a pair of tongs, dip a fresh corn tortilla into the hot oil for 2 to 3 seconds (just long enough for the oil to sputter). Let the excess oil run off into the pan, then dip the tortilla into the enchilada sauce to coat both sides.

Lay the sauce-coated tortilla on the dinner plate and spread a handful of cheese

in a thick line across the center (you're aiming for a cylinder about two fingers thick). Sprinkle the onions lightly over the cheese. Roll the tortilla into a cylinder and arrange in the baking dish, seam side down. Repeat until all the tortillas are used.

When the baking dish is full, ladle the remaining sauce over the enchiladas to cover them generously, and sprinkle additional cheese on top for garnish. Bake until the cheese is well melted, bubbling, and the enchiladas look slightly smaller and sunken, 25 to 30 minutes. Rest 10 minutes before serving.

Serve hot with lots of pico de gallo—a salsa made of fresh-cut tomato, onions, cilantro, and lime that makes a tasty, palate-cleansing accompaniment to a plate of cheesy enchiladas.

Notes

- *If using minced raw red peppers, start with 2 tablespoons and increase if you want more heat. If using chilies in powdered form, add a couple of pinches, allow the sauce to sit for 15 minutes, then taste and add more if desired.*
- *Monterey Jack cheese is a delicious addition to the enchiladas before putting them in the oven, but you can use more cheddar or any cheese of your choice.*
- *Enchiladas freeze well before baking. The tortillas break down slightly, resulting in more of a casserole, but given the work and mess involved in assembly, it's well worth the effort to double the recipe and put a few away for another day.*

Chapter 12

~⊗~

PIZZA AND PASTA

Roger and Bree's Pizza

Tortellini Portofino

Spaghetti and Meatballs with the Randalls

Roger and Bree's Pizza

"Pizza," he said.

She blinked, then laughed. It was one of their games; taking turns to think of things they missed from the other time, the time before—or after, depending on how you looked at it.

"Coke," she said promptly. "I think I could maybe do pizza—but what good is pizza without Coca-Cola?"

"Pizza with beer is perfectly fine," he assured her. "And we can have beer—not that Lizzie's homemade hell-brew is quite on par with MacEwan's Lager, yet. But you really think you could make pizza?"

"Don't see why not." She nibbled at the cheese, frowning. "This wouldn't do"—she brandished the yellowish remnant, then popped it in her mouth—"too strong-flavored. But I think. . ." She paused to chew and swallow, then washed it down with a long drink of rough cider.

"Come to think of it, this would go pretty well with pizza." She lowered the leather bottle and licked the last sweet, semi-alcoholic drops from her lips. "But the cheese—I think maybe sheep's cheese would do. Da brought some from Salem last time he went there. I'll ask him to get some more and see how it melts."

She squinted against the bright, pale sun, calculating.

"Mama's got plenty of dried tomatoes, and tons of garlic. I know she has basil—don't know about the oregano, but I could do without that. And crust—" She waved a dismissive hand. "Flour, water, and lard, nothing to it."

—*The Fiery Cross,* chapter 20, "Shooting Lessons"

No matter what you put on top, the key to a great pizza is the crust—crisp on the outside, with a chewy interior.

Makes one 14-inch pizza

Ingredients

2 cups all-purpose flour

1 teaspoon sugar

1 teaspoon instant yeast

½ teaspoon kosher salt

2 tablespoons olive oil

½ cup pizza sauce

8 ounces (225 grams or about 2 cups)
   shredded mozzarella

Toppings—sun-dried tomatoes, pesto,
   pepperoni, sausage, mushrooms,
   peppers, onions, garlic, etc.

1 ounce (30 grams or about ½ cup)
   shredded Parmesan cheese

Method

In the bowl of a standing mixer, combine the flour, sugar, yeast, and salt. Using the paddle attachment, mix on medium-low and add ⅔ cup of warm water and 1 tablespoon of olive oil, mixing well until a rough ball forms and the dough pulls away from the sides of the bowl. Change to the dough hook and knead on medium until you have a soft, smooth dough, about 5 minutes.

Alternatively, mix the dough by hand in a large bowl and knead on a lightly floured counter for 6 to 8 minutes.

Form into a ball, return to a clean bowl, cover with plastic or a plate, and set aside to rise in a warm place until more than doubled, about 1 hour.

Move a rack to the bottom rung and place a pizza stone or baking sheet on the rack. Heat the oven to 500°F for at least 30 minutes.

Transfer the dough to a large piece of parchment paper. Working from the center, gently stretch and flatten the dough with your fingertips to a 14-inch diameter, or a shape that fits the pizza stone heating in the oven, leaving the edges thicker than the middle. Cover the dough with plastic or a clean, dampened dishcloth and rest for 10 minutes.

Brush the edge of the crust with the remaining 1 tablespoon olive oil. Spread the pizza sauce over the dough and arrange the cheese and toppings on top. Finish with the Parmesan and transfer the pizza on the parchment to the pizza stone in the oven (see Notes). Bake until golden brown, 12 to 14 minutes. Rest the pizza on a cutting board for at least 5 minutes before slicing.

Notes

- *My favorite place to rise dough is in the oven with just the interior light on—a near-perfect proofing temperature within everyone's reach.*
- *Double the recipe and make one pizza to freeze for later. Set it on a cookie sheet, double wrap with plastic, and freeze up to 2 weeks. Defrost in the fridge overnight, and set it on the counter while you heat the oven. Bake as directed.*
- *Grab opposite corners of the parchment paper to move the pizza without spillage.*

TORTELLINI PORTOFINO

When Geillis Duncan had been condemned as a witch, Jamie had said to me, "Dinna grieve for her, Sassenach; she's a wicked woman." And whether she had been wicked or mad, it had made little difference at the time. Should I not have left well enough alone, and left her to find her own fate? Still, I thought, she had once saved my life. In spite of what she was—would be—did I owe it to her to try to save her life? And thus perhaps doom Roger? What right did I have to meddle any further?

It isna a matter of right, Sassenach, I heard Jamie's voice saying, with a tinge of impatience. It's a question of duty. Of honor.

"Honor, is it?" I said aloud. "And what's that?" The waiter with my plate of tortellini Portofino looked startled.

"Eh?" he said.

"Never mind," I said, too distracted to care much what he thought of me. "Perhaps you'd better bring the rest of the bottle."

I finished my meal surrounded by ghosts. Finally, fortified by food and wine, I pushed my empty plate aside, and opened Gillian Edgar's gray notebook.

—*Dragonfly in Amber,* chapter 48, "Witch Hunt"

A few years ago, while researching recipes, a search turned up Tortellini Portofino with Alfredo Sauce on the dinner menu of a restaurant in Phoenix. A few days after that, Diana coincidentally tweeted that she and her husband were headed out to a favorite Phoenix restaurant for a celebration, where she was looking forward to ordering, you guessed it, Tortellini Portofino.

This recipe is my interpretation of the description of the dish I found online—light-as-a-cloud, shrimp-filled tortellini tossed with a lavish, authentic, and lemony Alfredo sauce.

Serves 6

Ingredients

3 cups all-purpose flour

2 teaspoons kosher salt

4 large eggs

1 tablespoon olive oil

½ pound (225 grams) raw shrimp, shelled and deveined

¼ cup panko-style breadcrumbs

¼ cup sliced scallions (white and light-green parts only)

¼ cup chopped walnuts

2 tablespoons chopped fresh parsley

Pinch of crushed red pepper flakes

1½ cups whipping cream

2 to 3 tablespoons fresh lemon juice

6 tablespoons butter

2 ounces (60 grams or about 1 cup) finely shredded Parmesan cheese, plus additional

Zest of 1 lemon

¼ teaspoon ground white pepper

Pinch of freshly grated nutmeg (optional)

Method

For the pasta

IN A FOOD PROCESSOR: Pulse the flour and 1 teaspoon salt together three times to combine. In a small bowl, whisk together 3 eggs, the oil, and ¼ cup water. Pour this mixture down the chute in a continuous stream while pulsing the machine. Continue pulsing until the dough begins to pull away from the sides of the bowl. Knead into a smooth ball on the counter, split in half, and shape into two equal 1-inch-thick squares. Cover tightly with plastic and refrigerate for at least 1 hour.

BY HAND: In a large bowl, mix together the flour and 1 teaspoon salt. In a small bowl, whisk together 3 eggs, the oil, and ¼ cup water. Make a well in the flour, pour in the egg mixture, and gradually bring the flour into the liquid with your fingers or a fork until most of it is incorporated into a sticky dough. Pour onto the counter and knead until the dough ball is smooth, firm, and elastic, about 10 minutes. Split in half and shape into two equal 1-inch-thick squares. Cover tightly with plastic and refrigerate for at least 1 hour.

For the filling

Separate the remaining egg. In a food processor (clean the bowl if you used it to mix the dough), add the shrimp, breadcrumbs, scallions, walnuts, parsley, egg yolk, remaining 1 teaspoon salt, and the crushed red pepper. Pulse five to seven times, until finely chopped but not mushy. Scrape the filling into a bowl and stir in 2 tablespoons whipping cream. Cover and refrigerate while you roll out the pasta.

Cut each one of the squares of pasta into two rectangles. Rewrap three and roll out the first on a pasta machine, as if you were making sheets of lasagna. Follow the machine's instructions to roll each sheet out on the thinnest setting, or until you can see your hand through the dough. Dust the sheet lightly with flour, then cover with plastic wrap while you roll out the other pieces of dough. Use a cutter or sharp knife to cut 3-inch rounds or squares from the sheets.

Whisk the egg white with 1 teaspoon cold water to make an egg wash. Place 1 teaspoon of the filling in the center of each round or square, then use a pastry brush or your fingertip to spread egg wash on the bottom edge. Fold the top half over to form a half-moon or triangle, and seal the edges with your fingertips, making sure to squeeze out all the air pockets. Fold around your pinky finger and press the corners together, then fold down the top to form the collar of the tortellini. Keep unused

dough covered with plastic and work quickly to prevent the dough from drying out (this is a great project for two people). Wrap the finished tortellini tightly and refrigerate until just before serving.

In a stockpot, bring 6 to 8 cups of salted water to a rapid boil. Add the tortellini, stir once, and cook, boiling gently, until they float to the surface, 3 to 5 minutes. Drain and cover to keep hot.

In a large, heavy saucepan, stir 1 cup of the whipping cream and 2 tablespoons lemon juice together over medium heat. Add the butter and cook, stirring occasionally, until the butter is melted and the cream is just bubbling, 4 to 5 minutes. Reduce the heat to medium-low, add the cooked tortellini, and toss gently. Add the remaining 2 tablespoons of whipping cream, the Parmesan, lemon zest, white pepper, and nutmeg. Toss until the sauce thickens slightly, 3 to 5 more minutes. Taste and season with salt and additional lemon juice if desired.

Serve immediately with garlic bread and a salad on the side. Pass additional Parmesan and freshly ground pepper at the table.

Notes

- *Want less work? Use store-bought wonton wrappers instead of pasta—then you just have to make the filling and sauce.*
- *You will get more tortellini and waste less dough if you cut squares from the pasta sheets. Giant tortellini, using a 5-inch cutter, are very pretty and a little less work—use a scant 2 teaspoons of filling.*
- *Once the tortellini are folded, they can be wrapped tightly and frozen up to 2 weeks. Do not thaw before cooking—boil straight from the freezer.*

Spaghetti and Meatballs with the Randalls

"Oh, no, it's not!" she said quickly. "He hardly ever . . . well, he didna used to, but with so many . . . well, I couldna blame him, this time. It took him a terrible time to milk the goat, and then to have it all spilt and wasted—I would ha' shouted, too, I expect."

Her eyes were fixed on the ground, avoiding mine, and she was fingering the seam of her shift, running a thumb over and over the stitching.

"Small children can certainly be trying," I agreed, with vivid memories of an incident involving a two-year-old Brianna, a phone call that had distracted me, a large bowl of spaghetti with meatballs, and Frank's open briefcase. Frank normally exhibited a saintly degree of patience with Bree—if somewhat less with me—but on that particular occasion his bellows of outrage had rattled the windows.

And now that I recalled the occasion, I actually had thrown a meatball at him in a fury verging on hysteria. So had Bree, though she had done it out of glee, rather than vindictiveness. Had I been standing by the stove at the time, it might easily have been the pot I threw. I rubbed a finger under my nose, not sure whether to regret the memory or to laugh at it. I never did get the stains out of the rug.

—*A Breath of Snow and Ashes,* chapter 27, "The Malting Floor"

Mouthwatering meatballs in a fragrant and quick-cooking tomato sauce. A family meal that comes together in a little over an hour, because although Claire had an appreciation for good food, she wasn't one to spend all day over a hot stove.

Serves 6

Ingredients

1 large onion, chopped (see Knife Skills, page 11)

2 medium celery stalks, chopped

4 garlic cloves, grated or minced

1 pound (450 grams) lean ground beef

1 pound (450 grams) ground pork

1 cup toasted panko-style breadcrumbs

1 large egg

1 tablespoon Worcestershire sauce

1½ teaspoons ground fennel

2 teaspoons kosher salt, plus additional

1 teaspoon freshly ground pepper, plus additional

2 tablespoons olive oil

½ teaspoon crushed red pepper flakes

1 can (28 ounces or 796 ml) crushed tomatoes

1 can (28 ounces or 796 ml) diced tomatoes

1 cup Brown Chicken or Beef Stock (page 20)

1½ teaspoons sugar (optional; see Notes)

3 tablespoons finely chopped fresh parsley

3 tablespoons finely chopped fresh basil or oregano

2 tablespoons butter

1 to 1½ pounds (450 to 700 grams) dry spaghetti

Parmesan cheese, shredded

Method

Move a rack to the upper-middle rung and heat the oven to 450°F.

In a food processor, pulse the onions, celery, and garlic until finely chopped but not pureed, five or six 1-second pulses.

In a large bowl, combine one-third of the onion mixture with the beef, pork, breadcrumbs, egg, Worcestershire sauce, fennel, salt, and 1 teaspoon pepper. Use your hands to mix everything together well. Roll the mixture into 2-ounce balls (a little bigger than a golf ball) and arrange on a parchment paper–lined baking sheet. It makes 18 to 24 meatballs. Roast until cooked through, 12 to 15 minutes.

While the meatballs cook, start the sauce. In a large saucepan, heat the olive oil over medium flame. Add the remaining onion mixture and crushed red pepper. Cook until the onions are soft and translucent, about 5 minutes. Add the crushed tomatoes, diced tomatoes, and stock. Bring to a boil, reduce the heat, and cook at a gentle simmer for 15 minutes.

Add the sugar, if desired, the meatballs, parsley, basil or oregano, and butter and stir well. Simmer gently for another 15 minutes. Taste and adjust seasonings if necessary.

While the sauce simmers, cook the pasta according to the package directions. Drain, divide into bowls, ladle the sauce over, and give each person three or four meatballs. Serve immediately, passing shredded Parmesan and freshly ground pepper at the table.

Notes

- *If you have the time and the inclination, fry a small patty of the meatball mixture to test the seasoning before you form it all into balls.*
- *Sugar helps to cut the acidity of canned tomatoes, but not all brands and varieties of tomatoes need it. Taste your sauce and decide if it's too acidic before adding the sugar.*
- *On the same note, depending on the tomatoes you use, the amount of salt you need will vary widely. Season to your personal taste.*

Chapter 13

~∾⌒∿~

SIDE DISHES

Dumplings in Cross Creek

Auld Ian's Buttered Leeks

Oxford Baked Beans

Fergus's Roasted Tatties

Matchstick Cold-Oil Fries

Broccoli Salad

Honey-Roasted Butternut Squash

DUMPLINGS IN CROSS CREEK

She cut a dumpling in half and ate it slowly, savoring the rich warm juices of chicken and onion. She was grubby, travel-worn, starved, and exhausted, every bone in her body aching. They had made it, though, they were in Cross Creek, and tomorrow was Monday. Somewhere nearby was Jamie Fraser—and God willing, Claire as well.

She touched the leg of her breeches, and the secret pocket sewn into the seam. It was still there, the small round hardness of the talisman. Her mother was still alive. That was all that mattered.

—*Drums of Autumn,* chapter 41, "Journey's End"

Drop these soft dough balls onto Vegetable Stew (page 174) or Cock-a-Leekie (page 58) for a Scottish version of chicken and dumplings—cold-weather comfort at its most scrumptious.

Makes 12

Ingredients

1 cup all-purpose flour

1 cup stone-ground whole wheat flour

¼ cup chopped fresh chives

2 tablespoons chopped fresh parsley

2 teaspoons baking powder

1 teaspoon kosher salt

¼ cup (4 tablespoons) cold butter

1 cup whole milk

Method

In a medium bowl, mix together the flours, chives, parsley, baking powder, and salt. Grate in the butter and work it in with your hands until the mixture is well blended and the flour is the color of cornmeal.

Stir in the milk until combined into a loose, soft dough. With floured hands, form the dough into 12 balls (about the size of golf balls).

Place on top of a gently bubbling stew or soup, leaving space between. Cover and cook until the bottoms are no longer doughy, about 15 minutes.

Note

- *For a vegan version, substitute cold coconut oil for the butter and an almond or rice beverage for the milk.*

Auld Ian's Buttered Leeks

"I remember, when they were young, auld John told Ian it was his job to stand to Jamie's right, for he must guard his chief's weaker side in a fight. And he did—they took it verra seriously, the two of them. And I suppose auld John was right, at that," she added, snipping off the excess thread. "After a time, nobody would fight them, not even the MacNab lads. Jamie and Ian were both fair-sized, and bonny fighters, and when they stood shoulder to shoulder, there was no one could take the pair o' them down, even if they were outnumbered."

She laughed suddenly, and smoothed back a lock of hair behind her ear.

"Watch them sometime, when they're walking the fields together. I dinna suppose they even realize they do it still, but they do. Jamie always moves to the left, so Ian can take up his place on the right, guardin' the weak side."

—*Dragonfly in Amber,* chapter 33, "Thy Brother's Keeper"

Tender, mild leeks simmered gently in their own buttery juices—the perfect dish to guard the main's weaker side. Don't be surprised if this unassuming side, when fresh out of the pan and sitting beside a roast chicken or beef, emerges from the shadows to become a dinnertime star.

Serves 6

Ingredients

6 to 8 medium leeks, halved lengthwise (white and light-green parts only)

¼ cup (4 tablespoons) butter

1 teaspoon chopped fresh thyme

½ teaspoon kosher salt, plus additional

¼ teaspoon ground white pepper, plus additional

Method

Thinly slice the leeks on a diagonal and rinse them thoroughly in a bowl of cold water. Scoop out the leeks with a slotted spoon, leaving the silt and sand behind. Shake dry in a clean dishcloth or salad spinner.

In a large saucepan, melt the butter over medium heat. When bubbling, add the sliced leeks, thyme, salt, and pepper. Stir to coat well with butter. Cover, reduce the heat to low, and cook until tender, about 15 minutes, stirring once or twice. Taste and add more seasonings if required.

Serve hot, alongside Claire's Roast Chicken (page 106) or Roast Beef for a Wedding Feast (page 94).

Store leftovers in the fridge up to 3 days.

Notes

- *If you have leftovers, chop them finely and mix into butter for the next night's steak, stuff them into Trout Fried in Cornmeal (page 170) before frying, or add them to a pot of homemade soup bubbling on the stove.*

OXFORD BAKED BEANS

It was getting dark by the time he returned to his rooms. He could hear a clatter from the dining hall as he passed, and he smelled boiled ham and baked beans, but supper was the farthest thing from his mind.

He squelched up to his rooms and dropped his wet things in a heap on the floor. He dried himself, then sat naked on the bed, towel forgotten in his hand, staring at the desk and at the box that held Brianna's letters.

He would do anything to save her from grief. He would do much more to save her from the stones.

—*Drums of Autumn,* chapter 22, "Spark of an Ancient Flame"

English baked beans are cooked on the stovetop in a tomato sauce that is less sweet than molasses-based beans from North America. They are a traditional part of a full English breakfast, and make a quick lunch or dinner when served on toast with melted cheese.

Serves 6

Ingredients

1 pound (450 grams) dry white beans, such as cannellini, great northern, or navy

3 tablespoons vegetable oil

1 large carrot, grated

2 garlic cloves, minced or grated

1 can (14 ounces or 398 ml) tomato sauce

¼ cup dark brown sugar, lightly packed

1 tablespoon Worcestershire sauce

½ teaspoon smoked or sweet paprika

2 tablespoons butter

Kosher salt to taste

Method

Soak the beans overnight in a large bowl of cold water.

Drain the beans and add them to a large saucepan. Cover with cold water and bring to a boil over high heat. Once the beans have reached a rolling boil, reduce the heat to a simmer. Skim off any foam that has collected on the surface of the water and cook until tender, topping up the water as needed, 45 to 60 minutes, depending on the variety and age of the beans.

Meanwhile, in a medium saucepan, heat the oil to shimmering over medium flame. Add the carrot and garlic and cook, stirring constantly, until very soft but with no color, about 10 minutes. If necessary, reduce the heat to prevent the vegetables from coloring.

Add the tomato sauce, brown sugar, Worcestershire sauce, paprika, and 1 cup water to the pan. Stir well, bring to a boil, reduce the heat, and simmer for 20 minutes. Puree until smooth with an immersion blender.

Drain the beans and add them to the sauce, stirring to combine. Simmer for another 20 minutes while the flavors combine, adding a little more water if the sauce is too thick. Stir in the butter and season with salt.

Serve hot with a Bacon, Asparagus, and Wild Mushroom Omelette (page 45) for a savory and filling gluten-free breakfast.

Beans are always tastier the next day—keep leftovers in the fridge up to 5 days.

Notes

- *While any small white bean will work, I prefer the cannellini for their smooth texture.*
- *Use a countertop blender to puree the sauce if you don't have an immersion blender.*

FERGUS'S ROASTED TATTIES

"Och, aye?" The woman squinted censoriously at the basket. "Well, what d'ye do wi' them, then?"

"Well, you . . ." Jamie started, and then stopped. It occurred to me, as it no doubt had to him, that while he had eaten potatoes in France, he had never seen one prepared for eating. I hid a smile as he stared helplessly at the dirt-crusted potato in his hand. Ian also stared at it; apparently Sir Walter was mute on the subject of potato cooking.

"You roast them." Fergus came to the rescue once more, bobbing up under Jamie's arm. He smacked his lips at the sight of the potatoes. "Put them in the coals of the fire. You eat them with salt. Butter's good, if you have it."

"We have it," said Jamie, with an air of relief. He thrust the potato at Mrs. Murray, as though anxious to be rid of it. "You roast them," he informed her firmly.

—*Dragonfly in Amber,* chapter 32, "Field of Dreams"

If you are sitting around the campfire, by all means, wrap your tatties in aluminum foil and roast them in the coals. In lieu of an open fire, these oven-roasted spuds make a delightful side to Claire's Roast Chicken (page 106), as well as Cock-a-Leekie (page 58).

Serves 6

Ingredients

3 pounds (1.4 kilograms) russet
   potatoes (about 6 medium), peeled
   and quartered

1 large onion, cut into 8 wedges

⅓ cup vegetable oil

3 fresh thyme sprigs

1 teaspoon kosher salt, plus additional

¼ teaspoon freshly ground pepper

Method

Move a rack to the middle rung and heat the oven to 425°F.

Rinse the potatoes and cover them with cold salted water in a large pot. Bring to a boil, uncovered, over high heat. Reduce to medium-high and boil gently for 5 minutes. Drain the potatoes in a colander and allow to steam dry for 2 minutes.

In a metal baking pan, toss the potatoes with the onions, oil, thyme, salt, and pepper. Roast for 30 minutes, then flip the potatoes and squash slightly with the back of your fork or spatula. Return the pan to the oven until the potatoes are golden, crispy, and tender, about 15 more minutes. Serve hot.

Note

- *To cook these with Claire's Roast Chicken (page 106), put them in the oven at the chicken's 30-minute mark. (The higher oven temperature will be fine while the tatties share the space with the chicken.) Flip and squash the tatties at about the same time you take the chicken out of the oven, reduce the temperature to 425°F, and finish cooking the potatoes while the chicken rests and you make the gravy.*

MATCHSTICK COLD-OIL FRIES

Seized by the sudden desire to see her, he reached out, fumbling on the table by the bed. The little box was where she'd thrown it when they came back. She'd designed it to be used in the dark, after all; a turn of the lid dispensed one of the small, waxy sticks, and the tiny strip of roughened metal glued to the side was cool to his hand. A skritch! that made his heart leap with its simple familiarity, and the tiny flame appeared with a whiff of sulfur—magic.

"Don't waste them," she said, but smiled in spite of the protest, delighted at the sight as she'd been when she first showed him what she'd done.

Her hair was loose and clean, just washed; shimmering over the pale round of her shoulder, clouds of it lying soft over his chest, cinnamon and amber and roan and gold, sparked by the flame.

—*A Breath of Snow and Ashes*, chapter 21, "We Have Ignition"

If these were for Roger, I'd call them chips. But since these crisp golden sticks are all about our Boston Bree, they've just got to be fries. Because they start in cold oil, the potatoes first poach in the warming oil before it gets hot enough to fry and crisp up the outsides. The most succulent, least-hassle homemade fries you'll ever make.

Serves 1

Ingredients

1 large yellow potato   Kosher salt to taste
Vegetable oil

Method

Wash the potatoes and scrub off any dirt. Square off the sides and ends of the potatoes, then cut lengthwise into ⅜ x ⅜-inch sticks. Arrange the potatoes in a large saucepan (see Notes) and cover completely with the oil.

Cook over high heat, undisturbed, until the oil comes to a rolling boil, 8 to 12 minutes. Stir once with a slotted spoon, gently scraping the bottom of the pan to release any potatoes that stick. Continue to cook, stirring occasionally, until light golden and crisp, another 10 to 15 minutes.

Drain on paper towels, sprinkle with salt, and serve.

Notes

- *The high moisture content of Yukon Gold potatoes is essential for best results. Russets work, but the finished fries are much darker.*
- *Choose a pan that is large enough to hold the fries and oil with lots of room to spare, to avoid a spillover once the oil starts to boil. I use a tall, narrow pot, which uses about 2½ cups oil to cover two large potatoes.*
- *Once the oil has cooled, strain and store it in the fridge in a tightly closed container. You can use each batch of oil four or five times. Discard it before it becomes dark and smelly.*
- *For additional servings, use one potato per person.*

BROCCOLI SALAD

A hum of pleasant anticipation rose around me, as people began metaphorically to loosen their belts, squaring up to the tables with a firm determination to do their duty in honor of the occasion.

Jamie was still stuck fast to Mrs. MacDonald, I saw; he was helping her to a dish of what looked from the distance to be broccoli salad. He looked up and saw me, beckoned me to join them—but I shook my head, gesturing with my fan toward the buffet tables, where the guests were setting to in the business-like manner of grasshoppers in a barley field. I didn't want to lose the opportunity of inquiring about Manfred McGillivray, before the stupor of satiety settled over the crowd.

—*A Breath of Snow and Ashes,* chapter 54, "Flora MacDonald's Barbecue"

Crunchy and sweet, this raw broccoli and cauliflower salad looks quite different from the eighteenth-century version that would have adorned Jocasta's table, but it is an easy, make-ahead recipe that makes a delicious and colorful contribution to any modern-day potluck.

Serves 8 to 10

Ingredients

1 cup mayonnaise

¼ cup sugar

¼ cup white vinegar

3 large broccoli crowns (2 to 2½ pounds or 900 to 1,100 grams), cut into small florets (see Notes)

1 small cauliflower (1 to 1½ pounds), cut into small florets

1 pound (450 grams) bacon, cooked and crumbled (see Notes)

1 medium red onion, julienned (see Knife Skills, page 11)

4 ounces (115 grams or about 1 cup) shredded aged cheddar cheese

1 cup dried cranberries, chopped

Method

In a small bowl, stir together the mayonnaise, sugar, and vinegar until well combined.

In a large bowl, toss together the broccoli, cauliflower, bacon, onions, cheese, and cranberries. Pour over the dressing and toss well to coat evenly. Cover and refrigerate to allow the flavors to meld, 2 to 4 hours.

Store leftovers in the fridge up to 3 days.

Notes

- *You want about double the amount of broccoli to cauliflower by volume.*
- *For a vegan version, use an eggless mayonnaise and substitute chopped pecans for the cheese.*
- *The easiest way to cook a lot of bacon is in the oven, at 375°F, on a wire rack set in a baking pan. Cook for 12 to 15 minutes, until the bacon is crisped and darkening in color.*

Honey-Roasted Butternut Squash

Bird's wife Penstemon's nostrils flared delicately; Crombie was sweating with nervousness, and smelled like a goat. He bowed earnestly, and presented Bird with the good knife he had brought as a present, slowly reciting the complimentary speech he had committed to memory. Reasonably well, too, Jamie thought; he'd mispronounced only a couple of words.

"I come to b-bring you great joy," he finished, stammering and sweating.

Bird looked at Crombie—small, stringy, and dripping wet—for a long, inscrutable moment, then back at Jamie.

"You're a funny man, Bear-Killer," he said with resignation.

"Let us eat!" It was autumn; the harvest was in and the hunting was good. And so the Feast of the Guns was a notable occasion, with wapiti and venison and wild pig raised steaming from pits and roasted over roaring fires, with overflowing platters of maize and roasted squash and dishes of beans spiced with onion and coriander, dishes of pottage, and dozen upon dozen of small fish rolled in cornmeal, fried in bear grease, their flesh crisp and sweet.

—*A Breath of Snow and Ashes,* chapter 67, "The Last Laugh"

A sweet vegetable side that brings color to any plate, including Veal Patties in Wine Sauce (page 99), or Buttermilk Lamb Chops with Rosewater Mint Sauce (page 136).

Serves 6

Ingredients

2 tablespoons olive oil

2 tablespoons honey

1 garlic clove, grated or minced

1 teaspoon kosher salt

½ teaspoon crushed red pepper flakes

1 medium (2 to 2½ pounds or 900 to 1,100 grams) butternut squash, peeled and cut into 2-inch cubes

Method

Move a rack to the middle rung and heat the oven to 400°F.

In a small bowl, whisk together the olive oil, honey, garlic, salt, crushed red pepper flakes, and 2 tablespoons hot water.

Place the squash cubes in a large glass or ceramic baking dish, pour the honey mixture over the squash, and stir to coat the pieces. Roast until tender and just starting to brown, 35 to 40 minutes, tossing the squash once during cooking.

Toss in the sticky, but still wet, glaze one last time and serve hot.

Store leftovers in the refrigerator up to 3 days.

Notes

- *Any winter squash (acorn, Hubbard, pumpkin, et cetera) substitutes well. Adjust the cooking time as required.*
- *To make this vegan, substitute maple syrup for the honey.*
- *To give this side an Asian twist, add 1 teaspoon sesame oil to the honey mixture, and toss the hot cooked squash in 2 tablespoons toasted sesame seeds just before serving.*

Chapter 14

୨୦

BREADS AND BAKING

Mrs. Graham's Oatmeal Scones with Clotted Cream

Pumpkin Seed and Herb Oatcakes

Nettle Rolls

Brown Buns at Beauly

Fiona's Cinnamon Scones

Bannocks at Carfax Close

Honey-Buttermilk Oat Bread

Spoon Bread

Jocasta's Auld Country Bannocks

Raisin Muffins

Corn Muffins

Mrs. Bug's Buttermilk Drop Biscuits

Mrs. Graham's Oatmeal Scones with Clotted Cream

"I've brought but the two cups, for I thought perhaps Mrs. Randall would care to join me in the kitchen. I've a bit of—" I didn't wait for the conclusion of her invitation, but leapt to my feet with alacrity. I could hear the theories breaking out again behind me as we pushed through the swinging door that led to the manse's kitchen.

The tea was green, hot and fragrant, with bits of leaf swirling through the liquid.

"Mmm," I said, setting the cup down. "It's been a long time since I tasted Oolong."

Mrs. Graham nodded, beaming at my pleasure in her refreshments. She had clearly gone to some trouble, laying out handmade lace mats beneath the eggshell cups and providing thick clotted cream with the scones.

—*Outlander,* chapter 1, "A New Beginning"

Oatmeal Scones

As the caller at Craigh na Dun and fortune-teller at the town fair, Mrs. Graham undoubtedly believes in at least a few spirits beyond those with whom she communes in church on a Sunday. How much does she know? One thing's for certain—she'll never tell—practical, Presbyterian lips like hers don't crack easily.

I like to think, however, that she would have gladly shared her scone recipe with us. As traditional as the woman herself, and made hearty with oats and tender with butter, their slight sweetness is the perfect foil to the tang of clotted cream.

Makes 8

Ingredients

2 cups all-purpose flour

1 cup rolled oats

⅓ cup sugar

2 teaspoons baking powder

½ teaspoon kosher salt

¾ cup (12 tablespoons) cold butter

⅔ cup light cream

Method

Move a rack to the middle rung and heat the oven to 350°F. Line a baking sheet with parchment paper.

In a large bowl, combine the flour, oats, sugar, baking powder, and salt and mix well.

Set aside 2 tablespoons of the butter. Grate the remaining butter into the flour mixture and stir to distribute evenly.

Make a well in the center of the bowl and pour in the cream, mixing with a large spoon. Use your hands to bring the dough together into a rough ball, pour onto a lightly floured counter, and knead lightly until combined.

Lightly flour the top and bottom of the dough and pat it into a 1-inch-thick round. Use a 3-inch cutter to cut eight circles. Evenly space the scones on the prepared baking sheet.

Melt the remaining 2 tablespoons butter, use it to brush the tops of the scones, and bake until golden brown on the tops and bottoms, 20 to 25 minutes. Cool on a wire rack for at least 15 minutes.

Serve slightly warm with clotted cream or butter and jam.

Store in a covered container for 3 to 4 days.

Notes

- *Substitute buttermilk for the cream for a lower-fat scone with a tang.*
- *Optional additions: ½ cup raisins, currants, or dried cranberries. For a savory scone, ½ cup shredded cheese and/or 2 tablespoons chopped fresh thyme or rosemary.*
- *If you prefer, cut the dough into eight equally sized wedges; these are called farls.*

Clotted Cream

Ancient Britons may have clotted cream to lengthen its shelf life, but more recently, prior to agricultural industrialization, dairy farmers clotted their milk because it resulted in a higher yield of cream. Modern cream separators have eliminated the need for clotting, but the sweet, slightly nutty flavor of clotted cream remains popular in the UK and many Commonwealth countries. It is a traditional part of a formal tea, and usually accompanies scones and strawberry preserves.

Begin the recipe early in the morning to have clotted cream ready for the next day.

Makes 1 cup

Ingredient

2 cups whipping cream (not ultrapasteurized)

Method

Move a rack to the middle rung and heat the oven to 180°F.

Pour the cream into an ovenproof dish or saucepan, cover, and set in the oven until a thick, yellowish skin has formed on top of the cream, 8 to 12 hours.

Cool completely on the counter and refrigerate overnight.

Use a spoon to carefully skim the firm clotted cream from the surface. Stir until smooth, creamy, and the texture of whipped butter. Use the whey in the bottom of the dish for baking, in a smoothie, or discard.

Serve alongside freshly baked scones with a pot of Fraser Strawberry Jam (page 318).

Store covered in the fridge up to 3 days.

Notes

- *Ultrapasteurized cream will not work in this recipe.*
- *The fresher the cream, the better it will clot and the longer it will last.*
- *The greater the surface area of the cream, the faster and better it will clot. Choose a dish or pan so that the cream is 1 to 3 inches deep, and not deeper than 3 inches.*

PUMPKIN SEED AND HERB OATCAKES

I found what I supposed I had been looking for in the central drawer. A half-finished letter, written in a flowing hand rendered no more legible by the eccentric spelling and total lack of punctuation. The paper was fresh and clean, and the ink crisply black. Legible or not, the date at the top of the page sprang out at me as though written in letters of fire: 20 April, 1743.

When he returned a few moments later, Colum found his guest seated by the casement windows, hands clasped decorously in her lap. Seated, because my legs would no longer hold me up. Hands clasped, to hide the trembling that had made it difficult for me to stuff the letter back into its resting place.

He had brought with him the tray of refreshments; mugs of ale and fresh oatcakes spread with honey. I nibbled sparingly at these; my stomach was churning too vigorously to allow for any appetite.

—*Outlander,* chapter 5, "The MacKenzie"

Ubiquitous in eighteenth-century Scotland, oatcakes have made a resurgence in the early part of this century as a gluten-free alternative to bread and crackers. The herbs and pumpkin seeds in this recipe make a modern and flavorful addition to the traditional oatcakes Claire nibbled on with Colum.

Makes two 6-inch oatcakes (16 farls)

Ingredients

1½ cups coarsely ground rolled oats (see Grinding Grains, Nuts, and Seeds, page 10)

¼ cup finely ground unsalted pumpkin seeds (see Grinding Grains, Nuts, and Seeds, page 10)

1 tablespoon cornstarch or tapioca starch

1 tablespoon honey

1 teaspoon minced fresh thyme

1 teaspoon minced fresh rosemary

½ teaspoon kosher salt

2 tablespoons butter

Flour, for dusting

Method

Move a rack to the middle rung and heat the oven to 375°F.

In a large bowl, combine the ground oats and pumpkin seeds, cornstarch or tapioca starch, honey, herbs, and salt.

In a small saucepan, melt the butter in ¼ cup hot water over medium-high heat. When the water boils, stir it into the dry ingredients to make a stiff dough, adding more hot water sparingly if required.

Divide the dough in half and loosely tent aluminum foil over one piece to keep it warm. On an 8-inch square of lightly floured parchment paper, roll out the other piece into a circle ¼ inch thick. Loosen and turn the dough as you go to prevent it from sticking. Use a 6-inch plate and a sharp knife to cut out a large circular oatcake. If it is too cool and too stiff to roll, lightly knead 1 tablespoon boiling water into the dough first. Cut the circle into eight equal wedges, or farls, but do not separate. Repeat with the second half of the dough.

Bake both oatcakes on their parchment, on a single baking sheet until light golden, 15 to 20 minutes. Cool on a wire rack and gently separate.

Enjoy with Crowdie Cheese (page 31) and Tomato Pickle in the Manger (page 321), or serve with butter and honey.

Store in a covered container up to a week.

Notes

- *Not all oats are guaranteed to be gluten-free. Check the packaging before you buy.*
- *Grind extra oats and use them to flour the parchment to keep everything gluten-free.*
- *Use a 2- or 3-inch cutter to make individual round oatcakes instead.*
- *Mix it up with different seeds and nuts, herbs and spices, such as almonds and mint, sesame seeds and black pepper, cashews and caraway, and so on.*

NETTLE ROLLS

"The peasants of Gascony beat a faithless wife wi' nettles," he said. He lowered the spiky bunch of leaves and brushed the flower heads lightly across one breast. I gasped from the sudden sting, and a faint red blotch appeared as though by magic on my skin.

"Will ye have me do so?" he asked. "Shall I punish you that way?"

"If you . . . if you like." My lips were trembling so hard I could barely get out the words. A few crumbs of earth from the nettles' roots had fallen between my breasts; one rolled down the slope of my ribs, dislodged by my pounding heart, I imagined. The welt on my breast burned like fire. I closed my eyes, imagining in vivid detail exactly what being thrashed with a bunch of nettles would feel like.

Suddenly the viselike grip on my wrist relaxed. I opened my eyes to find Jamie sitting cross-legged by me, the plants thrown aside and scattered on the ground. He had a faint, rueful smile on his lips.

"I beat you once in justice, Sassenach, and ye threatened to disembowel me with my own dirk. Now you'll ask me to whip ye wi' nettles?" He shook his head slowly, wondering, and his hand reached as though by its own volition to cup my cheek. "Is my pride worth so much to you, then?"

"Yes! Yes, it bloody is!" I sat up myself, and grasped him by the shoulders, taking both of us by surprise as I kissed him hard and awkwardly.

—*Dragonfly in Amber,* chapter 29, "To Grasp the Nettle"

Nettles are native to Europe, Asia, northern Africa, and most of North America. Found in wetlands, forests, and meadows, they are at their culinary peak in early to mid-spring. When foraging, wear protective clothing to guard against stings, and clip only the top two to three sets of leaves, which are the most tender.

These soft rolls are full of savory, earthy flavor and are a wonderful accompaniment to Gypsy Stew (page 96) or to complete a breakfast of bacon and A Coddled Egg for Duncan (page 41).

Makes 12

Ingredients

2 cups all-purpose flour

½ cup stone-ground whole wheat flour

1¼ teaspoons instant yeast

1 teaspoon kosher salt

6 tablespoons cold butter

1 large egg

2 tablespoons honey

⅔ cup whole milk at room temperature

1 teaspoon vegetable oil

6 big handfuls (wear gloves!) fresh young nettle leaves

¼ cup shredded Parmesan cheese

Zest of 1 lemon, grated or minced

¼ cup pine nuts or slivered almonds

Method

In the bowl of a standing mixer, combine the flours, yeast, and salt. Using the paddle attachment, mix together on low. Add 2 tablespoons of the butter in small chunks and mix on medium-low until well blended.

In a separate bowl whisk the egg and honey into the milk and add it to the dry ingredients. Mix on medium-low until combined into a rough ball. Switch to the dough hook and knead on medium-low for 5 minutes until the dough is soft, supple, and tacky but not sticky.

Alternatively, combine the dough by hand and knead on a lightly floured counter for 6 to 8 minutes.

Pour the oil into a large bowl, roll the dough in the oil to coat, and cover with a plate or plastic wrap. Set in a warm place to rise until the dough is doubled, 1½ to 2 hours.

Meanwhile, blanch the nettles in boiling salted water for 2 to 3 minutes. Drain the nettles and immediately submerge them in ice water to stop the cooking process and maintain their bright green color. When cool, drain the nettles and wring them in a clean dishcloth to squeeze out as much moisture as possible. Chop finely.

Melt the remaining 4 tablespoons butter.

Line a 9-inch square or round baking pan with parchment paper.

Turn the proofed dough out onto a lightly floured counter and roll into a 12-inch square. Brush the dough with 2 tablespoons of the melted butter and spread the nettles evenly on top. Sprinkle the Parmesan, lemon zest, and pine nuts on top and press them lightly into the dough with the palm of your hand.

Roll the dough into a log, using a bench scraper or spatula to release the dough when necessary. Pinch the bottom seam to seal, and rock it, seam side down, to flatten the join.

Flour a knife or bench scraper and cut the log in half, then quarters. Cut each quarter into three pieces for a total of twelve buns. Gently transfer the slices to the parchment paper–lined pan, cover with plastic, and let rise on the counter until doubled, about 1 hour.

Move a rack to the middle rung and heat the oven to 350°F.

Dab the remaining 2 tablespoons melted butter onto the proofed rolls with a pastry brush and bake until light golden, 12 to 15 minutes.

Cool slightly on a wire rack before serving.

Keep leftovers in an airtight container up to 3 days.

Notes

- *Wash just-picked nettles in a bowl of tepid water with a splash of vinegar to kill any little bugs.*
- *If you don't want to pick your own, look for nettles at farmers' markets in spring, or substitute spinach, kale, chard, collards, mustard, or any favorite greens.*

BROWN BUNS AT BEAULY

Young Simon snorted and looked at Jamie for support. Over the last two months, his initial suspicious hostility had faded into a reluctant respect for his bastard relative's obvious expertise in the art of war.

"Jamie says . . ." he began.

"I ken well enough what he says," Old Simon interrupted. "He's said it often enough. I shall make up my own mind in my own time. But bear it in mind, lad—when it comes to declaring yourself in a war, there's little to be lost by waiting."

"Waiting to see who wins," Jamie murmured, studiously wiping his plate with a bit of bread. The old man looked up sharply, but evidently decided to ignore this contribution.

—*Dragonfly in Amber,* chapter 41, "The Seer's Curse"

A welcoming whole-meal loaf made with stone-ground whole wheat flour and oats.

Start the preferment the night before to add flavor and lift to whole-grain loaves that would otherwise be dense and heavy-tasting. The preferment is an easier, modern simulation of the more authentic yeast culture, which cooks in the past kept alive by feeding with flour and water.

Makes 12 buns or two 1½-pound loaves

Ingredients

3½ cups stone-ground whole wheat flour

1½ teaspoons instant yeast

1¼ cups lukewarm whole milk

1 cup coarsely ground rolled oats (see Grinding Grains, Nuts, and Seeds, page 10)

1½ teaspoons kosher salt

2 tablespoons honey

1 large egg

2 tablespoons melted butter, plus additional

2 tablespoons rolled oats

Method

Just before you go to bed, mix together in a medium bowl 1½ cups of the flour and ¼ teaspoon of the yeast. Stir in the lukewarm milk and cover with a plate. In a separate bowl, mix the coarsely ground oats with 1 cup water and cover with a plate. Set both bowls on the counter overnight.

The next morning, in the bowl of a standing mixer, combine the remaining 2 cups flour and 1¼ teaspoons yeast with the salt and mix thoroughly, using the paddle attachment on low speed. Add the frothy preferment, oat soaker, honey, and egg. Mix on medium-low until the dough forms a rough ball. Scrape down the bowl, change to the dough hook, and knead on medium until the dough is smooth, firm, and slightly tacky but not sticky, 10 to 12 minutes.

Alternatively, mix the dough by hand in a large bowl and knead on a lightly floured counter for 15 to 18 minutes.

Grease a bowl lightly with melted butter and roll the dough in the bowl to coat. Cover with a clean dishcloth and let rise in a warm, draft-free place until doubled in size, 1½ to 2 hours.

Divide the dough into twelve equal pieces and cover with plastic wrap or a clean dishcloth. On a lightly floured counter, working with one piece of dough at a time, draw the edges of the dough into the center, making a ball. Pinch the seam together tightly to seal, turn the ball over, and roll it under your palm in a tight circle on the counter five or six times, to tighten the surface tension of the dough and ensure an even rise (see photo on page 225). Flatten the ball slightly with your palm or a rolling pin and repeat with the remaining pieces of dough. Arrange on two parchment paper–lined baking sheets, cover with plastic wrap, and let rise on the counter until almost doubled in size, 60 to 90 minutes.

Move a rack to the middle rung and heat the oven to 350°F.

Gently brush the tops of the buns with the melted butter, sprinkle the rolled oats on top, and bake until the tops are golden brown and the loaves sound hollow when tapped on the bottom, turning and rotating the pans halfway, 30 to 35 minutes. Cool on a wire rack for at least 60 minutes before slicing.

Store in a paper bag or bread bin up to 3 days. Freeze baked buns or loaves up to 2 weeks.

Notes

- *Whole wheat flour takes a lot of kneading to develop the gluten, which is what reacts with the yeast and causes the dough to rise—if kneading by hand, it's helpful to have a friend who can take over when you get tired.*
- *For an even more flavorful loaf, substitute buttermilk for the milk. If you happen to make your own Crowdie Cheese (page 31) or Clotted Cream (page 218), use the resulting whey in this recipe instead of milk. Waste not, want not!*
- *For loaves, separate the dough into two equal pieces and follow the shaping and rolling instructions for Honey-Buttermilk Oat Bread (page 232). Bake for 50 to 55 minutes.*

FIONA'S CINNAMON SCONES

"A pound of best butter—that's what you told me to ask for, and I did, but I kept wondering whether there was such a thing as second-best butter, or worst butter—" Brianna was handing over wrapped packages to Fiona, laughing and talking at once.

"Well, and if ye got it from that auld rascal Wicklow, worst is what it's likely to be, no matter what he says," Fiona interrupted. "Oh, and ye've got the cinnamon, that's grand! I'll make cinnamon scones, then; d'ye want to come and watch me do it?"

"Yes, but first I want supper. I'm starved!" Brianna stood on tiptoe, sniffing hopefully in the direction of the kitchen. "What are we having—haggis?"

"Haggis! Gracious, ye silly Sassenach—ye dinna have haggis in the spring! Ye have it in the autumn when the sheep are killed."

"Am I a Sassenach?" Brianna seemed delighted at the name.

"Of course ye are, gowk. But I like ye fine, anyway."

—*Voyager,* chapter 3, "Frank and Full Disclosure"

Light, buttery scones rolled with cinnamon sugar. A sweet start to the day when paired with a cup of coffee, or a delectable afternoon snack alongside a soothing cup of tea.

Makes 8 scones

Ingredients

½ cup dark brown sugar, firmly packed

2 teaspoons cinnamon

2½ cups all-purpose flour

½ cup sugar

½ teaspoon kosher salt

2 teaspoons baking powder

½ teaspoon baking soda

½ cup cold butter, plus additional

½ cup whole milk, plus 2 tablespoons

½ cup yogurt

1 cup confectioners' (powdered) sugar

Method

Move a rack to the middle rung and heat the oven to 425°F. In a small bowl, stir together the brown sugar and cinnamon and set it aside.

In another bowl, mix together the flour, sugar, salt, baking powder, and baking soda. Grate the butter into the bowl and mix well.

In a third bowl, stir the milk and yogurt together. Add to the flour mixture and stir until combined into a slightly sticky ball.

Transfer the dough to a lightly floured counter and sprinkle with a little more flour. Quickly and lightly knead the dough five or six times. Return the dough to the bowl, cover, and chill in the refrigerator for 10 to 15 minutes.

On a lightly floured board, roll out the dough to a 12 x 12-inch square, loosening and turning the dough to keep it from sticking. Sprinkle the cinnamon sugar over the dough in a thick layer, pressing down lightly with your palms. Roll the dough up tightly into a log, using a bench scraper or spatula to lift the dough when necessary. Pat it out to approximately 4 x 12 inches long. Flour a sharp knife or bench scraper and cut the log into quarters. Cut each quarter in half on the diagonal, for a total of eight scones.

Carefully transfer to a parchment paper–lined baking sheet. Melt about 1 tablespoon butter and brush over the tops of the scones. Bake until the tops and bottoms are golden, about 18 to 22 minutes. Cool on a wire rack for 20 minutes.

In a small bowl, stir together the confectioners' sugar and the 2 tablespoons milk.

Drizzle the glaze over the scones and serve while still slightly warm.

Store in a sealed container up to 2 days and reheat slightly before serving.

Notes

- *For fresh scones in the morning without all the work, freeze unbaked scones on the pan. Transfer the frozen-solid scones to a freezer bag or sealed container and return to the freezer up to 2 weeks. Bake from frozen at 375 °F for 25 to 35 minutes and glaze as above.*
- *You may have trouble cleaning the pan without parchment paper. Use aluminum foil in a pinch, but watch carefully to make sure the bottoms don't burn.*
- *You can dress these up to your heart's content. Sprinkle 1 cup pecans or walnuts on top of the sugar before rolling. For a Highland treat, soak 1 cup raisins in ¼ cup scotch whisky for 20 minutes before sprinkling them on the dough and rolling. Not a fan of cinnamon? Press 1 cup blueberries into the rolled-out dough and sprinkle with ¼ cup granulated sugar and the zest of a lemon before rolling as directed.*

BANNOCKS AT CARFAX CLOSE

"Hungry, Sassenach?" Jamie asked, rather unnecessarily, I thought.

"Well, yes, now that you mention it. Do you still keep food in the top drawer?" When we were first married, I had developed the habit of keeping small bits of food on hand, to supply his constant appetite, and the top drawer of any chest of drawers where we lived generally provided a selection of rolls, small cakes, or bits of cheese.

He laughed and stretched. "Aye, I do. There's no much there just now, though, but a couple of stale bannocks. Better I take ye down to the tavern, and—" The look of happiness engendered by perusing the photographs of Brianna faded, to be replaced by a look of alarm. He glanced quickly at the window, where a soft purplish color was beginning to replace the pale gray, and the look of alarm deepened.

"The tavern! Christ! I've forgotten Mr. Willoughby!" He was on his feet and groping in the chest for fresh stockings before I could say anything. Coming out with the stockings in one hand and two bannocks in the other, he tossed the latter into my lap and sat down on the stool, hastily yanking on the former.

—*Voyager*, chapter 24, "A. Malcolm, Printer"

Traditional bannocks, such as Jocasta's Auld Country Bannocks (page 238), were dense round cakes of oat and/or barley meal, animal fat, and water or milk and were consumed, for the most part, while still warm.

This modern recipe yields light and flaky biscuitlike bannocks, thanks be to wheat and baking powder.

Makes 12

Ingredients

2 cups all-purpose flour, plus additional

1 cup coarsely ground rolled oats (see Grinding Grains, Nuts, and Seeds, page 10)

1 tablespoon baking powder

1 tablespoon sugar

1 teaspoon kosher salt

¼ cup (4 tablespoons) cold butter

¾ cup whole milk

½ cup yogurt

Method

Move a rack to the upper-middle rung and heat the oven to 400°F. Line a baking sheet with parchment paper.

Combine the flour, oats, baking powder, sugar, and salt in a large bowl. Grate in the butter and mix well. In a separate bowl stir together the milk and yogurt. Add to the dry ingredients and stir with a wooden spoon to make a slightly sticky dough.

Turn onto a floured counter and sprinkle with more flour. Knead dough lightly five or six times, working in just enough additional flour so that dough is no longer sticky.

Pat or roll into an 8 x 8-inch square, about ½-inch thick. Cut into twelve rectangles and arrange on the prepared baking pan. Bake until just golden, 12 to 15 minutes. Cool on a wire rack for 10 minutes.

Serve warm or cold with butter, cheese and jam, or beside a bowl of Geillis's Cullen Skink (page 56).

Keep in a covered container up to 3 days.

Notes

- *The quickest and easiest way to incorporate butter into a dough for bannocks, scones, biscuits, and pastry is to grate it cold.*
- *To cook your bannocks on the stovetop, heat a large cast-iron pan over medium-low for 5 minutes. Cook the bannocks in batches until golden brown on both sides, 6 to 8 minutes per side.*

HONEY-BUTTERMILK OAT BREAD

A knock at the door broke the tension. It was a small serving maid, with a tray of supper. She bobbed shyly to me, smiled at Jamie, and laid both supper—cold meat, hot broth, and warm oat bread with butter—and the fire with a quick and practiced hand, then left us with a murmured "Good e'en to ye."

We ate slowly, talking carefully only of neutral things; I told him how I had made my way from Craigh na Dun to Inverness, and made him laugh with stories of Mr. Graham and Master Georgie. He in turn told me about Mr. Willoughby; how he had found the little Chinese, half-starved and dead drunk, lying behind a row of casks on the docks at Burntisland, one of the shipping ports near Edinburgh.

We said nothing much of ourselves, but as we ate, I became increasingly conscious of his body, watching his fine, long hands as he poured wine and cut meat, seeing the twist of his powerful torso under his shirt, and the graceful line of neck and shoulder as he stooped to retrieve a fallen napkin. Once or twice, I thought I saw his gaze linger on me in the same way—a sort of hesitant avidity—but he quickly glanced away each time, hooding his eyes so that I could not tell what he saw or felt.

—*Voyager,* chapter 25, "House of Joy"

A slightly sweet, soft loaf made with oats and the finest milled flour, as only the sophisticated Madame Jeanne would serve.

Makes 12 buns or two 1½-pound loaves

Ingredients

2 cups buttermilk

½ cup whole milk

2 cups rolled oats, plus additional for the top

5 tablespoons honey

5 cups all-purpose flour

2 teaspoons kosher salt

2 teaspoons instant yeast

5 tablespoons softened butter, plus additional for the pans

Method

In a saucepan on the stove over low heat or in a dish in the microwave, warm the buttermilk and milk until lukewarm. Stir in the oats and 4 tablespoons of the honey. Set aside while you gather the rest of the ingredients.

In the bowl of a standing mixer, combine the flour, salt, and yeast. Using the paddle attachment, mix on low speed. With the machine running, add 4 tablespoons butter in small chunks. Pour in the buttermilk mixture and combine on medium-low until a rough ball forms. Switch to the bread hook, scrape down the bowl, and knead on medium until the dough ball is soft and dense, tacky but not sticky, about 6 minutes.

Alternatively, mix the dough by hand and knead on a lightly floured counter until soft, dense, and tacky but not sticky, about 10 minutes.

Place in a bowl and cover with plastic wrap or a plate. Rise in a warm, draft-free place until doubled in size, 1½ to 2 hours.

Move a rack to the middle rung and heat the oven to 375°F. Grease two loaf pans generously with butter.

Divide the dough into two equal pieces. On a lightly floured counter, press each piece into a rectangle measuring 5 x 8 inches. Starting on the shorter end, roll up the dough one section at a time, using your thumbs to pinch the seam closed after each roll. Pinch the final seam closed, then gently rock the loaf on the counter, seam side down, to even it out. Do not taper the ends.

Transfer to the prepared pans, ensuring that the loaf touches both ends of the pan for an even rise. Cover loosely with plastic wrap or a clean dishcloth and rise on the counter until the dough is doubled in size and cresting the top of the pans, 60 to 90 minutes.

Melt the remaining 1 tablespoon butter, and stir together with the remaining 1 tablespoon honey. Brush the tops of both loaves gently. Garnish with a few oats and bake, turning and rotating the pans halfway, until the tops are a dark brown and the loaves sound hollow when tapped on the bottom, 45 to 50 minutes.

Remove the loaves from the pans immediately and cool on a wire rack for at least 60 minutes before slicing.

Notes

- *My favorite place to rise dough is in the oven with just the interior light on—a nearly perfect proofing temperature within everyone's reach.*
- *Once the dough is shaped and in the pan, it will keep, tightly wrapped, in the fridge up to 2 days, or in the freezer up to 2 weeks. Loaves from the fridge need 2 to 4 hours of rising time on the counter before baking. Defrost frozen loaves, loosely covered on the counter, overnight, then bake as directed.*
- *For buns, separate the dough into twelve equal pieces and follow the shaping and rolling instructions in Brown Buns at Beauly (page 224). Bake buns 25 to 35 minutes.*

SPOON BREAD

"That's a fine wee book, Uncle Jamie," Ian said, with approval. "Does it say more about the snakes?" He looked hungrily over the expanse of table, in search of more food. Without comment, I reached into the hutch and brought out a plate of spoon bread, which I set before him. He sighed happily and waded in, as Jamie turned the page.

"Well, here's a bit about how the rattlesnakes charm squirrels and rabbits." Jamie touched his plate, but encountered nothing save bare surface. I pushed the muffins toward him.

"'It is surprizing to observe how these Snakes will allure and charm Squirrel, Hedge-Conneys, Partridges and many other small Beasts and Birds to them, which they quickly devour. The Sympathy is so strong between these, that you shall see the Squirrel or Partridge (as they have espied this Snake) leap or fly from Bough to Bough, until at last they run or leap directly into its Mouth, not having power to avoid their enemy, who never stirs out of the Posture or Quoil until he obtains his Prey.'"

His hand, blindly groping after sustenance, encountered the muffins. He picked one up and glanced up at me. "Damned if I've ever seen that, myself. D'ye think it likely?"

"No," I said, pushing the curls back off my forehead. "Does that book have any helpful suggestions for dealing with vicious pigs?"

He waved absently at me with the remnants of his muffin.

"Dinna fash," he murmured. "I'll manage the pig." He took his eyes off the book long enough to glance over the table at the empty dishes. "Are there no more eggs?"

—*Drums of Autumn*, chapter 25, "Enter a Serpent"

Corn was the mainstay of many colonial diets, along with pork. Upon arrival, colonists prepared corn dishes as the Native Americans taught them, but were soon replacing wheat with corn in their favorite recipes from home, and using eggs to leaven instead of yeast, which requires the gluten in wheat to produce a rise.

These new dishes were dense and creamy, more similar to English-style puddings than loaves of bread. Spoon bread was a favorite of George Washington, and was served regularly at his residence, Mount Vernon.

Ingredients

1 cup cornmeal

2½ cups whole milk

1 cup corn kernels (fresh, frozen, or canned)

2 tablespoons butter

1 teaspoon kosher salt

2 teaspoons lemon juice

3 large eggs

½ teaspoon baking soda

Method

Move a rack to the middle rung and heat the oven to 350°F. Butter a 9-inch square glass or ceramic baking dish.

In a large saucepan, stir together the cornmeal, milk, corn kernels, butter, and salt over medium flame. Heat until thickened, stirring constantly, 5 to 8 minutes. Remove from the heat and stir in the lemon juice.

Beat together the eggs and baking soda in a medium bowl. Add about 1 cup of the hot cornmeal mixture to the eggs to temper, then add that back to the saucepan and mix well before pouring the batter into the buttered baking dish.

Bake for 30 to 35 minutes, until the center has set.

Serve hot, with butter and honey, or with Rosamund's Pulled Pork with Devil's Apple BBQ Sauce (page 120).

Note

• *To use fresh corn, blanch a medium-size cob in boiling salted water for 3 minutes. Cool in an ice bath, then drain and pat dry before carefully slicing the kernels off the cob with a sharp knife. Use frozen corn or drained canned corn as is.*

JOCASTA'S AULD COUNTRY BANNOCKS

"I don't quite understand," Brianna said. "Did Mr. Browne not want to admit that a woman hit him?"

"Ah, no," Jamie said, pouring another cup of ale and handing it to her. "It was only Sergeant Murchison making a nuisance of himself."

"Sergeant Murchison? That would be the army officer who was at the trial?" she asked. She took a small sip of the ale, for politeness' sake. "The one who looks like a half-roasted pig?"

Her father grinned at this characterization.

"Aye that'll be the man. He's a mislike of me," he explained. "This wilna be the first time—or the last—that he's tried such a trick to cripple me."

"He could not hope to succeed with such a ridiculous charge," Jocasta chimed in, leaning forward and reaching out a hand. Ulysses, standing by, moved the plate of bannocks the necessary inch. She took one, unerringly, and turned her disconcerting blind eyes toward Jamie.

—*Drums of Autumn*, chapter 41, "Journey's End"

Bannocks are many different things to many different people. The bannocks I grew up with here on the Canadian west coast—an unleavened dough of wheat flour, water, and salt, molded over a stick and toasted over an open fire—came originally from our First Nations. In other regions of North America, cornmeal or baking powder might also be in the dough, and bannocks can be deep fried, cooked in a pit, or baked in the oven.

In Scotland, where the term originates from the Gaelic *bannach*, meaning cake, bannocks were originally round, medium-size flatbreads made from a wet dough of barley and/or oatmeal, and cooked on a girdle, or griddle. Today, the term refers to any baked item similar in shape and size to the original. Wheat flour and baking soda are included in most modern recipes, such as Bannocks at Carfax Close (page 230).

Makes one 8-inch bannock

Ingredients

¼ cup whole milk or water

2 tablespoons butter

½ teaspoon kosher salt

1 cup coarsely ground rolled oats or pearl barley (see Grinding Grains, Nuts, and Seeds, page 10), plus additional for rolling

Method

In a small saucepan, combine the milk, butter, and salt and heat over medium flame until the butter melts. Add the hot liquid to the ground oats or barley in a large bowl and stir to form a slightly sticky dough that pulls away from the sides of the bowl.

On a lightly floured counter, with lightly floured hands, roll the dough out to an 8-inch circle, about ¼ inch thick.

Heat a cast-iron pan over medium-low flame for 5 minutes. Cut the dough into quarters and cook in the pan until golden, about 5 minutes per side.

Serve warm from the pan with butter and honey.

Notes

- *Substitute any animal fat, such as bacon, or use coconut oil for a vegan alternative. The tastiest batch I recall is one I made with the fat left after frying pancetta.*
- *If you prefer a thicker bannock, double the recipe then roll the dough out to an 8-inch circle, ½ inch thick. Heat the pan over low and cook 10 minutes per side, until lightly browned and cooked through.*
- *Keep tightly wrapped, uncooked dough in the fridge up to 2 days.*

RAISIN MUFFINS

Ian didn't talk, but ate his way in a businesslike manner through half a loaf with butter and honey, three raisin muffins, two thick slices of ham, and a jug of milk. Jamie had done the milking, I saw; he always used the blue jug, while Mr. Wemyss used the white one. I wondered vaguely where Mr. Wemyss was—I hadn't seen him, and the house felt empty—but didn't really care. It occurred to me that perhaps Jamie had told both Mr. Wemyss and Mrs. Bug to stay away for a bit, feeling that I might need a little time alone.
—*A Breath of Snow and Ashes,* chapter 30, "The Captive"

English muffins, as they are known outside the Great Isles, are thought to have been introduced by French Huguenot immigrants to England in the seventeenth century. The word itself comes from the Low German *muffen,* meaning "little cakes."

Split one with a fork while it's still warm from the griddle, and spread it with Mrs. Bug's Cinnamon Toast (page 47) for a sweet, homemade start to the day.

Makes 10 to 12

Ingredients

4 cups all-purpose flour, plus additional
    for rolling
2 tablespoons sugar
2 tablespoons softened butter
1 tablespoon instant yeast

2 teaspoons kosher salt
1¾ cups whole milk
1¼ cups raisins
1 teaspoon vegetable oil
2 tablespoons cornmeal

Method

In the bowl of a standing mixer, combine the flour, sugar, butter, yeast, and salt. Using the paddle attachment, mix on low speed. Add the milk and mix on medium-low until a rough, sticky ball forms. Switch to the dough hook and knead on medium-low for 5 minutes until you have a soft, smooth dough.

Add the raisins gradually, until they are all incorporated into the dough, about 2 more minutes. Form the dough into a ball.

Alternatively, combine the dough by hand and knead for about 10 minutes on a lightly floured counter before adding the raisins gradually. Continue kneading until the raisins are fully incorporated. The dough will start out sticky, but by the time you have finished kneading, it should be soft and smooth with a good stretch.

Add the oil to a large bowl and roll the dough ball around in it to coat. Cover and set in a warm place to rise until doubled, 60 to 75 minutes.

Dust the counter with a mixture of 1 tablespoon cornmeal and 1 tablespoon flour. Dust two baking sheets lightly with 1 teaspoon cornmeal on each.

Roll the dough out into a rough circle 15 inches in diameter and ¾ inch thick. Be gentle, so you don't lose all the rise. Use a 4-inch round cutter to cut out twelve muffins. Space six muffins evenly apart on each sheet. Dust the top of the muffins lightly with the remaining cornmeal, cover with plastic wrap, and proof on the counter for another 45 to 60 minutes. The muffins should feel slightly puffy.

Heat a flat griddle on the low side of medium-low (see Notes) until the pan feels hot. Gently transfer the muffins to the pan and cook until dark golden, 6 to 8 minutes. Flip them and cook for another 6 to 8 minutes on the other side.

Cool on a wire rack for at least 20 minutes before splitting with a fork and spreading with butter.

Store in a closed container for 3 or 4 days.

Notes

- *Don't cook the muffins at too high a heat, or the outsides will burn before the insides cook through. Watch the heat, and reduce if necessary.*
- *Omit the raisins if you're not a fan, or replace them with another dried fruit chopped to a similar size. Muffins flavored with dried apple and cinnamon have become one of my favorite breakfast treats—add 1 to 2 teaspoons cinnamon to the flour at the beginning of the recipe and substitute chopped dried apple for the raisins.*

CORN MUFFINS

"Mmmphm!" said Mrs. Bug's voice, grimly satisfied at having routed the rioters. The door closed, and the clang of wood and clang of metal from below announced the commencement of the day's activities.

When I went down a few moments later, I found that good lady engaged simultaneously in toasting bread, boiling coffee, making parritch, and complaining as she tidied up the men's leavings. Not about the untidiness—what else could be expected of men?—but rather that Jamie had not waked her to provide a proper breakfast for them.

"And how's Himself to manage, then?" she demanded, brandishing the toasting-fork at me in reproach. "A fine, big man like that, and him out and doing wi' no more to line his wame than a wee sup of milk and a stale bannock?"

Casting a bleary eye over the assorted crumbs and dirty crockery, it appeared to me that Himself and his companions had probably accounted for at least two dozen corn muffins and an entire loaf of salt-rising bread, accompanied by a pound or so of fresh butter, a jar of honey, a bowl of raisins, and all of the first milking.

"I don't think he'll starve," I murmured, dabbing up a crumb with a moistened forefinger. "Is the coffee ready?"
—*The Fiery Cross,* chapter 22, "The Fiery Cross"

Moist, delicious muffins that make a homey accompaniment to any meal.

Makes 12

Ingredients

2 large eggs, slightly beaten

1½ cups buttermilk

2 cups cornmeal

1 cup all-purpose flour

2 tablespoons sugar

2 teaspoons baking powder

1½ teaspoons kosher salt

½ teaspoon baking soda

½ teaspoon cayenne pepper

1 can (14 ounces or 398 ml)
    creamed corn

¼ cup (4 tablespoons) butter,
    melted

Method

Move a rack to the middle rung and heat the oven to 400°F. Grease a twelve-cup, nonreactive (not aluminum) muffin tin with butter.

In a small bowl, lightly beat the eggs, then whisk in the buttermilk.

In a large bowl, combine the cornmeal, flour, sugar, baking powder, salt, baking soda, and cayenne pepper. Add the buttermilk mixture, creamed corn, and melted butter. Stir until just combined. Rest the mixture on the counter for 15 minutes.

Use a ½ cup measure to fill the muffin cups with batter. Bake in the oven until the edges are just starting to become golden and a toothpick inserted into the centers comes out clean, 20 to 25 minutes. Cool 10 minutes in the pan before transferring to a wire rack.

Serve warm with butter. Best when served shortly after baking, but day-old leftovers are delicious when lightly toasted under the broiler/grill and soaked with butter.

Notes

- *Overmixing the batter will result in tunnels in the finished muffins.*
- *Add your choice of 1 cup frozen blueberries, 4 thinly sliced scallions, 6 strips crisped and crumbled bacon, 1 cup shredded cheese, or ¼ cup chopped pickled jalapeños to the batter to pair these with your favorite breakfast, lunch, or dinner.*
- *Do not bake these in muffin liners. The warm muffins stick to the paper, and you want to eat these babies right out of the oven!*

Mrs. Bug's Buttermilk Drop Biscuits

It seemed rather a long time before Jamie reappeared, though the indignant cries of the searchers had been quickly stilled. If Jamie had got his bum smacked, Roger thought cynically, he appeared to have enjoyed it. A slight flush showed on the high cheekbones, and he wore a faint but definite air of satisfaction.

This was explained at once, though, when Jamie produced a small bundle from inside his shirt and unwrapped a linen towel, revealing half a dozen fresh biscuits, still warm, and dripping with melted butter and honey.

"I think perhaps Mrs. Bug meant them for the quilting circle," he said, distributing the booty. "But there was plenty of batter left in the bowl; I doubt they'll be missed."

—*The Fiery Cross,* chapter 108, "Tulach Ard"

Tender, southern-style biscuits ready in a flash; no kneading or rolling required.

Makes 12

Ingredients

1 cup cold buttermilk

2 teaspoons honey

½ cup (1 stick) plus 2 tablespoons butter

2 cups all-purpose flour

1 tablespoon cornstarch

1 tablespoon baking powder

1 teaspoon kosher salt

¼ teaspoon baking soda

Method

Move a rack to the upper-middle rung and heat the oven to 450°F.

In a bowl, combine the cold buttermilk and honey. In a saucepan over medium heat, or in a dish in the microwave, heat a stick of butter until just melted. Pour the butter into the buttermilk-honey mixture and stir until well combined.

In a large bowl, whisk together the flour, cornstarch, baking powder, salt, and baking soda for 1 minute to ensure that everything is evenly combined.

Add the lumpy buttermilk mixture to the dry ingredients and stir until just mixed and the batter pulls away from the side of the bowl. Use a lightly greased ¼ cup measure to scoop out level portions and drop onto an ungreased 9- or 10-inch cast-iron pan or cake pan—arrange three biscuits in the middle of the pan and nine biscuits around the outside.

Bake until the tops are golden, 15 to 17 minutes. Meanwhile, melt the remaining 2 tablespoons butter. Brush the tops of the biscuits with the melted butter immediately out of the oven. Cool at least 5 minutes on a wire rack before serving.

Serve warm, drizzled with honey and even more butter, if your hips can handle it.

Note

- *To make Mrs. Aberfeldy's Blueberry Biscuits from* The Fiery Cross *(chapter 33, "Home for Christmas"), push a few frozen berries into each biscuit just before baking.*

Chapter 15

SWEETS AND DESSERTS

Governor Tryon's Humble Crumble Apple Pie

The MacKenzies' Millionaire's Shortbread

Warm Almond Pastry with Father Anselm

Black Jack Randall's Dark Chocolate Lavender Fudge

Jam Tarts

Sweet Potato Pie

Chocolate Biscuits

Lord John's Upside-Down Plum Cake

Almond Squirts

Ginger-Nut Biscuits

Banoffee Trifle at River Run

Apple Fritters

Ulysses's Syllabub

Gingerbread and Fresh Crud

Jem's Bread Pudding with Maple Butterscotch Sauce

Stephen Bonnet's Salted Chocolate Pretzel Balls

Maple Pudding

GOVERNOR TRYON'S
HUMBLE CRUMBLE APPLE PIE

"It was a mistake! And one I have come to rectify, so far as I may!" Tryon was standing his ground, jaw tight as he glared upward.

"A mistake. And is the loss of an innocent man's life no more than that to ye? You will kill and maim, for the sake of your glory, and pay no heed to the destruction ye leave—save only that the record of your exploits may be enlarged. How will it look in the dispatches ye send to England—sir? That ye brought cannon to bear on your own citizens, armed with no more than knives and clubs? Or will it say that ye put down rebellion and preserved order? Will it say that in your haste to vengeance, ye hanged an innocent man? Will it say there that ye made 'a mistake'? Or will it say that ye punished wickedness, and did justice in the King's name?"

—*The Fiery Cross,* chapter 72, "Tinder and Char"

American history records Governor William Tryon as anything but humble. In this fictional scene, however, Diana affords him a sense of humility unlikely for an eighteenth-century man of his status.

His reward? Pie; lightly sweetened fruit in a crisp, flaky crust, topped with a rich, nutty streusel.

Makes one 9-inch pie

Ingredients

3 pounds (1.3 kilograms or 7 or 8 medium) firm, tart apples, such as Granny Smith

1 tablespoon lemon juice

½ cup dark brown sugar, lightly packed

¼ cup granulated sugar

6 tablespoons butter, diced, plus additional

2 teaspoons cornstarch or tapioca starch

1½ teaspoons cinnamon

¼ teaspoon freshly ground nutmeg

1 teaspoon kosher salt

½ cup walnut or pecan halves

½ cup all-purpose flour

½ recipe Short Crust Pastry (page 27), chilled

Method

Peel, core, and slice the apples into ½-inch wedges. Toss in a large bowl with the lemon juice, ¼ cup brown sugar, granulated sugar, 2 tablespoons butter, cornstarch, 1 teaspoon cinnamon, nutmeg, and ½ teaspoon salt. Set aside to macerate for about 1 hour.

Combine the nuts and the remaining ¼ cup lightly packed brown sugar in the bowl of a food processor and pulse five to seven times, until the nuts are coarsely chopped. Add the flour and the remaining 4 tablespoons butter and ½ teaspoon salt and pulse two or three times to combine.

Move a rack to the bottom rung and heat the oven to 425°F.

On a lightly floured counter, roll out the dough to a circle ⅛ inch thick. Transfer the dough to a 9-inch pie plate. Trim the excess, leaving an extra ½ inch beyond the plate's edge. Fold the excess under so the edges are a double thickness and crimp with your fingers or fork.

Mound the apple filling into the prepared pie shell, pouring the juices evenly over

the top. Cover lightly with foil brushed with butter and bake for 1 hour.

Remove the pie from the oven, reduce the heat to 375°F, and remove the foil. Top the pie evenly with the crumble topping and return to the oven for 15 minutes, until the apples are tender and the crust and topping are golden brown.

Cool completely and serve with ice cream or the whisky sauce from Jem's Bread Pudding (page 286).

Note

• *If your dough has been chilling in the refrigerator for longer than 30 minutes, allow it to soften on the counter for 10 minutes before rolling.*

The MacKenzies'
Millionaire's Shortbread

"I gave my word to Colum, not to you." So it was young Jamie MacTavish, and precisely three guesses as to what he was upset about.

"One and the same, man, and ye ken it well." There was the sound of a light slap, as of a hand against a cheek. "Your obedience is to the chieftain of the clan, and outside of Leoch, I am Colum's head and arms and hands as well as his legs."

"And never saw I a better case of the right hand not knowin' what the left is up to," came the quick rejoinder. Despite the bitterness of the tone, there was a lurking wit that enjoyed this clash of wills. "What d'ye think the right is going to say about the left collecting gold for the Stuarts?"

—*Outlander,* chapter 11, "Conversations with a Lawyer"

Caramel shortbread goes no further back than the 1970s, to a recipe most likely first published in the Australian *Ladies' Home Journal.* It first appeared as Millionaire's Shortbread in Scotland circa 1990.

The base layer, of course, is 100% Scottish, and delicious all on its own. Add caramel and chocolate and you've got a three-layered treat so sweet it can set brother against brother faster than the Jacobites' gold.

Makes 16 squares (one 9-inch pan)

Ingredients

1 cup (2 sticks) plus 2 teaspoons cold butter, plus additional for the pan

1½ cups all-purpose flour

½ cup granulated sugar

½ teaspoon kosher salt

½ cup light brown sugar, firmly packed

1 can (14 ounces or 396 grams) sweetened condensed milk

7 ounces (200 grams) milk or dark chocolate, chopped

Method

Move a rack to the middle rung and heat the oven to 300°F. Dot the sides and bottom of a 9-inch square baking pan with butter and line with parchment paper, sticking the paper to the butter and ensuring that the edges of the paper are higher than the pan.

Combine the flour, granulated sugar, and salt in a large bowl. Grate in ¾ cup (12 tablespoons, or 1½ sticks) butter and blend well using your fingertips, until everything resembles the texture of cornmeal. Press the dough into the bottom of the parchment paper–lined pan and prick lightly with a fork. Bake until firm and light golden, 30 to 35 minutes. Cool in the pan (see Notes).

In a saucepan, melt 4 tablespoons butter over medium heat. Stir in the brown sugar and sweetened condensed milk and bring to a gentle boil over medium heat, stirring frequently to prevent scorching. Reduce the heat to medium-low and continue to cook until slightly thickened, stirring occasionally, about 10 minutes. Pour over the shortbread in an even layer and cool completely.

Melt the chocolate and remaining 2 teaspoons butter in a double boiler over hot water until smooth. Pour over the cooled caramel in an even layer and cool completely. Use a sharp knife to cut into sixteen squares.

Store in the fridge up to 3 days.

Notes

- *The shortbread can still be warm when you pour the caramel over it. However, the caramel layer must be completely set before you cover it with the hot chocolate.*
- *You can stop at plain shortbread, if you prefer. Simply butter the pan instead of lining it with parchment paper and let it cool completely in the pan before cutting into squares or wedges (petticoat tails).*

WARM ALMOND PASTRY
WITH FATHER ANSELM

The kitchens of the abbey were warm and cavelike, the arching roof black-ened with centuries of grease-filled smoke. Brother Eulogius, up to his elbows in a vat of dough, nodded a greeting to Anselm and called in French to one of the lay brothers to come and serve us. We found a seat out of the bustle, and sat down with two cups of ale and a plate containing a hot pastry of some kind. I pushed the plate toward Anselm, too preoccupied to be interested in food.
—*Outlander*, **chapter 40, "Absolution"**

This buttery, puff-pastry braid filled with a traditional almond cream will be wel-come after deep and draining philosophical conversations beside the carp pool, or wherever you prefer to conduct your most important tête-à-têtes. Better paired with coffee than ale, in my opinion, but there's a time and place for everything.

Serves 6 to 8

Ingredients

¾ cup finely ground almond meal (see Grinding Grains, Nuts, and Seeds, page 10)

2 tablespoons all-purpose flour

2 tablespoons softened butter

5 tablespoons sugar

2 large eggs

1½ teaspoons vanilla

½ recipe Blitz Puff Pastry, chilled (page 29) or 1 14-ounce (396 grams) package frozen puff pastry, thawed

2 tablespoons sliced almonds

2 tablespoons confectioners' (powdered) sugar (optional)

Method

Move a rack to the middle rung and heat the oven to 375°F.

In a small bowl, stir together the almond meal and flour. In a large bowl, using a hand mixer on medium-high speed, cream the butter and ¼ cup (4 tablespoons) sugar together until pale and fluffy, about 1 minute. Beat in 1 egg and the vanilla, re-duce the speed to low, and beat in the almond meal and flour mixture until well mixed.

On a large cutting board, roll out the puff pastry to a rectangle measuring 14 x 16 inches. Cover with plastic and refrigerate for 10 minutes. Trim the rectangle to 12 x 15 inches and transfer it to parchment paper.

With a dull knife, score two light lines from the top to the bottom of the dough, 4 inches in from either long side. Spread the almond cream in the center column of the dough, leaving 1 inch clear on the top and bottom (see photo).

Use a sharp knife to cut the side margins of the dough into 1-inch strips on a diagonal. Cut off the excess dough from the top and bottom. Turn the 1-inch flaps at the top and bottom over the filling, then braid the diagonal strips over the filling at an angle, alternating left and right and pressing lightly in the middle to ensure that the strips stick.

Whisk the remaining egg with 1 teaspoon water. Brush the braid lightly with the egg wash and sprinkle with the almonds and the remaining sugar. Transfer the pastry on the parchment to a baking sheet. Bake for 25 to 30 minutes, or until a deep golden brown. Cool on the parchment on a wire rack for half an hour.

Cut on a diagonal with a serrated knife into 2-inch strips. Sift confectioners' sugar over the top of the slices if desired. Best served within 3 hours of baking.

Keep in a covered container at room temperature up to 2 days. Rewarm slightly before serving.

Notes

- *Spoon some strawberry jam on top of the almond cream for an extra treat.*
- *Turn the trimmed edges of the pastry into cheese sticks: brush with the egg wash, sprinkle with shredded Parmesan or Gruyère, and twist. Bake at 375°F until golden.*

BLACK JACK RANDALL'S
DARK CHOCOLATE LAVENDER FUDGE

The trembling did begin to ease within a minute or two, and Jamie opened his eyes with a sigh.

"I'm all right," he said. "Claire, I'm all right, now. But for God's sake, get rid of that stink!"

It was only then that I consciously noticed the scent in the room—a light, spicy floral smell, so common a perfume that I had thought nothing of it. Lavender. A scent for soaps and toilet waters. I had last smelled it in the dungeons of Wentworth Prison, where it anointed the linen or the person of Captain Jonathan Randall.

—*Outlander*, chapter 38, "The Abbey"

Easy, dark-chocolate, *cheater* fudge made with condensed milk and lightly scented with lavender.

Makes one 8- or 9-inch pan

Ingredients

½ teaspoon baking soda

¼ teaspoon kosher salt

1 can (14 ounces or 396 grams) sweetened condensed milk

1 pound (16 ounces or 450 grams) bittersweet or semisweet chocolate, chopped

2 tablespoons edible lavender blossoms (see Notes)

Method

Line an 8- or 9-inch pan with wax paper or parchment paper.

In a heavy saucepan, stir together the baking soda, salt, and sweetened condensed milk. Add the chocolate and melt over medium-low heat, stirring occasionally to start, then more frequently as it melts. When it is melted and smooth, remove from the heat and stir in 1 tablespoon lavender, crushing the buds between your

fingertips as you drop them into the pot. Stir to combine, pour into the prepared pan, and spread evenly.

Chill in the refrigerator until firm, about 2 hours. Remove from the fudge from the pan, peel off the paper, and cut into 1-inch squares.

To serve, garnish with the remaining lavender flowers. Perfect as an afternoon pick-me-up with coffee or tea.

Wrap and store in the fridge up to 1 week.

Notes

- *The better the quality of chocolate you start with, the richer and more decadent your fudge will be.*
- *While French lavender is great for sachets, English lavender is the only choice for culinary projects. Ensure the buds come from an unsprayed bush, or buy them online, or from a specialty food store in your area.*

JAM TARTS

A knock on the study door interrupted his thoughts. The door opened and Fiona Graham came in, pushing a tea cart, fully equipped with teapot, cups, doilies, three kinds of sandwiches, cream-cakes, sponge cake, jam tarts, and scones with clotted cream.

"Yum!" said Brianna at the sight. "Is that all for us, or are you expecting ten other people?"

Claire Randall looked over the tea preparations, smiling. The electric field was still there, but damped down by major effort. Roger could see one of her hands, clenched so hard in the folds of her skirt that the edge of her ring cut into the flesh.

"That tea is so high, we won't need to eat for weeks," she said. "It looks wonderful!"

—*Dragonfly in Amber,* chapter 2, "The Plot Thickens"

Buttery pastry and a simple, sweet filling make for an easy, home-baked treat adored by all.

Makes 12

Ingredients

½ recipe Short Crust Pastry (page 27), chilled

½ cup Fraser Strawberry Jam (page 318) or your favorite jam

Method

Move a rack to the middle rung and heat the oven to 375°F.

On a lightly floured counter, roll out the pastry to an even round, ⅛ inch thick. Use a 4-inch cutter to cut out twelve rounds. Gently press the rounds into a muffin pan, ensuring you work the pastry into the corners of each cup. Prick each of the bottoms three or four times with a fork before parbaking the pastry until dry, about 5 minutes.

Fill each tart with 2 teaspoons of the jam, then return to the oven until bubbling and golden, 12 to 15 minutes. Cool in the pan for 15 minutes, then gently remove the tarts to a wire rack to cool completely.

Keep in a covered tin on the counter up to 3 days.

Notes

- *Fluted cutters make even prettier tarts.*
- *For cinnamon sticks, brush the pastry scraps with egg wash, sprinkle with cinnamon sugar, twist, and bake at 375°F until golden.*

SWEET POTATO PIE

"I don't imagine it was much of a contest," I murmured, helping him to peel off the dusty coat. "William Tryon's not even Scots, let alone a Fraser."

That got me a reluctant half-smile. "Stubborn as rocks," was the succinct description of the Fraser clan I had been given years before—and nothing in the intervening time period had given me cause to think it inaccurate in any way.

"Aye, well." He shrugged and stretched luxuriously, his vertebrae cracking from the long ride. "Oh, Christ. I'm starved; is there food?" He relaxed and lifted his long nose, sniffing the air hopefully.

"Baked ham and sweet potato pie," I told him, unnecessarily, since the honey-soaked fragrances of both were thick on the humid air. "So what did the Governor say, once you'd got him properly browbeaten?"

—*The Fiery Cross,* chapter 73, "A Whiter Shade of Pale"

Likely developed by slaves from traditional African cuisine, the first recipe for sweet potato pie appeared in eighteenth-century cookbooks, where it was listed with vegetable side dishes. By the nineteenth century, sweet potato pie was more commonly classified as a dessert.

Makes one 9-inch pie

Ingredients

1½ pounds (700 grams or 2 medium) orange-fleshed sweet potatoes

½ cup (1 stick) butter

1 cup graham cracker crumbs

⅓ cup granulated sugar

½ cup finely ground pecans (see Grinding Grains, Nuts, and Seeds, page 10)

½ cup dark brown sugar, lightly packed

½ cup whole milk

2 large eggs

1 teaspoon cinnamon

1 teaspoon vanilla

Zest of 1 lemon, grated or minced

½ teaspoon kosher salt

Nutmeg, freshly grated

Method

Move a rack to the upper-middle rung and heat the oven to 400°F.

Poke the sweet potatoes a few times with the tip of a knife and roast until tender enough to be pierced with a fork, 45 to 60 minutes, depending on their size. Cool slightly before peeling.

Reduce the oven temperature to 350°F.

Meanwhile, melt 4 tablespoons (½ stick) of the butter on the stovetop or in the microwave. In a medium bowl, combine it with the graham cracker crumbs, granulated sugar, and ground pecans until all the crumbs are moistened. Reserve ½ cup for the topping, and press the remainder into a glass or ceramic 9-inch pie dish.

Mash together the warm sweet potato flesh and remaining 4 tablespoons butter in a large bowl. Stir in the brown sugar, milk, eggs, cinnamon, vanilla, lemon zest, salt, and nutmeg to taste. Beat well to combine.

Pour the filling into the prepared crust and smooth out the top. Bake for 30 minutes. Sprinkle on the reserved topping and return to the oven until lightly golden, another 20 to 25 minutes.

Cool completely before serving with whipped cream or Ulysses's Syllabub (page 281).

Notes

- *If you prefer a more traditional pastry crust, use a half recipe of Short Crust Pastry (page 27), or a store-bought frozen crust to make things easy.*
- *If you prefer, substitute ⅓ cup honey for the brown sugar and reduce the milk to ⅓ cup.*

Chocolate Biscuits

"Thought you might do with some tea, Mr. Wake—I mean, Roger." Fiona set down a small tray containing a cup and saucer and a plate of biscuits.

"Oh, thanks." He was in fact hungry, and gave Fiona a friendly smile that sent the blood rushing into her round, fair cheeks. Seemingly encouraged by this, she didn't go away, but perched on the corner of the desk, watching him raptly as he went about his job between bites of chocolate biscuit.

Feeling obscurely that he ought to acknowledge her presence in some way, Roger held up a half-eaten biscuit and mumbled, "Good."

"Are they? I made them, ye know." Fiona's flush grew deeper. An attractive little girl, Fiona. Small, rounded, with dark curly hair and wide brown eyes. He found himself wondering suddenly whether Brianna Randall could cook, and shook his head to clear the image.

—*Dragonfly in Amber,* chapter 2, "The Plot Thickens"

A traditional, down-to-earth recipe for homemade digestive biscuits, using basic, whole-food ingredients.

Makes 18 to 20

Ingredients

¾ cup coarsely ground rolled oats (see Grinding Grains, Nuts, and Seeds, page 10)

1 cup stone-ground whole wheat flour

½ cup light brown sugar, lightly packed

1 teaspoon baking powder

½ cup (1 stick) cold butter

2 tablespoons whole milk

3 ounces (85 grams) milk or dark chocolate

Method

Move a rack to the middle rung and heat the oven to 350°F.

In a large bowl, mix together the ground oats, flour, sugar, and baking powder. Grate in the butter and blend it all together with your fingertips until no big lumps remain. Add the milk and mix with your hands, pressing into a slightly sticky ball. Flatten to a disk, wrap in plastic, and chill in the fridge for 15 minutes.

On a lightly floured counter, roll the dough out to a 12-inch circle, ¼ inch thick, loosening and turning the dough to prevent sticking. Use a 2½-inch round cutter to cut out cookies, rerolling the scraps once.

Arrange on a parchment paper–lined cookie sheet, leaving about ½ inch between cookies. Bake for 12 to 15 minutes, until the edges are just golden. Cool for 5 minutes, then transfer to a wire rack to cool completely.

Melt the chocolate in a microwave or a double-boiler over simmering water. Brush the tops of the cooled biscuits with chocolate and cool to set the chocolate.

Store in a covered container up to 1 week.

Note

• *No round cookie cutters? Try a wineglass—or any other glass with a thinnish rim.*

Lord John's Upside-Down Plum Cake

He heard a small, stealthy sound, and sat up abruptly, his eyes popping open. A large brown rat sat on the corner of his desk, a morsel of plum cake held in its front paws. It didn't move, but merely looked at him speculatively, whiskers twitching.

"Well, God damn my eyes!" Grey exclaimed in amazement. "Here, you bugger! That's my supper!"

The rat nibbled pensively at the plum cake, bright beady eyes fixed on the Major.

"Get out of it!" Enraged, Grey snatched up the nearest object and let fly at the rat. The ink bottle exploded on the stone floor in a spray of black, and the startled rat leapt off the desk and fled precipitously, galloping between the legs of the even more startled MacKay, who appeared at the door to see what the noise was.

—*Voyager,* chapter 8, "Honor's Prisoner"

Early cakes in Britain were made from bread dough sweetened with honey or sugar and kneaded with dried fruits, nuts, and spices. They were dense, heavy rounds that often lasted many months, similar to modern fruitcake.

This cake, by comparison, is light and delicately spiced. Its upside-down nature reflects Lord John's own life at this juncture, recently arrived in mysterious disgrace from London to cold, dank Ardsmuir in the far reaches of nowhere.

Makes one 9-inch cake

Ingredients

1 pound (450 grams or 6 to 8 medium) plums

½ cup dark brown sugar, lightly packed

1½ teaspoons ground cinnamon

½ teaspoon ground cardamom

¼ teaspoon freshly grated nutmeg

1 cup (2 sticks) softened butter

½ cup whole milk

1 orange, zest removed and grated or minced, and squeezed for juice (see Notes)

1½ teaspoons vanilla

2 cups all-purpose flour

2 teaspoons baking powder

1½ teaspoons kosher salt

3 large eggs

1½ cups granulated sugar

Method

Move a rack to the middle rung and heat the oven to 350°F.

Cut the plums in half, remove the pits, and cut each half in two or three wedges. Toss the plums in a bowl with the brown sugar, cinnamon, cardamom, and nutmeg.

Melt 4 tablespoons (½ stick) of the butter and pour into the bottom of a 9-inch square or round pan. Tip and rotate the pan to ensure the butter covers the bottom and about ½ inch up the sides. Arrange the plum slices as artistically or randomly as you wish on the bottom of the pan.

In a small bowl, combine the milk, orange zest, orange juice, and vanilla. In another bowl, stir together the flour, baking powder, and salt.

In a large bowl, beat the remaining ¾ cup butter and granulated sugar together with a handheld mixer on medium speed until pale and fluffy, about 3 minutes (see Notes). Add the eggs one at a time, beating for 1 minute between each. Use a spatula or wooden spoon to stir in the dry ingredients and milk mixture alternately, one third at a time, beginning and ending with the dry. Mix until just combined.

Spread the batter evenly over the plums in the pan and smooth the top with a spatula. Bake until a toothpick inserted in the center comes out clean, 40 to 45 minutes.

Cool on a wire rack for 30 minutes before running a knife around the outside of the pan to loosen the cake and inverting it onto a large plate or cake stand.

Serve warm or at room temperature, with ice cream or whipped cream. Slice it up after a meal of Pheasant and Greens at Ardsmuir (page 109) for a mouthwatering, and unlikely, complete prison dinner.

Store, covered, on the counter up to 3 days.

Notes

- *Zest the orange before juicing it. If the orange yields less than ⅓ cup juice, top it up with milk.*
- *It's important to beat the butter and sugar together for the time indicated in order to incorporate air for a high, even rise.*
- *Test three or four spots near the center of the cake with your toothpick to ensure that the cake is baked through evenly.*

ALMOND SQUIRTS

It was Ned Gowan who had mentioned Laoghaire to Jenny, returning from Balriggan to Edinburgh. Pricking up her ears, Jenny had inquired for further details, and finding these satisfactory, had at once sent an invitation to Balriggan, for Laoghaire and her two daughters to come to Lallybroch for Hogmanay, which was near.

The house was bright that night, with candles lit in the windows, and bunches of holly and ivy fixed to the staircase and the doorposts. There were not so many pipers in the Highlands as there had been before Culloden, but one had been found, and a fiddler as well, and music floated up the stairwell, mixed with the heady scent of rum punch, plum cake, almond squirts, and Savoy biscuits.

Jamie had come down late and hesitant. Many people here he had not seen in nearly ten years, and he was not eager to see them now, feeling changed and distant as he did. But Jenny had made him a new shirt, brushed and mended his coat, and combed his hair smooth and plaited it for him before going downstairs to see to the cooking. He had no excuse to linger, and at last had come down, into the noise and swirl of the gathering.

—*Voyager,* chapter 37, "What's in a Name"

A crisp, almond meringue delicately flavored with rosewater. Adapted from an eighteenth-century Scottish cookbook, this fancy, gluten-free cookie with the unfortunate name is as at home on your kitchen table beside a cup of afternoon tea as it was on Lallybroch's hall table full of holiday treats.

Makes 24 to 36

Ingredients

2 egg whites
½ teaspoon rosewater
½ teaspoon white vinegar
½ cup sugar

1 cup finely ground almond meal (see Grinding Grains, Nuts, and Seeds, page 10)

Method

Move a rack to the middle rung and heat the oven to 300°F. Line a baking sheet with parchment paper.

In a large bowl, with a handheld mixer, beat the egg whites, rosewater, and vinegar together on medium-high for 1 minute. With the mixer still running, gradually add the sugar. Increase the speed to high and beat to stiff peaks, 2 to 3 minutes. Fold in the almond meal and gently transfer the meringue to a pastry bag fitted with a large tip (see Note).

Pipe kisses 1 to 2 inches in diameter onto the prepared baking sheet, leaving about 1 inch between each.

Bake until set and light golden, 22 to 25 minutes. Cool on a wire rack. Store in a tightly covered tin up to 3 days.

Note

- *In lieu of a piping bag, drop small spoonfuls of meringue onto the prepared pan and bake as directed.*

GINGER-NUT BISCUITS

He turned over a page, and stopped, feeling as though he'd been punched in the stomach.

May 1, 1945. Craigh na Dun, Inverness-shire, Scotland. Claire Randall, age 27, housewife. Seen last in early morning, having declared intention to visit the circle in search of unusual plant specimens, did not return by dark. Car found parked at foot of hill. No traces in circle, no signs of foul play.

He turned the page gingerly, as though expecting it to blow up in his hand. So Claire had inadvertently given Gillian Edgars part of the evidence that had led to her own experiment. Had Geilie found the reports of Claire's return, three years later?

No, evidently not, he concluded, after flipping back and forth through those pages—or if she had, she hadn't recorded it here.

Fiona had brought him more tea and a plate of fresh ginger-nut biscuits, which had sat untouched since he had begun reading. A sense of obligation rather than hunger made him pick up a biscuit and take a bite, but the sharp-flavored crumbs caught in his throat and made him cough.

—*Drums of Autumn,* chapter 32, "Grimoire"

Soft cakelike cookies spiced with ginger and cinnamon and studded with little bursts of salt—the perfect match with a cup of tea or coffee, to fuel another all-night review of Geillis's nasty book of horrors.

Makes 24

Ingredients

1 cup (2 sticks) softened butter

1⅓ cups light brown sugar, lightly
    packed

¼ cup honey

2 large eggs

3 cups all-purpose flour

4 teaspoons ground ginger

2 teaspoons baking soda

1 teaspoon cinnamon

1 teaspoon kosher salt

½ cup granulated sugar

Method

Move a rack to the middle rung and heat oven to 375°F. Line two baking sheets with parchment paper.

In a large bowl, either by hand or with an electric handheld mixer, cream together the butter and the brown sugar until fluffy. Beat in the honey and eggs until well combined and smooth.

In another bowl, mix together the flour, ground ginger, baking soda, cinnamon, and salt. Mix into the wet ingredients in two equal additions until just combined.

Shape into balls the size of golf balls and roll in granulated sugar to coat. Place on the prepared baking sheets 1 inch apart. Do not flatten.

Bake until the tops start to crack and are golden around the edges, 10 to 12 minutes. Cool on the baking sheets for 5 minutes before transferring to a wire rack.

Keep in a closed container up to 1 week.

Notes

- *Love ginger? Stir in ½ cup of chopped crystallized ginger before shaping into balls.*
- *These cookies freeze very well, either as dough or baked. Alternatively, the recipe is easily halved if you need only a dozen, or doubled for even more!*

BANOFFEE TRIFLE AT RIVER RUN

Hands—so many hands. Everything was done as if by magic, with soft murmurs as they passed her from hand to hand. She was stripped and bathed before she could protest, scented water poured over her, firm, gentle fingers that massaged her scalp as lavender soap was sluiced from her hair. Linen towels and a small black girl who dried her feet and sprinkled them with rice powder.

A fresh cotton gown and floating barefoot over polished floors, to see her father's eyes light at sight of her. Food—cakes and trifles and jellies and scones—and hot, sweet tea that seemed to replace the blood in her veins.

A pretty blond girl with a frown on her face, who seemed peculiarly familiar; her father called her Marsali. Lizzie, washed and wrapped in a blanket, both frail hands round a mug of pungent liquid, looking like a stepped-on flower newly watered.

—*Drums of Autumn,* chapter 41, "Journey's End"

Created by two English restaurateurs in 1971, Banoffee Pie became a part of the *Outlander* lexicon after Sam Heughan, who plays Jamie in the TV series, took to Twitter to tease Caitriona Balfe, who plays Claire, about her devotion to the dessert, as served by the production's catering service. Banoffee soon ballooned into a full-blown obsession that spread from the cast and crew in the UK to those of us following along on the other side of the pond.

The adaptation to a trifle makes for a showcase dessert that looks far more complicated than it really is to make. Bake the gingerbread the day before, and make the rest of the components the morning you plan to serve. Assemble it hours before your guests arrive, and let it rest in the fridge while you make the remainder of your preparations.

Serves 6 or more

Ingredients

¼ cup (4 tablespoons or ½ stick) butter

½ cup dark brown sugar, lightly packed

1 can (14 ounces or 369 grams) sweetened condensed milk

1 cup Grand Marnier liqueur

2 cups whipping cream

2 tablespoons vanilla

1 tablespoon granulated sugar, plus additional

5 to 6 medium bananas

½ recipe Gingerbread (page 283), cut into ½-inch cubes

11 ounces (300 grams) milk or dark chocolate, grated or shaved

Method

In a saucepan, melt the butter over medium heat. Stir in the brown sugar and sweetened condensed milk. Bring to a boil, stirring constantly to prevent scorching. Boil gently for 1 minute, stirring almost continuously. Stir in 2 tablespoons Grand Marnier off the heat. Cool completely.

In a large bowl, whip the cream, vanilla, and granulated sugar together to stiff peaks with a hand mixer on high speed. Add more sugar, if desired.

Slice the bananas ¼ to ½ inch thick, on the bias, and toss with 2 tablespoons Grand Marnier.

Line the bottom of a trifle dish or large glass bowl with a single layer of the gingerbread cubes, using about half. Soak the cake with 3 to 4 tablespoons of Grand Marnier and spread with half of the cooled toffee. Top with half of the bananas, one-third of the chocolate, and half of the whipped cream, making sure to cover the bananas completely to prevent them from browning.

Repeat with the remaining cake cubes, Grand Marnier, toffee, bananas, another third of the chocolate, and the remaining whipped cream. Garnish with the remaining chocolate.

Refrigerate for at least 1 hour, and up to 6 hours. Serve chilled.

Keep leftovers in the fridge up to 2 days.

Notes

- *If you prefer, replace the Grand Marnier with your favorite boozy soak, such as dark rum or brandy, or use orange juice for a nonalcoholic treat.*
- *For something different, instead of whipped cream with vanilla and sugar, try Fresh Crud (page 283) or Ulysses's Syllabub (page 281).*
- *If you don't have a trifle dish, make individual trifle cups out of glass bowls, wineglasses, parfait glasses, or sundae dishes. For easier-to-eat layers, slice the bananas on the thin side.*
- *Use chocolate chips in a pinch, but for a special treat, buy quality chocolate and savor the difference.*

APPLE FRITTERS

Roger was sweating from the exertion, his heart beating fast from the adrenaline of performance, and the air away from the fire and the crowd was cold on his flushed face. The baby's swaddled weight felt good against him, warm and solid in the crook of his arm. He'd done well, and knew it. Let's hope it was what Fraser wanted.

By the time Bree reappeared with a drink and a pewter plate heaped with sliced pork, apple fritters, and roast potatoes, Jamie had come into the circle of firelight, taking Roger's place before the standing cross.

He stood tall and broad-shouldered in his best gray gentleman's coat, kilted below in soft blue tartan, his hair loose and blazing on his shoulders, with a small warrior's plait down one side, adorned with a single feather. Firelight glinted from the knurled gold hilt of his dirk and the brooch that held his looped plaid. He looked pleasant enough, but his manner overall was serious, intent. He made a good show—and knew it.

—*The Fiery Cross,* chapter 24, "Playing with Fire"

Originally served as an accompaniment to savory meat dishes, especially pork, these scotch whisky–marinated balls of fruit and dough pair well with Ragoo'd Pork (page 126), either beside it on the main plate, or after, as a sweet finish served with your favorite single malt.

Makes 20 to 24

Ingredients

¼ cup blended scotch whisky or orange juice

¼ cup whole milk

2 tablespoons fresh lemon juice

Zest of 1 lemon, grated

¼ cup sugar, plus additional

1 teaspoon vanilla

½ teaspoon ground ginger

1 pound (450 grams or 2 or 3 medium) sweet, firm apples such as Granny Smith, Gala, or Pink Lady

1 cup all-purpose flour

1½ teaspoons baking powder

1 teaspoon cinnamon

1 teaspoon kosher salt

2 large eggs

1 tablespoon melted butter

Vegetable oil

Method

In a medium bowl, mix together the whisky, milk, lemon juice, lemon zest, sugar, vanilla, and ground ginger.

Peel and core the apples. Chop into ½-inch cubes and toss them in the whisky mixture. Marinate for 30 minutes, stirring occasionally.

Drain the apples, reserving the marinade juice. In a large bowl, stir together the flour, baking powder, cinnamon, and salt. Whisk in the eggs, melted butter, and ½ cup of the marinade juice to make a pancakelike batter. Stir the apples into the batter, mixing well to ensure good distribution.

In a large saucepan, bring 2 or 3 inches of vegetable oil to 350°F over medium-high heat.

Drop tablespoonfuls of the batter into the hot oil and fry until golden on both sides, about 5 minutes depending on the size. Do not crowd the pan. Drain on paper towels.

Sprinkle more sugar on top and serve warm.

Note

- *Do not use an expensive single-malt scotch whisky for the marinade; it's a waste of your money and the distiller's skill and labor, as all the subtle aromas and flavors are lost in deep frying. Instead, choose a blended whisky, which you can then use in Atholl Brose for the Bonnie Prince (page 299) or Jamie's Rusty Nail (page 310).*

Ulysses's Syllabub

"There's still the problem of how the ground glass was administered. Do you know what Betty was given to eat or drink, Ulysses?"

"Dr. Fentiman ordered her a syllabub," he said slowly. "And a bit of porridge, if she were awake enough to swallow. I made up the syllabub myself, and gave it to Mariah to take up to her. I gave the order for porridge to the cook, but I do not know whether Betty ate it, or who might have carried it."
—*The Fiery Cross*, chapter 55, "Deductions"

A syllabub in the first half of the eighteenth century was a mixture of milk and sweetened wine, whisked into a froth and allowed to separate overnight. The liquid on the bottom was sipped through a spout in the glass, the frothy cap eaten with a spoon. During the second half of the century, the quantity of alcohol was reduced and the syllabub was whipped up into a thick lather, known as an everlasting syllabub, much more like modern whipped cream.

This twenty-first-century syllabub is made with cider instead of wine. The addition of fresh citrus zest makes for a dressed-up whipped cream that makes a tasty dollop on top of a slice of Sweet Potato Pie (page 263).

Serves 6

Ingredients

½ cup hard cider

3 to 4 tablespoons sugar

Zest of 1 lemon, lime, or orange, plus additional for garnish

1 tablespoon fresh lemon, lime, or orange juice

1 pint (500 ml) whipping or double cream

Freshly grated nutmeg

Fresh mint sprigs

Method

In a small bowl, combine the cider, sugar, zest, and juice. Stir until the sugar is dissolved.

In a large bowl, whip the cream to soft peaks with a handheld mixer on high. Fold in the cider mixture, then whip again to combine and slightly firm up the cream. Do not overbeat the cream, as it may curdle.

Refrigerate for 1 to 4 hours to allow the flavors to combine. If the cream separates, stir gently to recombine before spooning into small bowls or glasses, or on top of your favorite dessert.

Garnish with nutmeg and mint to serve.

Notes

- *North American whipping cream hovers around 30 to 35% milk fat. Double cream can contain up to 48% fat, and therefore whips up thicker.*
- *Experiment with different ciders and citruses to find your favorite combination; try apple cider and lemon, elderflower cider and orange, or strawberry cider and lime.*

GINGERBREAD AND FRESH CRUD

Jamie leaned back from the table, sighing in repletion. As he started to get up, though, Mrs. Bug popped up from her place, wagging an admonitory finger at him.

"Now, sir, now, sir, ye'll be going nowhere, and me left wi' gingerbread and fresh crud to go to waste!"

Brianna clapped a hand to her mouth, with the muffled noise characteristic of one who has just shot milk up one's nose. Jamie and Mr. Bug, to whom "crud" was the familiar Scottish usage for "curds," both looked at her curiously, but made no comment.

—*The Fiery Cross,* chapter 80, "Creamed Crud"

A soft, delectable gingerbread cake with a texture reminiscent of an old-fashioned steamed pudding. Homey, after-dinner comfort in a bowl that is irresistible when served with Mrs. Bug's famous creamed crud.

Serves 8

Ingredients

2 cups all-purpose flour, plus additional

1 teaspoon baking soda

1½ teaspoons cinnamon

1½ teaspoons ground ginger

Zest of 1 lemon, grated or minced

½ teaspoon salt

Pinch of ground cloves

½ cup (1 stick) butter at room temperature, plus additional

½ cup dark brown sugar, lightly packed

2 large eggs

½ cup light, mild, or fancy molasses

1 cup whole milk

1 cup whipping cream

1 tablespoon granulated sugar

½ teaspoon vanilla

1 recipe Crowdie Cheese (page 31)

Method

Move a rack to the middle rung and heat oven to 350°F. Butter and flour an 8- or 9-inch square glass or ceramic baking dish (see Notes).

Stir together the flour, baking soda, cinnamon, ginger, lemon zest, salt, and cloves.

In a medium bowl, beat the butter and brown sugar together with a handheld mixer on medium-high until fluffy, 3 minutes. Add the eggs and beat for 2 minutes, then beat in the molasses for 1 minute, scraping down the sides of the bowl as needed. Beat in the dry ingredients and milk alternately, beginning and ending with the dry. Mix until just combined.

Pour the batter into the prepared pan and smooth with a spatula. Bake until a toothpick inserted in the center comes out clean, 40 to 45 minutes. Cool on a wire rack for 10 minutes before removing from the pan. Cool completely.

In a large bowl, beat the whipping cream, granulated sugar, and vanilla to soft peaks using a handheld mixer on high. Gently fold in the Crowdie Cheese. Taste and sweeten with more sugar, if desired.

Cut the cake into squares, and serve in bowls topped with the creamed crud.

Store the cake, covered, up to 3 days. The crud will keep in the fridge up to 2 days.

Notes

- *The cake does not rise as much in a metal pan, but the resulting dense cake is ideal for a Banoffee Trifle (page 277).*
- *For extra ginger taste, add ¼ cup finely chopped candied ginger, or 1 teaspoon grated fresh ginger.*

JEM'S BREAD PUDDING
WITH MAPLE BUTTERSCOTCH SAUCE

Excusing himself, he made his way into the house, and discovered Jem down below in the main kitchen, cozily ensconced in the corner of a settle, eating bread pudding with melted butter and maple syrup on it.

"That's never your dinner, is it?" he asked, sitting down beside his son.

"Uh-huh. Want some, Daddy?" Jem extended a dripping spoon upward toward him, and he bent hastily to take the offered mouthful before it fell off. It was delicious, bursting-sweet and creamy on the tongue.

"Mmm," he said, swallowing. "Well, let's not tell Mummy or Grannie, shall we? They've this odd prejudice toward meat and vegetables."

Jem nodded, agreeable, and offered him another spoonful. They consumed the bowl together in a companionable silence, after which Jem crawled into his lap, and leaning a sticky face against his chest, fell sound asleep.

—*A Breath of Snow and Ashes,* chapter 15, "Stakit to Droon"

Historically, bread pudding was a poor man's dish, developed in the eleventh or twelfth century as a way to use up stale loaves. Modern-day recipes, such as the one below, tend to be much more extravagant creations, loaded with butter, eggs, nuts, fruit, and cream to comfort and satisfy the most discriminating dessert connoisseurs.

Serves 6 to 8

Ingredients

1-pound (450 grams) loaf of bread, crust mostly removed, cut into cubes (about 12 cups)

1½ cups chopped dried apples

1½ cups chopped pecans

1 cup (2 sticks) butter, melted

1½ cups dark brown sugar, lightly packed

1 cup maple syrup

2 large eggs

2 large egg yolks

½ cup scotch whisky (optional)

2 teaspoons vanilla

1 teaspoon cinnamon

1 teaspoon ground ginger

2½ cups whole milk

2 cups whipping cream

½ teaspoon kosher salt

Method

Move a rack to the middle rung and heat oven to 350°F. Butter a 2-inch-deep 13 x 9-inch glass or ceramic baking dish.

In a large bowl, combine the bread cubes, dried apples, and 1 cup pecans. Drizzle in ½ cup of the melted butter and toss well to coat evenly.

In a large bowl, with a handheld mixer on high, beat together 1 cup brown sugar, ½ cup maple syrup, eggs, yolks, ¼ cup whisky (if desired), vanilla, cinnamon, and ginger until pale and light, 2 to 3 minutes. Beat in the milk and 1 cup of the cream until combined. Add to the bread mixture and mix well.

Pour into the buttered baking dish, tuck the dried apples under the bread so they don't burn in the oven, and top with remaining pecans. Bake until golden brown, about 1 hour. Cool for at least 30 minutes.

Meanwhile, make the butterscotch sauce. In a medium saucepan, combine the remaining melted butter, ½ cup brown sugar, and ½ cup maple syrup over medium-high heat. Stir until smooth, then bring to a boil and cook without stirring for 5 minutes. Stir in the remaining ¼ cup whisky (if desired), being careful of splatters. Stir in the remaining 1 cup cream and salt. Cook 1 more minute, stirring constantly, then remove from the heat to cool before serving.

Serve the bread pudding warm, with the butterscotch sauce in a jug alongside.

Notes

- *My favorite mix of bread for this recipe is half dark rye and half French loaf. Brioche, challah, or day-old cinnamon rolls are also delicious.*
- *One cup of chopped, candied ginger makes a sophisticated substitute for the dried apples.*

STEPHEN BONNET'S
SALTED CHOCOLATE PRETZEL BALLS

"A bit more tea, Doctor Fentiman?" I urged a fresh cup upon him, willing him to stay awake. "Do tell me more about it. The surgery must have been quite delicate?"

In fact, men never like to hear that the removal of testicles is a simple matter, but it is. Though I would admit that the fact of the patient's being conscious during the whole procedure had likely added to the difficulty.

Fentiman regained a bit of his animation, telling me about it.

"...and the ball had gone straight through the testicle; it had left the most perfect hole.... You could look quite through it, I assure you." Plainly he regretted the loss of this interesting specimen, and it was with some difficulty that I got him to tell me what had become of the gentleman to whom it belonged.

"Well, that was odd. It was the horse, you see ..." he said vaguely. "Lovely animal ... long hair, like a woman's, so unusual ..."

—*A Breath of Snow and Ashes,* chapter 56, "Tar and Feathers"

Chocolate-filled pretzel balls garnished with coarse salt. One is never enough.

Makes 24

Ingredients

2½ cups all-purpose flour

1½ teaspoons instant yeast

1 teaspoon coarse salt, plus additional
    for sprinkling

1 tablespoon softened butter

7 ounces (200 grams) milk or dark
    chocolate, in squares

3 tablespoons baking soda

1 large egg

Method

In the bowl of a stand mixer fitted with the paddle attachment, combine the flour, yeast, salt, and butter on medium-low.

With the machine running, slowly pour in ¾ cup warm water. Once the dough has formed into a rough ball, change over to the dough hook and knead on low for 5 minutes. Increase the speed to medium and knead for another 7 minutes. The dough should be hard and smooth—not sticky in the slightest.

Alternatively, mix the dough by hand in a large bowl and knead on a lightly floured counter for 20 minutes (see Notes).

Form into a ball, cover, and rise in a warm place until doubled in size, 60 to 90 minutes.

Divide the dough into twenty-four equal pieces. Working one piece at a time, flatten the dough into a circle with your fingertips. Place one square of chocolate in the center and gather up the edges, pinching them together to seal. With the seam side down on the counter, rock the ball gently under your palm to smooth and even out the seam. Cover with plastic wrap and repeat with the rest of the dough and chocolate pieces.

Set aside to proof until puffy, about 30 minutes.

Move a rack to the middle rung and heat the oven to 400°F. Line two baking sheets with parchment paper. Bring 1 quart of water and the baking soda to a rolling boil in a medium pot over high heat. Lightly beat the egg with 1 teaspoon water for an egg wash.

Reduce heat to medium-high and carefully drop the proofed pretzel balls in batches of five or six, top down, into the gently boiling alkaline water bath. Do not overcrowd the pot. Cook for a total of 1 minute, turning over halfway. Transfer with a slotted spoon to parchment paper–lined baking sheets.

Brush each ball with the egg wash, sprinkle with coarse salt, and bake until a deep golden brown, 15 to 18 minutes.

Cool at least 15 minutes on a wire rack before serving—that's near-molten chocolate in there!

These are best eaten the same day. They will keep overnight in a closed container, but you will notice some "sweating" the next day—that is completely normal, a reaction between the salt and baking soda bath. Warm slightly in the oven to refresh.

Notes

- *The dough is very stiff, so if you're kneading by hand, you may want to consider enlisting a kneading partner to trade off with every few minutes.*
- *To make these vegan, substitute margarine for the butter, ensure the chocolate you use is vegan, and brush the balls with almond milk before sprinkling them with salt and baking as directed.*
- *Once you've wrapped the dough around the filling, the balls can be wrapped tightly and frozen up to 2 weeks. Defrost, loosely covered, on the counter for 3 to 4 hours before boiling and baking as directed.*

MAPLE PUDDING

"Maple pudding," he announced, looking happy.

"Oh?" I had no appetite at all yet, but maple pudding sounded at least innocuous, and I made no objection as he scooped up a spoonful, guiding it toward my mouth with the concentration of a man flying an airliner.

"I can feed myself, you kn—" He slipped the spoon between my lips, and I resignedly sucked the pudding off it. Amazing revelations of creamy sweetness immediately exploded in my mouth, and I closed my eyes in minor ecstasy, recalling.

"Oh, God," I said. "I'd forgotten what good food tastes like."

"I knew ye hadn't been eating," he said with satisfaction. "Here, have more."

I insisted upon taking the spoon myself, and managed half the dish; Jamie ate the other half, at my urging.

—*A Breath of Snow and Ashes,* chapter 64, "I Am the Resurrection, Part 2"

Creamy, rich, and sweet, pudding is the perfect dessert for sharing. Nothing says love like ending a meal with one dish and two spoons, except maybe sharing the spoon too.

Serves 6 to 8 (about 4 cups)

Ingredients

2 cups whole milk

1 cup pure maple syrup

¼ cup cornstarch

2 large egg yolks

½ cup whipping cream

½ teaspoon salt

¼ cup (4 tablespoons) butter

1 teaspoon vanilla

Whipped cream

Method

In a saucepan, gently heat the milk and maple syrup over medium-low heat until simmering. DO NOT BOIL.

In a bowl, whisk together the cornstarch and egg yolks into a smooth paste. Slowly whisk in the cream and salt.

Remove about a cup of the heated milk and pour it into the egg mixture, whisking continuously. Pour this tempered mixture back into the pot and increase the heat to medium. Bring it to a boil, whisking regularly. Boil for 2 minutes, whisking, until the mixture thickens and coats the back of a spoon. Remove it from the heat and stir in the butter and vanilla until completely incorporated and smooth.

To prevent a skin from forming, pour the pudding into a bowl, lay a piece of plastic wrap directly on the surface, and refrigerate until cool. To serve, spoon into dishes and top with whipped cream.

Alternatively, if you would like to keep the skin, spoon the pudding directly into serving dishes and chill, unwrapped, in the refrigerator. Top with whipped cream when ready to serve.

Store the leftovers covered in the fridge up to 3 days.

Notes

- *No cornstarch? Substitute the same amount of tapioca starch or arrowroot. You can also use the same amount of all-purpose (regular) flour, but be sure to boil the pudding for 4 minutes to cook off the raw taste of the flour and whisking continuously to prevent scorching.*
- *The recipe halves easily; use a small saucepan to ensure it doesn't cook too quickly.*

Chapter 16

❦

DRINKS AND COCKTAILS

The Comte St. Germain's Poison

Frank's Sherry Tipple

Atholl Brose for the Bonnie Prince

Hot Chocolate with La Dame Blanche

Laoghaire's Whiskey Sour

Mamacita's Sangria

Cherry Bounce

Jamie's Rusty Nail

THE COMTE ST. GERMAIN'S POISON

"Drink, Monsieur," said the King. The dark eyes were hooded once more, showing nothing. "Or are you afraid?"

The Comte might have a number of things to his discredit, but cowardice wasn't one of them. His face was pale and set, but he met the King's eyes squarely, with a slight smile.

"No, Majesty," he said.

He took the cup from my hand and drained it, his eyes fixed on mine. They stayed fixed, staring into my face, even as they glazed with the knowledge of death. The White Lady may turn a man's nature to good, or to destruction.

The Comte's body hit the floor, writhing, and a chorus of shouts and cries rose from the hooded watchers, drowning any sound he might have made. His heels drummed briefly, silent on the flowered carpet; his body arched, then subsided into limpness. The snake, thoroughly disgruntled, struggled free of the disordered folds of white satin and slithered rapidly away, heading for the sanctuary of Louis's feet.

All was pandemonium.

—*Dragonfly in Amber,* chapter 27, "An Audience with His Majesty"

A sophisticated cocktail made from gin and tonic, lightly sweetened with St-Germain elderflower liqueur. Poison never tasted so good.

Makes 1

Ingredients

1½ ounces gin

½ ounce St-Germain elderflower liqueur, or more to taste

Ice

Tonic water

Lime twist

Method

Add the gin and St-Germain to an ice-filled glass. Top up with tonic, stir, and serve with the twist.

FRANK'S SHERRY TIPPLE

After a peaceful and not unpleasant sit with Mrs. Baird, I made my way up-
stairs, to ready myself before Frank came home. I knew his limit with sherry
was two glasses, so I expected him back soon.

The wind was rising, and the very air of the bedroom was prickly with elec-
tricity. I drew the brush through my hair, making the curls snap with static
and spring into knots and furious tangles.

—*Outlander,* chapter 1, "A New Beginning"

A cocktail I can imagine Frank indulging in after Claire's disappearance; after all,
when your wife vanishes, a double is what's needed to calm the old nerves.

Serves 1

Ingredients

2 ounces fresh orange juice

6 large fresh mint leaves

1 teaspoon sugar

1 cinnamon stick

4 ounces dry sherry

Ice cubes

Method

Muddle the orange juice, mint, and sugar with the cinnamon stick in an old-
fashioned glass. Add the sherry and ice cubes, stir, and serve.

Atholl Brose for the Bonnie Prince

"If I may present my wife, Your Highness?" he said. "Claire, my lady Broch Tuarach. Claire, this is His Highness, Prince Charles, son of King James of Scotland."

"Um, yes," I said. "I'd rather gathered that. Er, good evening, Your Highness." I nodded graciously, pulling the bedclothes up around me. I supposed that under the circumstances, I could dispense with the usual curtsy.

The Prince had taken advantage of Jamie's long-winded introduction to fumble his trousers into better order, and now nodded back at me, full of Royal dignity.

"It is my pleasure, Madame," he said, and bowed once more, making a much more elegant production of it. He straightened and stood turning his hat in his hands, obviously trying to think what to say next. Jamie, standing bare-legged in his shirt alongside, glanced from me to Charles, seemingly at an equal loss for words.

—*Dragonfly in Amber,* chapter 11, "Useful Occupations"

Atholl Brose has a long, colorful past—including the quelling of a rebellion—stretching back to 1475. Its fascinating history and satisfying finish far outshine that of its better-known cousin, Baileys Irish Cream, which first came to market in 1974.

Sweet, creamy, and delicious, Atholl Brose is the perfect after-dinner digestif, with a smooth finish the Bonnie Prince could only pull off in his dreams.

Makes about 2 cups

Ingredients

1 cup steel-cut or rolled oats

1 cup blended scotch whisky

1 tablespoon honey

½ cup light cream

Method

Soak the oats in 2 cups of water overnight.

Drain the oats in a strainer lined with cheesecloth or muslin, and squeeze the

cloth to extract all the liquid. Mix 1 cup of the strained oat milk with the whisky in a pitcher. Gently whisk in the honey until dissolved, and stir in the cream.

Serve chilled or over ice. The flavor improves on the second or third day, once the flavors have had a chance to combine.

Keep in the refrigerator up to 1 month.

Notes

- *Choose a midpriced blended whisky for a smooth result. If you decide on a more expensive single malt, stay away from those heavy on the peat, as it will overpower the sweetness of the honey and the richness of the cream.*
- *Dairy-free? Skip the cream. For slightly "creamier" oat milk, pulse the oats and their soaking water in a blender a few times before straining.*
- *Because it has no emulsifiers, Atholl Brose will separate if left to sit for a few days. Stir or shake gently to recombine.*

Hot Chocolate with La Dame Blanche

"The White Lady," he murmured. "She is called a wisewoman, a healer. And yet . . . she sees to the center of a man, and can turn his soul to ashes, if evil be found there." He bobbed his head, turned, and shuffled off hastily in the direction of the kitchen. I saw his elbow bob, and realized that he was crossing himself as he went.

"Jesus H. Christ," I said, turning back to Jamie. "Did you ever hear of La Dame Blanche?"

"Um? Oh? Oh, aye, I've . . . heard the stories." Jamie's eyes were hidden by long auburn lashes as he buried his nose in his cup of chocolate, but the blush on his cheeks was too deep to be put down to the heat of the rising steam.

I leaned back in my chair, crossed my arms, and regarded him narrowly.

"Oh, you have?" I said. "Would it surprise you to hear that the men who attacked Mary and me last night referred to me as La Dame Blanche?"

"They did?" He looked up quickly at that, startled.

—*Dragonfly in Amber,* chapter 20, "La Dame Blanche"

Chocolate first came to France in 1643, a gift from Spain, whose conquistadors brought the luxury item back from Mesoamerica. Europeans added sugar to the previously bitter drink to create a thick, luscious treat far and above anything to come from a packet of instant today.

Serves 4

Ingredients

2 cups whole milk

5 ounces (140 grams) finely chopped
    bittersweet or semisweet chocolate

1 to 2 tablespoons sugar (optional)

Fleur de sel (optional)

Method

In a medium saucepan, heat the milk over medium-low flame.

When the milk is warm, whisk in the chocolate, stirring until melted and steaming hot. To thicken, increase the heat to medium and cook at a low boil for 2 to 3 minutes, whisking constantly. Taste and sweeten with sugar, if desired.

Serve warm, in demitasses or small coffee cups, sprinkled with fleur de sel if desired.

Notes

- Fleur de sel, *meaning "flower of salt," is hand-harvested, small-crystal salt that is used to finish a dish just before serving.*
- *Add a drop or two of Grand Marnier, or even crème de menthe—just make sure the cask is clean of bodies if you choose the latter.*

LAOGHAIRE'S WHISKEY SOUR

"It's true!" She whirled toward Jamie, fists clenched against the cloak she still wore. "It's true! It's the Sassenach witch! How could ye do such a thing to me, Jamie Fraser?"

"Be still, Laoghaire!" he snapped. "I've done nothing to ye!"

I sat up against the wall, clutching the quilt to my bosom and staring. It was only when he spoke her name that I recognized her. Twenty-odd years ago, Laoghaire MacKenzie had been a slender sixteen-year-old, with rose-petal skin, moonbeam hair, and a violent—and unrequited—passion for Jamie Fraser. Evidently, a few things had changed.

She was nearing forty and no longer slender, having thickened considerably. The skin was still fair, but weathered, and stretched plumply over cheeks flushed with anger. Strands of ashy hair straggled out from under her respectable white kertch. The pale blue eyes were the same, though—they turned on me again, with the same expression of hatred I had seen in them long ago.

"He's mine!" she hissed. She stamped her foot. "Get ye back to the hell that ye came from, and leave him to me! Go, I say!"

—*Voyager*, chapter 34, "Daddy"

The sour's origins are most likely born from a British sailor's rations of lemons or limes and alcohol, which was often watered down over a long voyage to extend the supply; citrus juice was added to the alcohol to mask its watery taste.

Although more commonly a North American drink made from bourbon, this refreshing cocktail has a natural sourness reflective of the bitter Laoghaire, a woman most Outlanders love to hate.

Serves 1

Ingredients

1 tablespoon honey

2 ounces bourbon

½ ounce fresh lemon juice

Crushed ice

Citrus twist

Method

Dissolve the honey in 1 ounce hot water and stir to cool. Add the bourbon and lemon juice, and serve over crushed ice, garnished with a citrus twist.

Mamacita's Sangria

"Have you ever drunk sangria, Mrs. Fraser?"

I opened my mouth to say "Yes," thought better of it, and said, "No, what is it?" Sangria had been a popular drink in the 1960s, and I had had it many times at faculty parties and hospital social events. But for now, I was sure that it was unknown in England and Scotland; Mrs. Fraser of Edinburgh would never have heard of sangria.

"A mixture of red wine and the juices of orange and lemon," Lawrence Stern was explaining. "Mulled with spices, and served hot or cold, depending on the weather. A most comforting and healthful beverage, is it not, Fogden?"
—*Voyager,* chapter 50, "I Meet a Priest"

Hot or cold, it's refreshing, delicious, and dangerous; if you've never had sangria, proceed with caution. The brandy can sneak up on you and make you senseless before your second glass—and Mamacita doesn't strike me as one to tiptoe around a hangover, if you know what I mean.

Serves 2 to 4

Ingredients

1 bottle (750 ml) dry red wine

2 ounces brandy, Triple Sec, or Grand Marnier

½ orange, sliced

½ lemon, sliced

½ lime, sliced

1 cup orange juice

2 to 4 tablespoons sugar

1 2-inch cinnamon stick, plus additional

1 teaspoon whole cloves

1 teaspoon whole peppercorns

1 teaspoon whole allspice

½ teaspoon fennel seeds

Club soda or sparkling water (optional)

Method

Pour 2 cups of wine and the brandy into a pitcher. Add the sliced orange, lemon, and lime. Set aside on the counter for 1 to 2 hours.

In a small saucepan, combine the remaining wine with the orange juice and 2 tablespoons of sugar. Add the cinnamon stick, cloves, peppercorns, allspice, and fennel and heat over medium-high flame until just boiling. Remove from the heat, cover, and steep for 15 minutes. Strain and discard the spices.

To serve warm or hot, pour the wine and brandy (not the fruit) into the saucepan with the steeped wine and warm gently. Taste and add more sugar if needed. Pour everything back over the fruit in the pitcher, stir, and serve immediately in mugs or cups, garnished with a cinnamon stick.

To serve cold, add the cooled, steeped wine to the wine, brandy, and fruit in the pitcher. Refrigerate for at least 1 hour, and up to 1 day, before serving. Taste and add more sugar if needed. Serve with or without ice in wineglasses or tumblers topped up with club soda or sparkling water, if desired.

Note

- *This recipe stays true to the story and uses only the citrus fruits Claire described, but apples, melon, mango, pears, grapes, and kiwi all add wonderful flavor and color.*

CHERRY BOUNCE

Roger leaned forward and sniffed at his offspring's red-stained lips.

"Cherry Bounce, at a guess. There's a vat of it, round by the barn."

"Holy God!" She'd never drunk Cherry Bounce, but Mrs. Bug had told her how to make it: "Tak' the juice of a bushel o' cherries, dissolve twenty-four pound o' sugar ower it, then ye put it into a forty-gallon cask and fill it up wi' whisky."

"He's all right." Roger patted her arm. "Is that Germain over there?"

"It is." She leaned over to check, but Germain was peacefully asleep, also smiling. "That Cherry Bounce must be good stuff."

Roger laughed.

"It's terrible. Like industrial-strength cough syrup. I will say it makes ye very cheerful, though."

—*A Breath of Snow and Ashes,* chapter 6, "Ambush"

After years of experimentation with Mrs. Bug's rather vague "receipt," I've concluded that, though it's inconceivable that Jamie handed over a cask of the aged single malt to Mrs. Bug for her bounce, a midprice or better blended scotch whisky results in a much smoother finished product than a cheap bottle of hooch.

I've also cut way back on the sugar. Apparently George Washington liked his bounce extra-sweet, but I'll take his dentures as a sign to travel a different path. If you can't find sour, use the deepest, reddest cherries you can find and add a little lemon juice into the mix.

Makes about 3 cups

Ingredients

¾ pound (340 grams) sour cherries, stems removed, pitted

⅓ cup sugar, plus additional

2 tablespoons fresh lemon juice (optional; not necessary if you have sour cherries)

Zest of 1 lemon, grated

25 ounces (750 ml) blended scotch whisky

Method

Stir together the cherries, sugar, lemon juice, if desired, and lemon zest in a 2-quart jar until the sugar is dissolved. Pour the whisky over top and stir again before covering with a tight-fitting lid.

Store in a cool, dark place for 6 to 8 weeks. Taste for sweetness and add 1 to 2 tablespoons more sugar, if desired. Close the jar and return to its waiting place up to 2 more weeks.

Once it's to your liking, strain the bounce through a strainer lined with a few layers of cheesecloth or a clean linen or cotton tea towel that you don't mind permanently staining.

Store in a glass container in a cool, dark place.

Notes

- *A cherry pitter is an inexpensive and very useful tool. Work in a bowl to avoid cherry juice all over your backsplash and walls. You can also use the cherries with their pits, but if you intend to use the booze-soaked fruit after the whiskey is strained, it's easier to pit them first.*
- *Bourbon, vodka, and brandy also make tasty bounces. (Then there was that mango-rum bounce that took my small island's mojito circuit by storm in summer 2013.)*
- *The booze-soaked cherries are wonderful coated in chocolate for giftworthy bonbons, made into a batch of homemade ice cream, or eaten one by one, just as they are. Keep them in the freezer until ready to use.*
- *Drink your bounce straight, or get creative and mix up a few cocktails. One of my favorites is to drop a shot glass of Cherry Bounce into a pint of dry cider, christened a Cherry Bomb by fans on Facebook.*

Jamie's Rusty Nail

Technically, I supposed, it was a splinter. It was a two-inch sliver of cedar wood, and he'd driven it completely under the nail of his middle finger, nearly to the first joint.

"Jesus H. Roosevelt Christ!"

"Aye," he agreed, looking a little pale. "Ye might say that."

The protruding stub was too short to grip with my fingers. I hauled him into the surgery and jerked the sliver out with forceps, before one could say Jack Robinson. Jamie was saying a good deal more than Jack Robinson—mostly in French, which is an excellent language for swearing.

"You're going to lose that nail," I observed, submerging the offended digit in a small bowl of alcohol and water. Blood bloomed from it like ink from a squid.

"To hell wi' the nail," he said, gritting his teeth. "Cut the whole bloody finger off and ha' done with it! *Merde d'chevre!*"

—*A Breath of Snow and Ashes,* chapter 30, "The Captive"

Drambuie is from the Scottish Gaelic phrase *an dram buidheach,* meaning the drink that satisfies. Made from scotch whisky, honey, herbs, and spices, the liqueur adds a spiced sweetness that flavors the cocktail without overpowering it.

Traditionally made with blended scotch, you create a different Rusty Nail every time you try a different scotch whisky or whiskey. Switch to bourbon and you've got a Rusty Bob; use a peaty whisky and you're toasting with a Smoky Nail.

Makes 1

Ingredients

1½ ounces scotch whisky

½ ounce Drambuie, or to taste

Ice

Lemon twist

Method

Pour the whisky and Drambuie into an ice-filled glass. Stir and serve with a twist of lemon.

Chapter 17

PRESERVES AND CONDIMENTS

Quick Pickles
for a Hasty Escape

It was hunger that brought me unwillingly back to life the next day. I had not paused to eat through all the day before, nor when rising in the morning, but by noon my stomach had begun to register loud protests, and I stopped in a small glen beside a sparkling burn, and unwrapped the food that Jenny had slipped into my saddlebag.

There were oatcakes and ale, and several small loaves of fresh-baked bread, slit down the middle, stuffed with sheepmilk cheese and homemade pickle. Highland sandwiches, the hearty fare of shepherds and warriors, as characteristic of Lallybroch as peanut butter had been of Boston. Very suitable, that my quest should end with one of these.
—*Voyager,* chapter 35, "Flight from Eden"

A mix of zucchini and cucumber coins in a sweet, zesty brine that adds a spark to an otherwise boring sandwich or potato salad and makes a tasty palate cleanser when served beside the rich meats and cheeses of a charcuterie board.

Makes about 1 quart

Ingredients

½ pound (225 grams) zucchini, cut into ⅛-inch-thick slices

½ pound (225 grams) English cucumber, cut into ⅛-inch-thick slices

1 small onion, sliced paper thin

1 tablespoon kosher salt

1 cup white vinegar

½ cup white wine vinegar

½ cup sugar

1½ teaspoons pickling spice

1 teaspoon mustard powder

Method

In a large colander set over the sink or a bowl, toss the zucchini, cucumber, and onion slices with the salt. Set aside for 30 minutes to expel as much moisture as possible.

Pour out the vegetables onto a dry, clean dishcloth and gently but thoroughly pat them dry. Fill a clean 1-quart jar with boiling water and cover the jar's lid with boiling water in a small bowl for 5 minutes to sterilize. Drain both. Fill the jar with the zucchini, cucumber, and onion slices.

In a small saucepan, combine the vinegars, sugar, pickling spice, and mustard powder. Bring to a boil over high heat, reduce the heat, and simmer for 2 minutes. Pour this mixture over the vegetables in the jar and cool completely on the counter.

Cover with the lid and refrigerate up to 2 weeks.

Stuff these into your own Highland sandwiches of Crowdie Cheese (page 31) on Brown Buns at Beauly (page 224).

Notes

- *An inexpensive mandoline is the fastest way to slice raw veggies thinly and consistently.*
- *The pickles are ready to eat as soon as they've cooled, but they become even more flavorful after a night or two in the fridge.*
- *Mix up your vinegars for slightly different pickles with each batch. Other options include red wine, cider, or rice vinegar. In the same vein, combine different whole spices to make your own signature pickling spice.*

PICKLED MUSHROOMS

"Such a fine braw appetite as ye have, Mr. Fraser!" Mrs. MacIver exclaimed admiringly, seeing his loaded plate. "It's the island air does it, I expect."

The tips of Jamie's ears turned pink.

"I expect it is," he said, carefully not looking at me. "This minister . . . ?"

"Och, aye. Campbell, his name was, Archie Campbell." I started, and she glanced quizzically at me. "You'll know him?"

I shook my head, swallowing a pickled mushroom. "I've met him once, in Edinburgh."

"Oh. Well, he's come to be a missionary, and bring the heathen blacks to the salvation of Our Lord Jesus." She spoke with admiration, and glared at her husband when he snorted. "Now, ye'll no be makin' your Papist remarks, Kenny! The Reverend Campbell's a fine holy man, and a great scholar, forbye. I'm Free Church myself," she said, leaning toward me confidingly.

"My parents disowned me when I wed Kenny, but I told them I was sure he'd come to see the light sooner or later."

"A lot later," her husband remarked, spooning jam onto his plate. He grinned at his wife, who sniffed and returned to her story.

—*Voyager,* chapter 57, "Promised Land"

Right at home on a large plate of antipasto, served with your favorite cocktail or beverage, these tart, herby bites won't last through happy hour.

Makes about 1 quart

Ingredients

1 pound (450 grams) small button
    mushrooms, wiped clean

¼ cup plus 2 tablespoons olive oil

2½ teaspoons kosher salt

1½ teaspoons chopped fresh thyme

1 garlic clove, grated or minced

¼ cup white wine vinegar

1 shallot, julienned (see Knife Skills,
    page 11)

1 tablespoon dark brown sugar, firmly
    packed

Zest of 1 lemon, grated

½ teaspoon freshly ground pepper

½ teaspoon smoked or sweet
   paprika

½ teaspoon crushed red pepper flakes

2 tablespoons finely chopped fresh
   oregano

Method

In a large bowl, toss the mushrooms with ¼ cup olive oil, 1 teaspoon salt, the thyme, and garlic. Heat a large frying pan over medium-low flame for 5 minutes. Arrange the mushrooms in a single layer, cover, and cook, stirring occasionally, until tender but not darkened, 10 to 15 minutes.

Use the same large bowl to mix together the remaining 2 tablespoons olive oil and 1½ teaspoons salt with the vinegar, shallot, brown sugar, lemon zest, pepper, paprika, red pepper flakes, and oregano.

Pour the hot mushrooms and any liquid into the bowl and toss well. Cool completely, transfer to a glass jar or container, and refrigerate, tightly covered, up to 2 weeks.

Notes

- *These are even more flavorful after a night or two in the fridge.*
- *Red wine or cider vinegar make for a different, but equally delicious, flavor.*

Fraser Strawberry Jam

"Fréselière, eh? Mr. Strawberry? He grew them, did he, or was he only fond of eating them?"

"Either or both," he said dryly, "or it was maybe only that he was red-heided, aye?"

I laughed, and he hunkered down beside me, unpinning his plaid.

"It's a rare plant," he said, touching the sprig in my open hand. "Flowers, fruit and leaves all together at the one time. The white flowers are for honor, and red fruit for courage—and the green leaves are for constancy."

My throat felt tight as I looked at him.

"They got that one right," I said.

—*Drums of Autumn,* chapter 16, "The First Law of Thermodynamics"

An old-fashioned, compote-style jam made with naturally pectin-laden green apples.

Makes 12 half-pint jars

Ingredients

4 pounds (1.8 kilograms) strawberries

2 pounds (1 scant kilogram or about 3 medium) Granny Smith apples

½ cup fresh lemon juice

5 cups sugar

Method

Cover twelve clean half-pint canning jars with water in a boiling water canner and bring to a boil. Boil 10 minutes to sterilize the jars. Turn off the heat and cover.

Add twelve canning lids and rings to a medium saucepan and cover with water. Bring to a boil then turn off the heat and cover while you make the jam.

Gently wash the strawberries, discarding any spoiled fruit. Hull and cut the strawberries in half or quarters, depending on their size. Peel, core, and chop the apples into smaller than ½-inch pieces.

In an 8-quart or larger stainless steel or enamel pan, stir together the strawberries, apples, and lemon juice. Bring the fruit to a full boil over medium heat, stirring constantly to avoid scorching.

Add the sugar and stir until it is dissolved. Boil somewhat gently, stirring frequently, until the jam reaches 212°F on an instant-read thermometer, 15 to 25 minutes.

Use tongs to remove the jars from the hot water. Carefully ladle the jam into the jars to within ¼ inch of the rim. Wipe the jar with a damp paper towel to remove any spilled jam. (A canning funnel makes this process go more smoothly.) Cover each jar with a lid and ring as you fill it. Screw the lids finger-tight only.

When all the jars are filled, use the tongs to place the jars back in the canner. Cover and return the water to a boil. Process (boil) 5 minutes, then remove the jars. Process any remaining jars that didn't fit in the first batch. Cool completely. Check the lids to ensure they have all sealed. (Sealed lids curve downward and don't give when pressed. You should hear the telltale "pop" shortly after removing the jars from the canner.)

Wipe down the jars, label, and store in a cool, dark place up to 1 year.

Notes

- *This recipe is easily halved, but I like to make big batches of jam so I've always got a selection of homemade gifts I can give at the drop of a hat.*
- *You can reprocess any unsealed jars, but it's easier to just refrigerate or freeze those jars and use them first.*
- *The timing and temperatures in this recipe will work at altitudes of up to 1,000 feet. For those who live at higher altitudes, consult the website of the National Center for Home Preservation (http://nchfp.uga.edu), a great resource for all things preserved.*

TOMATO PICKLE IN THE MANGER

"Your mother's not back yet?" She was clearly alone, but he glanced briefly over her shoulder as though hoping to see Claire materialize out of the darkness.

Brianna shook her head. Claire had gone with Lizzie as escort to attend a birth at one of the farms at the far side of the cove; if the child hadn't arrived before sunset, they would stay the night at the Lachlans'.

"No. She said if she wasn't back, I was to bring you up some supper, though." She knelt and began to unpack the small basket she had brought, laying out small loaves of bread stuffed with cheese and tomato-pickle, a dried-apple tart, and two stone bottles—one of hot vegetable broth, the other of cider.

"That's kind, lassie." He smiled at her and picked up one of the bottles. "Will ye have eaten yet, yourself?"

"Oh, yes," she assured him. "Plenty." She had eaten, but couldn't resist a quick look of longing at the fresh rolls; the early faint sense of malaise had left her, replaced by an appetite mildly alarming in its intensity.

He saw her glance, and with a smile, drew his dirk and sliced one of the rolls in half, handing her the bigger piece.

—*Drums of Autumn,* chapter 48, "Away in a Manger"

A sweet, yet savory, whole-fruit jam with a kick. Makes a great alternative to ketchup on a grilled cheese, or served with Stovie Potatoes (page 182).

Makes about 2 cups

Ingredients

3 pounds (1.4 kilograms) tomatoes

¾ to 1 cup light brown sugar, lightly packed

⅓ cup honey

⅓ cup apple cider vinegar

1½ teaspoons kosher salt

½ teaspoon ground ginger

½ teaspoon cinnamon

¼ teaspoon crushed red pepper flakes

¼ teaspoon ground cloves

Method

Core and slice the tomatoes into 1-inch wedges. (Leave grape or cherry tomatoes whole.)

Combine the tomatoes, brown sugar, honey, vinegar, salt, ginger, cinnamon, red pepper flakes, and ground cloves in a large saucepan and bring to a rolling boil over medium-high heat. Reduce flame to medium-low and simmer until thick and syrupy, 1 to 2 hours.

Cool completely, transfer to a glass jar or container, and refrigerate, tightly covered, up to 1 month.

Notes

- *Some tomatoes need more sugar than others, so be sure to taste yours before and during cooking. Sweet heirloom varieties found at your local summertime farmers' market will need less added sugar than out-of-season specimens from the grocery store.*
- *If you want to store this over the winter, double, or even triple the recipe and preserve by following the canning technique described in the recipe for Fraser Strawberry Jam (page 318).*
- *To make this vegan, substitute maple syrup for the honey.*

STRAWBERRY–WHITE BALSAMIC SHRUB

"Lemon shrub, ma'am?" A wilting slave, gleaming with sweat, offered me yet another tray, and I took a glass. I was dripping with perspiration, my legs aching and my throat dried with talking. At this point, I didn't care what was in the glass, provided it was wet.

I changed my opinion instantly upon tasting it; it was lemon juice and barley water, and while it was wet, I was much more inclined to pour it down the neck of my gown than to drink it. I edged unobtrusively toward a laburnum bush, intending to pour the drink into it, but was forestalled by the appearance of Neil Forbes, who stepped out from behind it.

—*A Breath of Snow and Ashes,* chapter 54, "Flora MacDonald's Barbecue"

A colorful, sweet-and-sour, twenty-first-century fruit syrup that will leave you feeling refreshed on a hot summer day; a vast improvement on the sour-only beverage Claire was unable to stomach.

Makes about 3 cups

Ingredients

2 cups hulled and chopped strawberries

1 to 1½ cups sugar

2 cups white balsamic vinegar

6 whole peppercorns (optional)

Method

In a large jar, combine the strawberries and 1 cup of sugar. When the sugar has dissolved, stir in the vinegar and peppercorns. Cover and refrigerate for 5 days, stirring once a day.

Taste. Add more sugar, if desired, stir to dissolve, and return to fridge for 2 more days. When to your taste, strain through a fine mesh strainer, pressing on the fruit to extract the juice.

Stir into water or soda and serve over ice. Experimental cocktails with vodka or gin are also strongly encouraged.

Store in the refrigerator up to 6 months.

Note

• *Shrub also makes a very tasty Basic Salad Dressing (page 33) used in place of vinegar.*

ACKNOWLEDGMENTS

My first, and biggest, thank-you belongs to Diana Gabaldon, because, quite simply, there wouldn't be an *Outlander Kitchen* without you. Thank you for all the support and enthusiasm you showed me along the way, including allowing me to include your recipe for Cheese Enchiladas. The generosity you show with your fans inspires us all.

Susan Finesman, my agent. Fate brought us together at the last minute, but I will always remember it as perfect timing. A thousand gratitudes for every time you listened, and every great suggestion you made.

Rebecca Wellman, cook, food stylist, photographer. I'm a little in awe of you, and all that you have brought to *Outlander Kitchen*. You made it easy to relinquish control, and the beauty of this book is in great part due to you. I would be honored to do this all over again, one day very soon.

Anne Speyer, my editor at Penguin Random House. You have a wonderfully light and effective guiding touch. Thank you for giving me the space I needed to deliver what has been growing inside of me for five years.

Russell Galen and Anne Behar, for all of your help in putting this together.

Lori Zachary, blogger at *Little White Apron* (littlewhiteapron.com) and creator of the recipe for Peppery Oyster Stew. We've come a long way from that first batch of cross-continental salt-rising bread. Love you to the moon and back.

Kate Johnston, Donna Rubino, Aaron Brown, Gisela Giussi, Jeanie Oliver, Shana Jensen, Shannon Leblanc, Bridget Heihs, Claire MacDonald, Coralie Collins, Emily Kearns, and Lori Zachary. The most extraordinary coven of friends a woman could have on- or offline, and the women I run to first, whether I need to rant or to smile.

Anna Lapping, Janet Lee Anderson, Darcy Gagne, Jennifer Broughton, Rhiannon McVean, Brianne Begley, Helen Bullard, Becky Inbody, Lee Ann Monat, and Jen and Jason Davis, collectively known as the *Outlander Kitchen* recipe testers. A dedicated and helpful group with whom I was very privileged to work with. Thank you all.

Jessica Fraser, my oldest friend, for always being there.

Vlad Konieczny, author and adult educator extraordinaire. A gold star goes to you for your advice to hook myself to a star after that mean literary agent told me there would never be another Julia Child, nor any other unknown chef, to publish a cookbook. Success often comes from following trusted counsel. I am in debt to you for yours.

Surya and Patricia of Rolling Meadows Retreat in Maine. Thank you for placing that Adirondack chair *just so* in the far field. The view that day opened up a forgotten world to me, and in a single moment, forever altered my path.

Lara Oselsen, my first real-life meet-up with another Outlander. Thanks for not being crazy, and for turning out to be a pretty fabulous online friend.

Summer and Ginger, creators of the original *Outlander* podcast (outlanderpod .com). It's been a blast to watch you grow right along beside *OK*. A wild ride with friends is always the most fun.

JJ and Hildy, champion book reviewers at *The Book Bosses* (thebookbosses.blogspot .com). Appreciation for filling a whole lot of nothing time with some laughs, and for near-instantaneous book recommendations on demand.

Renate Wellman, cover model, for braving the elements of late October in the Pacific Northwest in nothing more than an eighteenth-century replica dress, to help create one of the most beautiful cookbook covers I have ever seen.

OK's thousands of fans on outlanderkitchen.com, Facebook, Twitter, and Instagram. Thank you for gathering around my virtual hearth to share your recipes and stories. You have made my life bigger and richer than I ever could have imagined.

My mom, who read to me as a baby; it has made all the difference. And my dad, who inspired my love of food, and who taught me the pleasure of a life filled with experiences rather than possessions—I owe you for the unencumbered simplicity of my life—I miss you every day.

Howard, for everything. I can't imagine a life without your love.

RECISE INDEX

Boldface indicates primary recipe page.

A food lover and bookworm from birth, THERESA CARLE-SANDERS grew up exploring the multicultural restaurant mecca that was, and still is, Vancouver, British Columbia, with her parents and two brothers. After years of travel as an early adult, she settled down and married the Englishman of her dreams, only to find herself, a few years later, blindly pursuing an unwanted corporate dream.

She and her husband, Howard, gave up the city life in 2003 and moved to the rain forests of Pender Island, BC, for a quieter, gentler life at a less hurried pace. In 2008, Theresa returned to Vancouver temporarily to follow her lifelong dream of culinary school, and graduated at the top of her class in 2009.

Back on Pender, between cooking for local restaurants and catering private functions, she began writing, cooking, and photographing her own recipes for her first blog, *Island Vittles*. In 2011, she began her second blog, *Outlander Kitchen*, a collection of writing and recipes based on her favorite Outlander series, by Diana Gabaldon.

Today, Theresa and Howard are happily ensconced in their little cabin in the woods on Pender, accompanied by their twelve-year-old Shiba Inu, Koda.

A visual artist from an early age, REBECCA WELLMAN has surveyed the world through a camera lens for most of her life. She has also always had a strong love for beautiful food and all things culinary. Eventually, the two passions collided into a joyful career.

Rebecca has worked as a professional photographer in the Victoria, British Columbia, area for more than fifteen years, specializing in food and lifestyle, creating images for magazines, cookbooks, packaging, and fine art.

In her spare time, she can be found in the kitchen experimenting with new recipes and creating visually stunning dishes, perusing thrift stores for that perfect prop, and enjoying all the West Coast has to offer.

Rebecca has been an avid fan of the Outlander series since the '90s.

rebeccawellman.ca